T5-CQB-141

CHANCES ARE

CHANCES ARE

A New Age Survival Guide

CATHERINE LILLY, Ph.D.
AND
DANIEL R. MARTIN, Ph.D.

TAYLOR PUBLISHING COMPANY
DALLAS, TEXAS

The authors wish to thank the following for their permission to reproduce the lyrics and artwork on pages 37, 69, 87, 88, 90, 102, 105, 114, 119, 128, 130, and 143.

"FIELD OF OPPORTUNITY" by Neil Young
c. 1978 Silver Fiddle
Used by permission. All rights reserved.

Marle, Raimond Van, "La Roue de la Fortune" from *Iconographie de l'Art Profane* (The Netherlands, Martinus Nujhoff publishers, 1932)
Reproduced with permission from the publisher.

"La Fortune et la Sagesse" from Petrarch's *Des rêmèdes de l'une et l'autre Fortune prospère et adverse*" (Paris, Gailot du Pré, 1523)
Reproduced with permission from the Beinecke Rare Book and Manuscript Library, Yale University.

Line art reproduced with permission from the artists, Margot E. Schmidt and Margaret Ryalls.

Library of Congress Cataloging-In-Publication Data

Lilly, Catherine.
Chances are.
1. Success. 2. Chance I. Martin, Daniel R.
II. Title.
BF637.S8Z484 1987 158 87-1873
ISBN 0-87833-559-5

Printed in the United States of America

9 8 7 6 5 4 3 2 1

There is a tide in the affairs of men
Which, taken at the flood, leads on to fortune;
Omitted, all the voyage of their life
Is bound in shallows and in miseries.
On such a full sea are we now afloat;
And we must take the current when it serves
Or lose our ventures.

SHAKESPEARE
Speech by Brutus in *Julius Caesar*, (Iv. iii.)

Contents

1 / The Return of Fortuna *1*
2 / Chance Is Not Fate *8*
3 / Planning Versus Preparation *22*
4 / Mistakes *30*
5 / Opportunity *37*
6 / Coincidence *56*
7 / Time *64*
8 / Fortuna the Woman *72*
9 / Contingency Planning *83*
10 / Luck *92*
11 / The Wheel of Fortuna *100*
12 / The Mystery of Life *117*
13 / Randomness and Social Machines *127*
14 / Romantic Fortuna *140*
15 / Probability *154*
16 / Accident *166*
17 / The Politics of Fortuna *175*
18 / The Good Life *200*
19 / The Fortunate Individual *217*
20 / Let Us Know *241*

1

THE RETURN OF FORTUNA

Ours is an age of uncertainty. The eighties in the United States began with a presidential election campaign between Jimmy Carter and Ronald Reagan. Some commentators said that the most interesting participants in this electoral process were the undecided voters who, in unprecedented numbers, could not decide on a favorite candidate — even until the very last days of the campaign. Another more worrisome manifestation of today's uncertainty is seen in the attitude of many troubled young people. They are alienated and restless, full of feelings of despair and hopelessness generated by uncertainty about whether there will even be a future to prepare for. What will it be like? Will there be an atomic war? Will they find jobs and security? Is it even worth trying? Is suicide the answer? Social workers sum up this all too familiar picture with the thought that the impotency that young people feel encourages them to live for the moment. "They have no idea what will happen to them in ten or twenty years — and they no longer care."

Change has become the normal state of affairs; individual lives are tossed to and fro in a sea of powerful, uncontrollable forces. The future is unknowable. Almost every week a new, dangerous conflict appears somewhere on the international scene. Was anyone expecting the Falklands war? Grenada? The bombing of the marines' barracks in Beiruit/Chernobyl? The continuing terrorist attacks all over the world? In times like these, we're worried about whether or not we will even survive; who knows if we can find a way to be happy and successful.

Today's uncertainty is a problem we must face and come to terms with. We cannot begin to seize the myriad opportunities that lie ahead of us until we break through and understand the nature of uncertainty. Ours is not the first age to try to do this. In troubled times people have always asked themselves these same questions. In other historical periods of tumult, transition and accelerating change, people were faced with these same problems and, over the centuries, developed answers and resources, many of which have been lost, but which we need today. These answers unlocked rich worlds of opportunity for them.

The purpose of this book is to resurrect some of these time-honored solutions, which people before us discovered when they were also faced with problems which are endemic today. Their collective wisdom, tailored to our present needs, is called throughout this book, "the Fortuna philosophy," a collection of personal traits which are advocated as tools for increasing our personal luck and our ease and comfort in today's uncertain world. The person who practices this advice will be called "lucky" or "a fortunate individual." By searching through history, literature, and science, we will uncover a way of living that makes sense today and which allows us to live happily, successfully, and without despair.

Two especially fruitful historical periods for this investigation were the height of the Roman Empire and the European Renaissance. It was in these periods, not surprisingly, that the idea of the goddess Fortuna, the goddess of chance and uncertainty, flourished. Originating in the East in ancient legends of a Great Mother goddess, the personality of Fortuna, the entity who is responsible for bringing all accidental things into our lives, from prosperity and wars to birth and death, was first clearly delineated in ancient Greece, and the idea of Fortuna has been revived whenever times have been uncertain and fearful.

Two thousand years ago, the Roman Empire stretched from Britain to Asia Minor. The Roman legions were unbeatable in warfare. The Roman citizen could travel thousands of miles and still have his citizenship and rights acknowledged. The Romans were strong, powerful, and had come to this position largely because of their pragmatic wisdom and commonsense way of dealing with the world and the forces surrounding them. Their philosophers created gems of commonsense wisdom that have been quoted for centuries; their builders pushed roads (which can still be seen today) through thousands of miles of wilderness. The Roman Empire and its people have always been very appealing to Americans, who see themselves as sharing similar values, desires, and virtues.

On the other hand, to modern eyes, the Roman religious practices before the rise of Christianity seem to be frivolous and highly impractical. There were dozens of gods and goddesses, each with its own temple, ritual, and devotees. There were gods for the home, for the harvest, for war, for the emperor, for sailing, etc. One of the most powerful goddesses of this time was the willful eldest daughter of Jupiter, Fortuna. She was the specific goddess for bringing whatever

comes and for determining the outcome of that which is uncertain. She came to be associated with material success or failure, adventure, gambling, commerce, war, success, or failure in love and many other aspects of life. There were eighteen temples honoring her in Rome alone. The fact that the serious, pragmatic Romans seemed to waste their time on this cult, possibly better spent out fighting Visigoths or protecting their borders, hints to us that the rituals and ceremonies surrounding these gods and goddesses might not be complete frivolities. We are now beginning to understand that these religions had specific, helpful societal functions. Conventional wisdom of the day concerning how to deal with powerful abstract forces was put into rituals, stories, images, and patterns of observances surrounding a god or goddess. Forces were personified to make it easier to conceptualize these abstractions. Stories, and the descriptions of appearance or personality of each god or goddess encapsulated the best knowledge of the time as to the nature of these forces and how to deal with them. They also made that information easy to transmit to others. A good example of this phenomenon is Cupid, the juvenile son of Venus, the goddess of love. He is seen carrying a bow and a quiver of arrows, mischieviously aiming darts at unsuspecting men or women. This image collects and represents in an unforgettable way many facts about love. That love is playful and irresponsible is shown by the fact that Cupid is an infant. Falling in love can happen anytime, any place, unexpectedly: an arrow from the hidden archer. The swiftness of the arrow tells us that falling in love can occur in a moment, and the arrow's sharpness symbolizes the fact that love can pierce even the hardest heart and can be painful. Some pictures showed Cupid and Lady Opportunity, one of the guises of Fortuna, with an hourglass between them. This reminds us that love hinges on finding the right time, the right place and, of course, the right person. All of these aspects make up what is called an opportunity for love.

At the height of the Roman Empire, there was great sophistication concerning the relationships among uncertainty, chance, and luck. It was a period of great change, adventure, opportunities, and possibilities. The people of that time had generated many ideas about how to cope with the psychological stress of uncertainty and how to achieve material success in its presence. This knowledge was an integral part of the religious practices surrounding the worship of the goddess Fortuna and it is something we could use today! Unfortunately, many insights into the nature of Fortuna were lost during the centuries long battle between Christianity and paganism, when Christian truths about the nature of the world dominated and erased the older pagan imagery of personalized forces. Not everything was lost. The process was slow and insights about uncertainty were still valuable even in a static medieval society. And also, since this wisdom is not

inconsistent with the essence of Christianity, many of the traits of Fortuna came to be attributed to the Virgin Mary.

Later, Fortuna enjoyed a brief revival during the Renaissance as a literary figure, where she was known as Fortune or Opportunity. Then the rise and success of modern science, and the feelings of control and certainty it engendered, again eclipsed her role in the popular culture. The methodology of science concerned itself with regularity and pattern, rather than disorder and irregularity, and the force represented by Fortuna was rarely discussed or incorporated into scientific models of reality. After a while even the existence of chance came to be disputed.

But in our century science has re-introduced randomness as a fundamental aspect of life. Quantum mechanics, which is based on probabilities and which probes the essential uncertainty of our knowledge of the physical world, is the modern foundation of physics, our most exact science. Statistics and probability underlie modern social science. The Atomic Age has introduced a new uncertainty into politics. Everyday life is touched by the changes in the family and other social structures. But although chance has been reestablished as a natural force in the modern world, we find ourselves ignorant of its nature and uncertain about how to deal with it. Wide-spread fear of change and nostalgia for "the good old days" and other signs of rigidity show that we are uncomfortable about integrating the force of uncertainty into our daily lives. Even though bountiful opportunities may lie behind the door of uncertainty, we are fearful of unlocking it. The idea of personifying abstractions such as chance, opportunity or uncertainty into a deity does not sit well with modern Americans, religious or not. However, embedded in old descriptions of Fortuna and in exhortations concerning how to deal with the opportunities she brings, we can find some still valid truths which can be helpful to us. We don't have to believe in the actual existence or presence of a pagan goddess, tooling around on a wheel or a ball, as she is often pictured. Let's give the ancient thinkers more credit than that! By personifying the forces which they noticed operating around them, they created a linguistic tool which allowed them to discuss these forces. What they noticed was that chance or uncertainty was a fundamental aspect of the physical world, and for this reason she was personified as a deity. We now know that, like space, time, matter, gravity, and light, chance is one of the fundamental actors whose actions and interactions create the substance of scientific reality and of everyday life.

We are sorely lacking a means of talking about chance. Author Betty Rollin, writing about events in her life says, "God makes such monkeys out of us. Cockily, we gear up for what we assume is in store. We chart our little courses, rig up our little boats; then, three miles offshore, wham! And what manner of wham it is depends on whether,

on that particular day, He feels like wiping you out or just scaring the hell out of you." Rollin ends up ascribing to God attributes which no theologian would accept as part of His essence. What she seems to be striving to express is the impact of uncertainty on her life. This is one of the major reasons we are attempting to revive discussion of the goddess Fortuna. Fortuna is the name of the force which Rollin means to describe. The name, Fortuna, is a convenient peg on which we can hang attributes to transmit information. And like the Romans, we do not hesitate to employ it.

The nature of Fortuna is revealed in several ways. Through literature we can rediscover how she was perceived in the Roman age and in the Renaissance and tap the reserves of their wisdom. If we look at our spoken language, we see that it contains traces of words and concepts relating to uncertainty. When these are pieced together, they re-create a rich complexity of traditional beliefs and wisdom which can prove helpful today. Fortuna's modern face is revealed in twentieth century science and mathematics. These ideas can be related to the historical Fortuna and can also be made useful in everyday life by showing us how to unlock the world of opportunities. In order for the wisdom of Fortuna, in all its aspects, to serve us today, a Renaissance scholar and a mathematician have joined forces to unearth these ideas and tailor them to suit today's needs in today's uncertain world.

In times like these we need a means of understanding and coming to terms with the dark "fearful" forces of uncertainty. It doesn't make any sense to talk about "harnessing" this force, as we would the force of the sun or tides, as it is Fortuna's nature to be fickle. But there is some established wisdom for getting on her best side and staying there as long as possible. Some people are favored by Fortuna. They are called lucky. You can be called "lucky" too, if you learn about her, understand the nature of this force, learn to appreciate and share in the bounty she brings us, learn how to swim strongly in that feminine sea of uncertainty, and, most importantly, learn to desire her, rather than fear her; then you too can unlock the rich world of opportunity and become a lucky person. And we all can use a bit of that in these precarious times!

HOW TO READ THIS BOOK

Everyone knows that knowledge isn't naturally arranged in a linear fashion, one fact following another, one idea leading into just one other idea. But a book necessarily is so ordered. Most often the author must decide what to put first, middle, and last. He or she decides when to look forward, previewing new ideas; when to refer back to something mentioned earlier; and when to repeat themes. At best, a fixed structure is thereby created which reflects the author's opinion of what themes and developments are most important. Sometimes it just reflects the order in which the author came to learn the subject or it merely recapitulates the facts in chronological order. However a natural body of knowledge is rich with interconnections, not all of which are known to the author working on the subject. The complexity of an organic subject cannot be arranged in a linear way without losing some of its subtleties. When you think about various aspects of a complex situation, each idea casts shadows on every other related idea. Like in a daydream, random firings of brain synapses trigger free associations as the mind wanders from thought to thought. Each exploration of the subject matter is different and unique. We want to make a book like that.

At the end of each chapter you will find a table of numbers with each row and column preceded by a single letter. Look on page 7 for an example. Tables like this appear at the end of each chapter. We suggest that you use these tables to guide your passage through this book. To do so, choose a pair of letters such as your initials, or a friend's. For example, if your letters are JS, then at the end of each chapter, you should next read the chapter whose number appears in the place of the table where row J crosses column S. If you were using the table on page 7 and your choice of letters was JS then you would proceed next to Chapter 10. This book is not intended to be read from beginning to end. And for good reason.

There are 676 different pathways through this book, made possible by following the tables at the end of chapters. These paths were chosen at random by a computer. If you follow the path suggested by your choice of two letters, your reading of the book will be a rare, different, almost unique occasion — an individually tailored happening, an event which is not likely to be repeated for anyone else. This is our way of introducing Fortuna to you, by offering you an opportunity, a sample of the rich abundance and variety which she characteristically brings our way. Your experience on your chosen path* through this book is her gift to you.

*(You may choose not to play this game, thinking it contrived and awkward, and instead choose to read the chapters in order, as in any other book. But, you will still be stepping into the world of chance as you read. The chapters were arranged randomly so even reading them in order from 1 through 20, you will be enjoying a unique encounter with chance.)

THE MATRIX FOR CHAPTER 1

	A	B	C	D	E	F	G	H	I	J	K	L	M	N	O	P	Q	R	S	T	U	V	W	X	Y	Z
A	12	17	9	11	10	8	9	7	16	8	6	5	12	6	4	7	8	5	13	13	4	15	9	9	13	10
B	8	9	4	10	7	6	5	6	10	8	12	13	5	2	15	17	16	4	18	16	14	9	3	16	3	16
C	8	15	5	13	12	3	4	3	14	16	2	6	9	19	19	9	4	19	8	7	19	7	12	9	9	18
D	12	14	7	10	10	16	6	18	5	14	10	12	10	16	3	2	10	11	8	10	9	5	17	2	7	18
E	2	15	7	19	5	17	16	19	8	18	10	16	4	14	11	13	6	16	19	14	7	8	19	8	8	6
F	17	4	14	12	10	3	2	3	14	2	10	10	5	9	19	17	12	4	12	13	10	15	11	9	8	9
G	17	16	3	3	2	19	6	12	4	19	6	2	2	2	5	15	2	15	8	10	3	9	8	13	10	18
H	11	6	11	16	11	13	16	4	11	14	15	5	11	9	14	19	2	5	13	12	7	6	11	13	4	17
I	18	9	19	18	7	15	15	12	18	10	4	2	12	13	18	19	7	8	10	19	6	4	13	4	16	3
J	18	2	2	12	16	5	16	2	2	9	7	19	12	8	3	7	6	5	10	11	5	11	2	4	7	3
K	5	14	18	11	13	5	15	16	7	16	11	8	7	6	2	4	2	7	17	7	18	12	12	6	13	8
L	10	9	14	19	6	7	18	18	2	19	7	15	3	4	16	17	13	14	6	6	9	16	4	9	19	19
M	13	13	15	17	10	14	18	4	15	8	10	19	12	5	7	4	4	9	17	3	8	16	17	11	18	11
N	12	11	15	4	13	6	10	3	5	13	15	5	10	18	10	14	12	12	5	11	3	8	9	8	15	5
O	2	16	3	2	17	13	13	11	13	11	6	7	3	10	8	2	5	8	8	17	6	3	19	17	14	2
P	13	10	18	7	10	11	12	2	4	14	17	15	17	3	4	7	17	8	4	13	5	5	11	7	8	5
Q	9	7	17	3	6	10	9	14	5	6	3	3	4	6	15	17	10	9	10	7	2	5	12	2	18	15
R	17	7	8	18	10	13	18	8	2	13	14	12	18	10	17	19	17	8	13	14	3	13	4	12	19	7
S	8	3	3	2	13	11	18	17	3	17	10	7	4	3	8	17	17	6	9	19	5	2	13	11	5	12
T	9	15	14	15	18	3	15	6	17	7	18	12	8	9	15	11	19	3	16	12	4	6	5	3	6	7
U	19	4	19	8	10	10	2	6	6	11	17	13	11	3	5	14	13	17	10	18	8	9	14	19	5	6
V	10	5	2	8	12	8	4	9	6	14	12	16	15	5	9	16	2	14	9	10	11	14	7	9	15	17
W	17	10	6	8	8	15	11	10	4	17	14	9	2	12	4	11	16	13	16	3	14	19	4	17	3	14
X	11	17	4	11	10	18	17	8	9	17	19	5	2	18	12	16	6	9	18	17	15	3	16	14	13	19
Y	3	16	5	2	8	18	16	4	4	16	17	5	2	7	5	5	8	5	6	14	6	12	3	2	7	14
Z	4	3	9	19	18	12	11	19	3	9	18	5	19	15	9	16	7	11	17	8	4	4	16	6	12	14

On the chart, find the place where the initials you've chosen intersect. Read the chapter whose number appears at that intersection.

2 CHANCE IS NOT FATE

Petrarch, one of the most learned people of all times and certainly the greatest of all Italian poets, was in Paris in 1360 when King John of France returned from England where he had been a prisoner of the English king. A few weeks after the return of the French king, some time in January, a great reception was given in Paris to celebrate his liberation and Petrarch was invited to make a speech before the monarch. In this speech, he offered consolation for what the king had suffered in prison and also rejoiced at the king's escape from adversities, asserting that all that had happened to the king was due to Fortuna. The audience was made up of many high ranking church dignitaries and scholars who apparently became disturbed by the repeated mention of the word Fortuna in the king's presence.

Later on that same evening, three doctors of theology came as a committee to Petrarch's apartment to discuss Fortuna with the great poet. The inquiry lasted late into the night and only his quick mind and his calm appraisal of the delicate situation saved him from a fatal danger. On this occasion, Petrarch came very close to being accused of heresy, a charge which, in those times, inevitably meant death if sustained. The times were dangerous and people were burned at the stake in public, right in the center of Paris, for much lesser crimes. In a letter to one of his friends, Petrarch later tells about his encounter with the inquisitors and states that he was finally able to conform to the orthodox position of the church by denying any belief in the existence of Fortuna.

The church had forbidden even the mention of Fortuna. In a dictionary published in 1566 by Ximénez, we can read under the term Fortuna: "There is no goddess Fortuna; instead, in whatever happens, there is only the will of God." The church was so afraid to see a return of Fortuna as a competing divinity that it forbade not only any mention of the ancient goddess but also any acknowledgement of the existence of chance, even in abstract terms. And yet people could see in everyday life that chance played a large role. The unsatisfactorily rigid answers provided by the church eventually led people to form many splinter groups, some of which adopted systems asserting that Fate was the answer (the doctrines of predestination) and some of which simply advocated skepticism or plain atheism.

Most religions and all traditional philosophical systems are at odds with the notion of chance. Even though people have some idea of what chance is, their religious beliefs or the way they interpret reality leads them to think that chance is either something evil or the product of ignorance. In other words, if there is a God, then nothing is left to chance. For example, most people believe that if we cannot tell whether or not it is going to rain next month, it is because we are still too ignorant about the weather. They discount the role of chance.

Discussions of chance and fortune are immediately linked to superstition, to palm reading, to astrology, and are rejected as heretical in religious circles. At the same time, references to chance by the man on the street are seen as uneducated chatter in much scientific discussion, particularly in the least advanced sciences. In the 1930s most physicists eventually came to believe that randomness was a fundamental aspect of physical matter. But even in the face of evidence, some scientists could never accept it. Einstein said: "God does not play dice with the universe." His fervent desire was to find a theory which would have no cracks for chance. He was not successful.

The idea of chance has been chased out of the houses of God whether they be churches, synagogues, mosques, or other temples of worship. This exclusion is the result of chance being misunderstood throughout history. There is definitely a place for chance in a religious view of the world but because it is hard to explain and easily misunderstood, many established religious leaders have always discouraged talking seriously about it. The view that chance and God don't mix represents what many people presently believe.

As we shall see later in more detail, chance can be interpreted as the gift that God gave mankind in order to make us free. In very simple terms, our happiness depends on our ability to make choices. There is no happiness without freedom. And there is no freedom without chance.

There is no happiness without freedom and no freedom without chance.

It is also widely believed, mistakenly, that chance has no place in the University. People think that as far as experts are concerned nothing really happens by chance. After all, experts are there to find out the reasons why things happen. This simplistic view of nature holds that everything that happens must have a cause. So, according to popular lore, if you still think that some things happen by chance, all you have to do is to go to the university, get yourself a Ph.D. and you will be cured forever of your ignorant habit of believing that something may have happened by chance. Moreover, such utterances as "How fortunate!", "What a coincidence!", "How lucky can you get!" are disregarded as ignorant superstition.

In brief, what we are attempting to do throughout this book is to rehabilitate the idea of chance. We intend to reinstate both its religious and scientific respectability. Far from being an anti-religious notion, the idea of chance forms the basis of both free-will and salvation. It also serves as the Christian foundation of Charity or divine love (demonstrated among Catholics by the intercession of the Virgin Mary, which is explained more fully in Chapter 8). At the same time, from a scientific point of view, we illustrate and defend the role of chance in the physical world and particularly in human affairs. Once we have understood more fully what chance really is, and more importantly what it is not, we will be prepared to unlock the door to happiness.

Primarily, we must understand that chance is not fate. Cicero wrote: "Fate is only a fiction born in the brain of philosophers; common sense shows us that nature exists and that chance *(fortuna)* also exists but not fate *(fatum).*" Suppose you are having a discussion with friends about chance. If you tell them that you believe in chance they will think you are a weird, superstitious fellow, a mystic at best. And if you tell them that you can lead a happy life by making friends with uncertainty, instability, and unpredictability, they will think that you are a little strange. If you tell them that you are doing research on chance, they will ask you if you can read palms. They may mention some friend of theirs who owns a set of tarot cards. The conversation will turn then to astrology, to the powers of the stars, to destiny, and other such things, all of which are only superficially related to the idea of chance.

Once the conversation turns to such things as fortune-telling and reading one's fate from the stars it becomes impossible to get most people to listen seriously. This does not mean that chance does not have a long and rich association with the occult and the mysterious. We find it hard, however, at casual meetings in social gatherings to lead the discussion about chance along more scientific and seriously religious paths. It shows clearly that a great many people have a very confused idea of what chance is. And when this happens, the serious business of dealing with life's opportunities is neglected.

The most common mistake is to confuse chance or Fortuna with Fate or Destiny. In this book we talk about chance and Fortuna making little or no distinction between them. For the sake of simplicity we will also view Fate and Destiny as being very closely related notions. In any case, we will see that both Fate and Destiny are concepts which can be discarded as soon as we start investigating seriously the notion of chance. In the meantime, let us examine the difference between Fortuna and Fate.

OEDIPUS AND THE MULTINATIONAL CORPORATION

Suppose we are all working in a large multinational corporation, a metaphor for our world, of which the chairman of the board is God. Immediately under Him we would find the president of the corporation, better known as Divine Providence. Working under both God and Divine Providence we find Fate. Now, Fate would be like an office manager who transmits to the employees the orders coming from above.

Fate will say to Mr. Oedipus, a young, dashing, and proud executive trainee: "It has been decided upstairs, in the front office, that you are not to be promoted to account executive because you will kill the Greek deal and you will screw up the Jocasta account." Fate is merely the spokesperson for management. He is a middle-level manager. He will simply tell you what is written up there in the board room, what has already been decided in stone. There is generally no engraved recourse to the dictates of Fate. People who work for this type of corporation feel the heavy hand of management pressing down on them and have no other outlet but to react like rats trapped in a cage. Under Fate, people are locked inside and out and opportunity vanishes.

Now, if young Mr. Oedipus were to rebel against this harsh decision to deny him an opportunity for promotion and if, on top of that, he were to finagle his way into the position which was denied to him, by showing his great ability at solving riddle-like problems, the lesson would be that he still would kill the Greek deal and mess up the Jocasta account. In this case, management would come down very hard on the young man. He would get fired. How dare he attempt to unlock the opportunity that was closed to him by Fate? Reflecting upon the whole series of events, young Oedipus would wonder how he could have been so blind. He was blind indeed to believe that he had any chance at all in that corporation which employs such nasty people as Mr. Fate. He was blind to believe that he would be given a chance. There is no chance, no opportunity to better one's lot in that corporation; the door of opportunity is tightly locked; there is no Fortuna; there is only Fate.

As you read these words you may be convinced of the fact that the best policy under this set-up is to always obey Mr. Fate. If you wish to be happy in such an organization, you will convince yourself that it is indeed wiser to obey the orders from above. However, if you agree to work under Fate, you may lead a very miserable life, unable to do much of what you want. You will not be free to choose. Also, as we have already pointed out, you will not be able to bargain effectively with Fate. It would be nice to bargain directly with management but Fate gets in the way. Fate will tell you that he is just carrying out orders.

Now, this does not mean that the chairman of the board is evil. The corporation is man-made; it exists only in the brains of people. Under the by-laws of that corporation, if you are obedient and submissive, everything will go smoothly for you. If you could only talk directly to the Chairman of the Board (God) or at least to the President (Divine Providence) everything would be fine.

All this was very clearly explained by Sophocles, author of the Greek play, *Oedipus Rex.* In this play, Sophocles attempts to demonstrate that people should not count on Fortuna (chance), but should, on the contrary, obey the dictates of Fate. In the beginning of the play, Oedipus, a proud young man, tells the audience boldly and without shame that Fortuna, the goddess of chance, is his mother. "Fortuna is my mother and I am not ashamed to declare it," says he. He tells the audience that Fortuna loves him. This is to say that it is possible for Oedipus to be lucky when he makes an effort to change his life for the better. Oedipus believes that he has a chance. He thinks he can change the world. He is confident that he can solve the problems that plague his country.

His brashness is punished, horribly, when the oracle's prediction — that Oedipus will unknowingly kill his father and marry his mother — is realized. The terrible lesson that was taught to him and, in turn, to the audience, is that when you attempt to "unlock opportunity," you may unknowingly commit adultery by penetrating into the forbidden places belonging to the father. In any case, we see that the dictates of Fate are inescapable and self-fulfilling. Oedipus punished himself by plucking out his eyes. Supposedly, his new physical blindness allowed him to gain divine insight. The ancient public who attended these plays was thus taught not to trust Fortuna, that woman whom Oedipus called his mother, but instead to believe in and obey Fate. The lesson, simply put, is that one should not make waves, but should instead passively accept one's fate.

We see that Fate is inflexible and rigid while Fortuna is unstable. Because of this unstable nature and because of the fact that she does change her mind, Fortuna is more accessible to men and women in negotiating their own freedom. The play *Oedipus Rex* was subsidized by the state and by the people in power who had an interest in teaching citizens to stay in their places. They were trying to reduce the number of troublemakers like those who would start thinking that things could be changed, that things could be different, that they could be other than what they were, and that they would have a chance, an opportunity to improve their lot. Such revolutionary ideas would render unsteady the position of those at the top.

The playwrights who propagated these ideas about Fate were not evil men; they just thought that this was the best way to keep the peace and to prevent social unrest. The system worked well. However, the problem here is not whether the system works well or not. The question for the individual is whether we are ready to accept a system which is incompatible with our expectations. Are we willing to accept one in which we cannot act freely to improve our circumstances? If we like to see things change, at least once in a while, we would not be happy living in the Iran of the Ayatollahs or in present-day Poland, where change is by itself a political threat to the state. There, one lives according to rigid rules which were written by revered bearded thinkers.

The important thing to keep in mind is that, in this conception of the way things work, once we believe in the authority of Fate we can't go past him in the chain of command. A completely different set of circumstances prevails once we recognize Fortuna as a major influence in the situation. Actually, if we view both concepts from a historical perspective we can see that Fate is the more ancient or primitive notion. Fortuna is a more advanced and modern development of the basic idea of pure chance. Originally, chance was that entity which brings our destiny, and much later Fortuna came to mean the one who acts in a way which makes change possible. Fortuna operates in a fluid, nonrigid way. This is why men and women may deal, bargain, and find happiness with her.

Life for us, in this multinational corporation will be a lot happier under an organizational system which includes Fortuna and excludes Fate. It is up to us to decide how we want to imagine the organizational chart of the corporation and the people who work in it. Let's fire the office manager, Fate, and deal with Fortuna, who is none other than the first-born daughter of the Chairman of the Board. In Ancient Greece, when she was called Tyche, she was the daughter of Zeus (the Jupiter of the Romans), king of all the gods.

Fortuna, as the daughter of the boss, is a very powerful and influential ally even if she herself does not hold a steady job in any particular office of the corporation. She comes and goes as she pleases (like

Playboy's Christie Hefner). She can walk into any office and have her say, for all things in the universe are subject to chance. If you think of Fortuna as a personified entity, you may wish to think of her also as a generous woman, as a benevolent mother, as a possible bride, as a lover, or simply as a friend and ally.

When people say "Let's take a chance," they are trying to say that they are free to change the future. On the other hand, people who believe in Fate or who are, as we say, fatalistic about life, feel that they have no influence in shaping the future and, subsequently, no chance of improving their own lives. Fatalism has even led to the destruction of entire civilizations. Why work indeed, if it's written up there that you are going to be poor all your life? Why take precautions in battle, if the hour of your death was written down by Fate at the moment you were born? An army made up of fatalistic minded soldiers can be a powerful instrument of the state but, in the end, the society that espouses a belief in Fate will destroy itself. People who see no need for initiative or incentive often will be overwhelmed by events and swept away.

These examples, of course, are of extreme positions. Most people today do not think or act like that. They are not completely fatalistic. However, if you examine the idea more closely, you come to realize that many people are at least somewhat fatalistic and, because of this, lead unhappy existences, resigned as they are to their lot in life and afraid to take chances. Even when they know of the existence of an opportunity somewhere, they are afraid to unlock the door that could lead to it. They are afraid to deal face to face with Fortuna.

Going back to our example of the multinational corporation, many of us are resigned to blindly obey Fate and we do not dare talk to rich, beautiful, and bountiful Ms. Fortuna. Many of us won't even dare look her in the eye, much less seize her by the forelock, when she passes by in the form of Opportunity, one of her many guises. Since the corporation we have been talking about is man-made, merely a convenient shorthand way of talking about more complex issues, it is up to each one of us to choose whether we place Fortuna or Fate in our mental picture of reality. That choice is among the many that we make in our lives.

RECONCILING FORTUNA AND RELIGION

We wish to insist that the philosophy of Fortuna is not anti-religious. Having chosen to believe in the presence of Fortuna (chance) in the corporation (nature) does not deny the ultimate authority of God. It is necessary to insist on this point because the idea of chance has been little understood for centuries and is still viewed in fundamental or orthodox religious circles as contrary to belief in a supreme being. Their reasoning goes like this: If things happen by chance, then, not even God can tell what will happen next. So, if we admit chance, we have to limit the power of God. Since God, by definition, is all-powerful, then there is no such thing as chance.

The flaw in this apparently logical string of reasoning is in the very first statement: "If things happen by chance, then God cannot tell what will happen." This statement is not only illogical; it is also heretical. Without going into too many details, let us point out that the clause "God cannot" is a contradiction. If God is all-powerful, then, by definition, He can — universally, eternally, and absolutely. If we believe in God, we must also conclude that nothing is impossible to Him, including the supervision of the workings of chance.

To deny God the use of chance as an ingredient of His creation is to bring God down to the level of humans — the height of insolence and pride. An article in the *Christian Science Monitor* (12-28-81), however, tries to deny chance. "The realization of God's supremacy enables us to overcome a sense of chance existence. It enables us to find safety." On the contrary, we think that to tell people that chance does not exist, when anyone can see that it is a concrete element of daily life, creates confusion. Taken to the extreme, this idea has led fanatics to go recklessly into the thick of battle with only a Bible or a Koran in their pockets. Wisdom dictates that God helps those who help themselves. He will ultimately come to our aid, but first He has given us the means to take care of ourselves.

Most of the time, however, it is not out of insolence and pride that some people deny the existence of chance. Since chance is incomprehensible to the man or woman who assumes a "rational" basis for the universe, it is reasonable to deduce that it is that very incomprehensibility, that very misunderstanding, that breeds fear and that causes the exclusion of chance from religion and science. We have written the word "rational" inside of quotation marks in order to point out that rationalization is a human activity which is neither flawless nor divine.

This exclusion of chance was quite unfortunate because great theologians like St. Augustine and St. Thomas Aquinas had been able to reconcile chance and God. They wrote that chance is necessary in order to make room for freedom of choice in human actions. Simply stated: We may not wish to go as far as to pray to Fortuna but, at the very least, we must admit that chance is a fact of life and deserves an explanation. The explanation that these church fathers provided was based on what Aristotle said about chance. He made chance respectable in religious and scientific circles by defining it as an "accidental cause." Calling chance "a cause" gave it a rational explanation and made people feel less anxious about uncertainty. For more inquisitive minds the definition was not completely satisfactory because it avoided a real answer and did not explain the meaning of "accidental." But, in any case, the weight of Aristotle made it legitimate to talk openly about Fortuna, the Latin name for chance.

According to St. Thomas, there are two kinds of chance: one is simple chance and the other is Fortuna. Chance governs the inanimate things, while Fortuna rules over those animate creatures which are endowed with elective consciousness. In simpler terms, a person can make choices while a rock cannot, and so, chance is for things while Fortuna is for people. Notice however that the place of animals in all this is problematic and has been a source of constant argument. Even today, the theory of evolution by Darwin, which closely links animals and humanity, is being attacked by fundamentalists. One reason is that behind Darwin lies Fortuna.

The idea of separating rocks and animals in order to explain Fortuna is still fruitful. Carl Jung, the contemporary and one-time friend of Freud, had a special word for such things as rocks. He called them pleroma and had another word for animate creatures which he called creatura. Gregory Bateson, the husband of better-known Margaret Meade, more recently picked up the same dichotomy between animate and inanimate things. "If you kick a stone," writes Bateson, "it moves with the energy which it got from your kick. If you kick a dog, it moves with the energy which it got from its metabolism." The point that St. Thomas was making is that one cannot predict how a human being may react to a kick. The idea of Fortuna helps to explain the many ways a person reacts to kicks. Good and bad fortune, according to St. Thomas, depend merely on the way Fortuna (the total event) suits individual taste and desire. Unlike the rock, the individual reacts in a multiplicity of ways, depending on such variables as the force of the kick, the reason for the kick, previous experience with kicks, and depending, of course, on who is doing the kicking, a factor the rock has no interest in. One subject may react violently, another may love it, and yet another may do nothing.

The point is that the kicking of creatura becomes an event of insurmountable complexity quite impossible to duplicate. It is a unique event in the universe. Even if you kicked the same person again, the event would be completely unique since a human being has the ability to remember and would thus be a different person from the one who was kicked the first time. That person may hit you back after the next kick. When an event cannot be duplicated we say that it is unpredictable. Another, more poetic way of saying this is that it falls under the realm of Fortuna. A religious person may accept this and say that God allows Fortuna to operate in the world in order that humans may make choices among an array of ever changing and novel possibilities.

The richness of human experience stems from that very possibility — open to us by God through Fortuna — to make individual choices and to become unique individuals. Our differences, acquired through our ability to make individual choices and to seize opportunities in life, contribute to our uniqueness and hence to our humanity.

The existence of Fortuna in human affairs began to be accepted not only by the church fathers, but also by some Christian writers of great fame. In *The Divine Comedy,* Dante introduced a remarkable conception, the Christian Fortuna, who plays a role as God's handmaiden. She is a figure both satisfying to the intellect and appealing to the imagination. Independently from Dante, the figure of the Christian Fortuna appears also in many medieval writers in France, England, and Spain. The late Howard Patch, a scholar on the subject of Fortuna, wrote that in these works written by pious and faithful authors, "God and Fortuna do not work in opposition, or without some measure of concord. In the *Roman de Renard,* a medieval French novel, God punishes some sinners on the wheel of Fortuna."

For Dante, Boethius, and many Christian writers — although God is always in control of things Fortuna plays a role in making things a little loose, unstable, variable, and uncertain in order that humans may make decisions, may make choices, may seize opportunities, may feel free to do so, and, more importantly, may feel morally responsible for their actions. If we were not responsible for the possible alternatives of stealing or not stealing, of killing or not killing, we could run into the sad conclusion of having to accuse God for our sins. The role of Fortuna is to prevent that conclusion from ever being made.

God and Fortuna can be reconciled:

- human actions are fundamentally unpredictable
- Fortuna allows for moral responsibility
- God is powerful enough to encompass chance
- St. Augustine and St. Thomas write that chance is necessary for human freedom of choice

---

A philosophy which includes Fortuna is thus acceptable to people who believe in God. It is also acceptable to skeptics and others who only see chance as a force in the universe, in purely scientific terms. The intrinsic variety of Fortuna allows for the same variety of religious stands among its adherents. In other words, because Fortuna is in favor of variety, it fosters religious tolerance. Fortuna thrives in political, social, and religious plurality. The French essayist Michel de Montaigne, who is known for his moderate skepticism in religious matters, dealt extensively in his writings with the uncertainty of human affairs and the role of chance in life. He wrote: "The uncertainty of my judgement (I have so much trouble making up my own mind) is so evenly balanced (and I care so little which way it goes) in most occurences that I would willingly submit to the decision of chance and of the dice."

Having thus evoked the role of Fortuna in his own decision-making process, Montaigne may have feared that he was opening himself up for scrutiny by the ecclesiastical authorities of his own intolerant times (1580). Wanting to protect himself, he proceeded to give an example from the Scriptures where Fortuna is allowed a role in decision making. Consequently, in the next sentence he added "that even sacred history (The Bible) has left us this custom of entrusting to Fortuna and chance the determination of choice in doubtful cases: 'The lot fell upon Matthias (Acts).' "

In the end, whether we are believers or not, our language is full of expressions and allusions to Fortuna. The skeptic who at one moment denies the existence of the goddess, at the next moment shows that he or she believes in chance by using words like "perhaps," "it just happened," or "fortunately." As Patch wrote, "In one way or another she goes on (as lady and princess of change), a favorite of romanticists, and a phantom of delight to pique the intellect of everybody."

Our attitude toward Fortuna depends on the kind of life we live. If we feel strong and powerful in the face of events, we may decide to be adventuresome, seek out opportunities, and go into areas full of uncertainty and danger. If an individual continues being successful he may come to be like Caesar who, it is generally believed, had profound faith in his personal Fortuna. In the words of another scholar, T. R. Holmes: "Caesar believed with the faith of a devotee, that above himself there was a power, without whose aid the strongest judgment, the most diligent calculation, might fail. That power was Fortuna; and Caesar was assured that Fortuna was always on his side."

On the other hand, people who feel weak may think that they are not capable of taking chances in life. Such people may then forego any hope of living with Fortuna and submit resignedly to Fate. People who give up and the ones who behave like Caesar are, of course, extreme examples. Most of us fit somewhere in between the two.

Fate, viewed in a purely mechanical way like rocks being kicked by measurable forces and moving in predictable ways, is still present in the minds of modern men and women who believe in determinism. But with people, no such things happen. Life within the brain escapes the constrictions imposed by time and space. Through memory we can bring back the past to impact upon the present. The memory of a past mistake may prevent us from repeating it. The ability to visualize future situations can enable us to take preventive measures which in effect control and modify the future. We are encouraged to do this when we are assured that the future contains a variety of possible outcomes. This does not mean that because we reject Fate, all kinds of determinism must be rejected. A modern determinism is possible which works in concert with chance. Determinism can be probabilistic and not necessitating, synthetic and not analytic.

Humanity may hope to achieve happiness by gaining more and more control over the world. "But when all is said," wrote Montaigne, "it is hard, when dealing with the life and actions of human beings, to arrive by rationalization at any rule so exact as to exclude Fortuna from her rights in the matter."

HAPPINESS

As we have seen, chance, a much misunderstood concept, is the key to happiness. The world of opportunity will remain locked until we understand the link that exists between happiness and chance. Most people have an idea of what happiness is, and they seek it. In fact, all religious and philosophical systems are to some extent inquiries into the nature of happiness or attempts at making us happy. How is chance the key to happiness? In two ways: First, our definition of happiness takes into account the fact that chance is an undeniable aspect of life. Second, chance becomes nonthreatening when we remove fear that erroneously accompanies it. We fear the idea of chance when we fail to understand it. Once we understand the nature of chance, we begin welcoming opportunity and finding happiness.

Happiness, indeed, can be of two kinds: One is absolute happiness; the other is episodic happiness, the kind that is lived and experienced. The latter is the one we are promoting in this book. The first kind of happiness, the absolute kind, is unattainable and many people lead miserable lives trying to achieve it. One attribute of this type of happiness is that it comes packaged with a fear of the uncertainities that chance brings. For instance, people who seek absolute happiness will tell you that men and women cannot consider themselves happy until they have lived the last minutes of their lives. They will tell you old tales about people who were once happy but who were subsequently visited by great misfortune. Their business seems to be to frighten people. In other words: We can't count ourselves happy until we are dead! They say this because, until the last moment of one's life there is a chance that one will be made miserable, one may be dishonored, and ultimately unhappy.

But this is only playing with words for every life must have some unhappy moments in its past, its present, and its future. Absolute happiness is a myth. This book doesn't attempt to deal with absolute happiness but, instead, tries to show how we all can achieve episodes of happiness as often as possible by learning to adapt to the necessary up-and-down flows of ever present chance. This will prepare us to unlock the opportunities that lead to happiness.

Differences between Fate	and Chance
inflexibility	flexibility
powerlessness	freedom
despair	happiness
predestiny	change is possible
your future is fixed	you can make choices
people who feel weak	people who feel strong
absolute happiness	episodic happiness

The choice is up to you which way you conceive the universe!

THE MATRIX FOR CHAPTER 2

	A	B	C	D	E	F	G	H	I	J	K	L	M	N	O	P	Q	R	S	T	U	V	W	X	Y	Z
A	6	19	5	5	3	6	16	9	6	16	13	19	4	7	8	4	5	14	11	5	6	8	14	19	17	14
B	6	17	7	6	5	3	3	5	8	11	10	15	10	13	5	11	6	19	17	6	8	18	19	15	18	15
C	7	16	7	20	9	10	20	12	11	19	5	19	10	18	11	20	13	7	9	6	18	4	10	3	7	11
D	19	17	6	18	8	9	18	3	7	4	15	19	14	4	12	8	14	15	5	4	12	6	3	16	18	8
E	14	13	19	18	11	12	17	12	4	13	16	8	18	11	19	6	17	6	4	5	12	5	15	10	16	20
F	4	7	4	14	18	19	4	11	9	16	9	18	19	18	11	12	11	12	18	6	20	18	7	11	17	20
G	15	12	20	15	16	20	8	7	3	9	5	15	15	15	17	17	8	13	17	19	7	18	20	18	11	4
H	7	7	6	9	8	3	5	20	4	6	13	13	5	7	10	17	4	12	6	10	13	10	7	3	14	11
I	6	18	4	13	4	12	18	18	19	19	10	3	9	10	5	20	13	10	3	10	18	20	16	18	12	17
J	13	6	4	17	4	3	3	8	4	8	12	3	5	5	8	3	9	16	18	6	9	15	4	11	8	5
K	18	13	4	15	4	12	7	12	19	19	5	15	15	13	16	15	9	9	14	8	7	9	10	20	16	20
L	20	4	7	17	15	4	8	4	14	5	4	20	11	13	15	6	19	7	20	14	16	10	12	10	17	18
M	16	15	5	10	20	7	9	6	9	12	14	3	6	15	13	3	14	19	15	20	6	10	19	5	9	4
N	4	16	11	6	17	10	6	19	14	4	7	3	7	15	16	18	13	3	13	13	8	11	13	13	3	18
O	4	6	16	11	9	15	19	17	8	3	12	14	14	19	9	14	19	6	4	15	3	13	16	18	11	18
P	18	14	9	19	11	7	10	13	5	3	8	19	13	10	10	6	5	4	5	10	9	8	8	16	5	9
Q	13	18	8	8	7	3	11	15	7	20	6	16	8	3	5	7	3	15	4	9	15	19	11	5	15	9
R	12	19	4	9	19	20	10	15	14	6	15	4	14	8	18	10	10	20	8	17	11	10	5	7	8	9
S	3	9	8	6	12	20	12	14	7	3	16	5	12	8	9	18	10	16	3	4	12	9	4	16	15	9
T	3	12	6	5	5	16	13	13	19	20	16	20	6	11	5	15	12	12	4	3	7	16	10	16	15	14
U	20	7	4	7	8	4	12	10	8	13	15	16	3	14	4	20	5	16	3	19	7	18	19	6	18	5
V	16	19	6	5	5	4	16	11	12	11	4	17	14	17	11	7	7	3	7	6	10	15	10	12	11	19
W	19	5	4	20	3	10	6	7	18	11	11	13	8	5	19	5	15	12	12	4	17	14	19	16	18	18
X	14	3	11	16	17	4	8	13	19	14	12	13	14	6	7	9	16	20	11	11	12	16	9	17	4	5
Y	4	7	8	8	10	4	20	18	14	18	3	12	10	6	8	16	9	19	5	10	15	20	20	8	8	13
Z	16	8	17	7	13	17	16	8	19	17	7	7	8	20	3	7	18	17	12	10	3	20	6	3	15	16

On the chart, find the place where the initials you've chosen intersect. Read the chapter whose number appears at that intersection.

3

PLANNING VERSUS PREPARATION

We ask five-year-old children, "What do you want to be when you grow up?" and urge them to choose. We applaud the young couple who struggles for years pinching pennies and saving, and finally accumulate enough money for a down-payment on their own home. According to popular wisdom, careful planning for the future will bring safety and rewards. We're told that people who look ahead prosper while foolish people often get burned when they don't anticipate the possible consequences of their action.

That's why uncertain times provoke so much anxiety. We want to plan but we can't. If we can't determine what the future will be, how can we prudently make provisions for it? Is it wise to buy a house with a variable interest rate on the mortgage? When the payments increase with inflation, can I be sure my income will? Even so, will it be good investment if the major industry in town unexpectedly leaves for the sunbelt? Can two young people marry, honestly promising " 'Til death do us part," knowing how much people change and that they may have 50 years more to live? What can we teach our children to make them successful, productive citizens of the twenty-first century?

Uncertainty about the future makes absolute plans impossible. Young people in college are anxious about job security. They want to be guaranteed a job when they graduate. They're looking for rigid, but certain, pathways to future happiness. They study pre-law, premedicine, business, computer science, or communications because it's easy to see there will be a need for these professions in the future. The more a course teaches them exactly what they will be doing on the job, the more they like it. They hate electives because they feel they're a waste of time. These sincere, hard-working students, trying to plan in the best way they can, end up spending four years of education limited to mastering the necessities of just that first year in their first hard-won job.

But wait. There's something wrong here. People live longer. Skills are rapidly outmoded. We read that new unforeseen career possibilities open up every year and that the average worker will have several different careers in his or her lifetime. These four years would have been better spent getting a deeper understanding of our culture (history, literature, science, languages), sharpening analytic skills (philosophy, mathematics, composition), and learning how people tick (psychology, sociology, economics, anthropology). College years provide a golden opportunity for acquiring general knowledge and skills. It's foolish to take a two-semester course in "The Operating System of the XYZ-21 Computer" when the XYZ-21 will be obsolete even before graduation day! But the anxious, paralyzing fear of making mistakes, given our uncertain future, has unfortunately locked many of today's students into narrow, rapidly obsolete curriculums.

Instead of rigidly planning in anticipation of stability, we must somehow learn to continually prepare for change. The keyword here is preparation. Planning is based on exact knowledge of what the future will bring and involves adjusting oneself accordingly. If this was ever possible, it no longer is in the modern world of constant flux. But the wise person still has recourse to preparation. Preparation means taking actions now, today, which will make it easier to take advantage of unforeseen opportunities that present themselves in the future. Preparation is one of the key elements in the process of unlocking the world of opportunity and enjoying its gifts. Preparation has always been an aspect of planning, but today it is the most important part of it.

Think of a nineteenth century explorer, about to travel into uncharted lands. He prepares for his adventure by packing guns, Bibles, food, water, trade goods, warm clothing, light clothing, tools, medicines, tents, and so on. Some of these he may never use, but they're part of his preparations, part of what he can do now to make his perilous future journey safer. In addition, he talks to people who have travelled through these lands and consults journals of earlier travellers. It's not that he expects that his journey will be exactly like theirs. Instead he hopes that when opportunities come his way he will be informed and recognize them. This is a good model for the way we should pass through life in uncertain times. Instead of counting on marriage and children as the only way to avoid loneliness in later years, we should prepare ourselves for any contingency by having, as well, a rich social life and many friends of both sexes. Instead of being frustrated by obstacles in our path as we plan on a career, say, as an airplane pilot, we can prepare by studying hard in school, doing well in technical areas, taking flying lessons, learning about flying, finding out how others came to be pilots. If opportunities come along that lead in the desired direction, we should take them. If one gets turned down by the Air Force because of bad eyesight, at least there will be contingency plans, ideas of other related paths to follow, and the ability to respond to related opportunities.

We must be familiar with our equipment (by knowing ourselves and our basic values and needs), be familiar with the possibilities of what might happen and be ready to take actions and make decisions as opportunities arise.

Preparation involves:

- being familiar with your resources
- learning about what might happen — future possibilities
- being ready to make decisions as the moment arises
- being adaptable
- being courageous
- mastering yourself — accepting the past and moving forward in your life — not looking back in regret

---

Some kinds of planning are limiting and constricting when considered in light of the uncertainty we must face, and hence they tend to decrease happiness. Other kinds are liberating. For an example of the first kind, imagine an eighteen-year-old youth entering college whose one primary career goal is to become a lawyer. All her plans revolve around this decision, freely made. Every opportunity that comes along will be measured against the standard, "Will this help me get into law school?" and later on, "Will this help me succeed in law school?" This plan can become a tyranny in a life which should be growing and changing. From the moment a fixed decision of this sort is made, options and possibilities vanish. Opportunities that could lead to other careers or opportunities to develop new interests are turned down. These opportunities are put under lock and key. Her best strategy becomes a conservative one of not even considering anything that might get in the way of the goal, and thus youthful experimentation is squelched. A great deal of anxiety is generated because no matter how carefully one plans one's life, it is impossible to know what is going to happen. It is possible that by being a drummer in a rock band she could develop exactly the contacts one would need to get into law school, whereas working on the school paper may prove to be a dead end. She can't know in advance, and every decision which must be made generates anxiety for her. Through her lack of knowledge of the future she may be making big mistakes, and yet, it's impossible to get the information which would tell her exactly what she should do. Finally, even if this young person succeeds in finally graduating from law school and getting her first job with a law firm, she may find herself a totally different person, shaped by the previous years of struggle, and, possibly, with no present interest in being a lawyer. She's no longer that eighteen-year-old who made that decision, and after spending her youth chasing a narrow, limited goal, she may be a much less happy person.

On the other hand, consider a young person who experiments widely, seeking diverse and varied experiences, hoping to discover his own values. Perhaps after involvement in local politics, college course work, social activities, and working on the school newspaper, he discovers that he is often drawn to and interested in discussions of justice and freedom. He may also have interests in music and mathematics, which he does not neglect. If he seeks variability, expands his interest, eventually he may find that he has a real vocation for law, and will take the steps necessary to become a lawyer. His progress toward this goal is not the result of rigid planning, but his final state develops out of an awareness and acceptance of his present circumstances. He is fully involved in the process of living, growing, and changing. His goals and values are constantly being reexamined in light of personal growth. No decisions are fixed. Without doubt, this person will have a much better chance of being happy in our uncertain world.

A broadly based liberal arts education, which unlocks the world of ideas and opportunities to a student, can be the path to more happiness than a narrow career-oriented education. Being exposed to a wide number of opportunities is better than rigidly pursuing just one. The liberally educated student might appear to struggle a bit more to achieve his first job but, in the long run, if he learns to be receptive to uncertainty and relish variety, his long-run life satisfactions will be greater. Fortuna brings many unexpected surprises, both pleasant and unpleasant, into our lives. A liberal arts education will acquaint us with this fact and can teach us how to positively respond to all of them.

We may not like uncertainty and we may attempt to control it by rigid planning, but it is futile to try to erase the impact of this force, Fortuna, which comes from outside ourselves and from outside our control. The only "planning" that makes sense is in learning how to master ourselves. If events to not adapt themselves to us, we must learn how to adapt ourselves to them. We can cultivate an attitude of acceptance. We can act with courage so as to increase the randomness around us, because when more things are happening, the more likely it is that events will occur which will be to our benefit. We must abandon ourselves into the arms of uncertainty, not just tolerating it but relishing it.

"I ride an uncertain chariot
to an uncertain destiny,
adoring each surprise."
private communication from a young poet

A specific plan for the future more often gets in the way than it helps. A young woman who grew up in the fifties usually had a firm plan in her mind of what her future would be like. She would be engaged by her senior year in high school, married shortly after graduation. She would have studied typing and maybe shorthand and would probably work in a clerical job for a few years to help buy furniture or make a down-payment on a house. Then she'd get pregnant, leave her job, have three or four children and devote the rest of her life to her children, her home, and husband. Perhaps after her children were grown she might become active in social or church affairs. This is a dream of "living happily ever after," but even then, in the much more static fifties, not every life fit into those narrow confines. And when it didn't work out, the women caught in these unplanned for situations really suffered. One woman of this generation told us her story. She wasn't really attracted to any of the boys at her high school and didn't accept one pimply-faced young man's invitation to the prom. She didn't get engaged and she has never left her original post-high-school clerical job. She's never married and still lives with her parents. An almost daily subject of conversation between her and her mother, even now, is whether she should have been less choosey and accepted that invitation to the prom. She's haunted by the fear that she made a mistake and thinks that because of her foolish error the automatic film of her life story has ground to a halt at the first frame. Not being able to progress in her anticipated plan, she does nothing. She finds little happiness in her real life because she cannot relate it to her fixed plan.

When we plan so rigidly for the future, we destroy freedom and we lock out opportunity. We don't see possibilities. A definite expectation for the future becomes a subtle, built-in obligation on our actions. Freedom from fixed life-plans is what the "lib" in "women's lib" was originally all about. Fixed expectations are a tyranny we impose on ourselves.

Women today in particular should not be trapped into the type of planning where one visualizes a path and then automatically proceeds along it. No one can really tell what they'll be doing five or ten years hence. There are not enough role models to show women all the possibilities ahead; women need the freedom to create roles that have never even been conceived before. How to be successful in the business world? How to combine career and family? How to manage if your husband dies or leaves you? How to be a friend to other women, who have traditionally been seen as competition? Some women have done each of these things, but each of these lives is so individualized and idiosyncratic that they could hardly be called role models. They can't be used as patterns. All they do is illustrate that some solutions are possible, but not what our own solutions will be. Women need the freedom to discover these solutions themselves.

All of us, not only women, must learn to sail in uncharted waters. We have to create our individual lives, moment by moment, actively moving into an unknown future. We can approach with relish the points in our life where the future is unknowable, a place where there is a fork in the road. At these forks, many critical variables are out of our control and we cannot accurately foresee the future. The potential for paralyzing anxiety is there because any action could be a mistake. But if we know and accept the impossibility of planning in these situations then our anxiety will be diminished. We will know that we cannot make a mistake and that we are not responsible for failure. All that is possible is to prepare, make the best of whatever comes, and accept the gifts of Fortuna in our lives. This is what we will be judged on.

Planning
- is rigid
- involves fear of making mistakes
- makes success or failure of future plans our responsibility
- is not really possible in light of future uncertainties
- is stressful

Preparation
- is flexible
- makes mistakes tolerable
- allows us to share responsiblity for outcomes with Fortuna
- allows us to take advantage of change and unexpected opportunities
- is not stressful

We are given choices and faced with opportunities. At those forks in the road we must act and contribute to what will happen. The various possible outcomes may not be completely clear. Uncertainty may play a major role. But, trusting in the adequacy of our preparations, we should choose. At no other time are we more alive; at no other time are we expressing more fully a fundamental human capacity: to experience the present and influence the future. If we were to try to plan, we would just be pruning the tree of future possibilities down to one branch, unnecessarily limiting ourselves to those future options which can be imagined today. No one can foresee the unique and unexpected ways men and women will live their lives in the future. But lifestyles are being forged today by people who accept themselves, who are prepared, who relish the freedom that uncertainty brings, who seize opportunities, and who thereby move confidently into the future.

Once we are free from the tyranny of our plans, we will be happier. The anxiety of attempting to responsibly plan the details of one's life in uncertain times is incredibly stressful. Preparation and contingency planning (a more systematic form of preparation — the subject of Chapter 9) should replace planning. We need to recognize those times when we can act and distinguish them from those times when the variables are out of our control and all we can do is react. It's just like teaching children to ride a bike: "Relax. If you're too stiff and rigid, then you'll hurt yourself if you fall." We can't depend on rigid planning in these changing times to keep us safe. Active and flexible preparation, on the other hand, will allow us to handle the situation, no matter what happens.

How a planner can become a preparer:

- think of life as an adventure
- acknowledge the uncertainties in your future path
- make many contingency plans, not one specific plan
- relax — share responsiblity with Fortuna
- be accepting of whatever happens and move forward from there

---

THE MATRIX FOR CHAPTER 3

	A	B	C	D	E	F	G	H	I	J	K	L	M	N	O	P	Q	R	S	T	U	V	W	X	Y	Z
A	13	11	4	18	15	19	4	2	10	2	20	20	7	8	16	5	7	9	8	11	8	18	2	20	14	18
B	5	13	8	9	20	4	14	13	2	15	20	5	11	17	18	12	18	2	7	8	7	10	5	19	16	8
C	17	17	17	2	17	7	19	2	8	17	16	13	11	13	18	15	11	2	19	4	11	9	11	13	11	2
D	20	9	16	11	18	14	10	14	16	19	8	17	12	13	4	6	4	14	11	8	13	13	7	9	11	13
E	8	2	15	16	19	15	18	13	5	2	11	4	2	19	2	18	11	5	13	15	14	20	9	18	17	18
F	16	13	7	11	9	7	19	13	2	14	11	6	12	2	13	6	15	9	5	14	14	7	2	13	15	12
G	7	4	15	16	17	6	16	17	11	18	15	14	17	16	12	7	9	17	6	14	5	2	7	9	8	8
H	20	19	20	13	4	8	2	15	8	11	14	20	16	16	8	15	20	16	11	9	8	9	10	6	20	16
I	17	6	5	12	19	19	2	13	6	9	6	9	14	15	14	8	10	11	4	14	19	12	20	9	18	6
J	12	12	15	11	7	18	6	9	18	14	16	7	6	20	18	19	10	6	16	14	8	16	16	12	6	6
K	2	10	14	14	12	4	2	8	15	12	8	7	4	9	11	12	13	4	2	5	4	20	17	2	19	5
L	19	15	15	16	7	14	12	17	10	10	16	14	10	14	13	14	12	9	17	18	18	18	14	17	18	12
M	8	8	18	9	8	6	6	10	10	9	19	11	15	2	15	11	19	8	18	5	2	2	2	15	11	14
N	11	9	10	20	9	7	19	18	2	9	19	7	4	4	13	20	6	4	7	8	7	7	16	7	13	9
O	18	13	2	19	18	12	14	7	6	12	14	16	19	13	14	12	4	4	7	13	19	6	4	2	13	20
P	19	2	7	17	18	14	6	4	18	15	16	17	5	13	15	4	7	16	16	14	4	7	2	15	20	10
Q	7	20	6	11	8	17	20	8	14	9	19	15	17	10	17	12	12	7	9	13	12	2	13	11	11	13
R	13	12	7	19	8	17	7	5	12	9	4	17	17	13	10	2	7	13	18	6	10	7	7	13	17	18
S	18	11	2	16	2	16	8	15	19	18	13	13	17	14	6	12	5	5	8	9	15	16	19	18	7	6
T	8	2	9	18	11	10	6	17	7	13	6	19	13	14	11	16	8	11	12	17	17	10	19	2	14	11
U	6	17	12	11	7	11	16	7	19	12	5	10	9	17	17	2	11	5	6	16	15	13	2	14	11	16
V	4	11	14	17	20	13	12	17	7	4	2	14	6	18	16	6	15	4	8	15	5	7	6	7	5	18
W	4	12	13	9	16	7	5	6	8	14	10	10	10	14	2	7	6	8	10	8	20	4	20	12	7	7
X	19	5	16	4	6	6	2	19	11	18	5	9	12	16	2	4	11	8	9	7	6	9	4	10	5	7
Y	7	12	7	6	13	12	12	11	5	17	13	17	19	4	13	20	2	2	7	17	8	7	19	18	4	8
Z	19	6	6	15	6	18	7	12	15	19	11	11	9	8	8	5	14	13	14	6	9	18	9	9	5	9

On the chart, find the place where the initials you've chosen intersect. Read the chapter whose number appears at that intersection.

4

MISTAKES

There are far too many people who don't like mathematics. This attitude develops in school. It's no fun to sit in a classroom and struggle over a problem for fifteen minutes (whether it be adding a column of digits or integrating a product of transcendental functions) just to have the teacher glance momentarily at our hard-won solution and say sneeringly, "Wrong!" It's humiliating to make a mistake. We're supposed to do things right. "Be careful, Johnny. Keep your colors inside the lines. Don't make a mistake and ruin the picture. Do it right." When we do make a mistake, it seems to imply that we're careless, lazy, or worst of all, stupid. And nobody likes to feel that way about themselves. Doing math is especially painful because the teacher sees the right answer so quickly and, when it's explained well to us, we also see how simple the problem was. The obviousness of our mistakes convinces us that we're "terminally stupid." A lot of people believe firmly, because of this, that they are incapable of doing mathematics at any level. "I don't have the head for it," they say. Students resist taking math classes and when forced to by school requirements, many are convinced in advance that they will fail. They sit in the classroom passively, or sometimes rebelliously, afraid to even try. To try is to court failure; if one doesn't try at all then there is at least some excuse, other than base stupidity, for the failure which will surely come to him. But it doesn't have to be this way. Teachers of mathematics have been aware of this syndrome for years. Recently, because of the increased need for mathematical skills in many modern careers, a lot of attention has been focused on the problem, this paralyzing fear of making mistakes, which has been labelled "math anxiety." A majority of the population is affected by it to some degree.

In uncertain times like today, when precise planning becomes impossible and things often don't turn out the way they're supposed to, a similar thing happens in a general sense. An inhibiting fear of making mistakes leads many people into living passively and fatalistically, letting life drift out of their control. We put off making decisions for the fear of making mistakes and we're afraid to make commitments. Young couples who love each other dearly and are devoted to one another, and yet who shy away from the permanent commitment of marriage and settle for the temporary expedient of living together, are a good example of this syndrome in personal relationships. They're afraid to make a mistake and so don't really want to take chances. A failed marriage is much more traumatic than a relationship that just didn't work out. Sadly, their fear often becomes self-fulfilling, because a relationship built without the glue of mutual commitment can easily fall apart over relatively small difficulties.

But there is a cure for "math anxiety" and it is directly applicable to "life anxiety." We begin by stripping the word "mistake" of some of its negative emotional baggage.

The things we learn in elementary mathematics classes are often long, connected strings of processes, called algorithms. Do you remember the first time you did long division or added two fractions? The teaching of algorithms involves an apprenticeship. The teacher does it over and over, explaining each step one by one. The first time through, different students will grasp different portions of the process, depending on individual strengths and weaknesses. Some students need to see examples more often than others. But the best teaching method is to give the student a brief explanation and then let him or her try a problem. The wise teacher can diagnose what the student has and has not understood by the type of error committed and can individually tailor an explanation which will allow the student to patch up that mistake and successfully complete the problem. It would be foolish to keep lecturing and demonstrating because, if a student has misinterpreted the instructions, more instruction of the same sort won't ferret out his error but will just bore him. The most successful math student is the one who is willing to make mistakes, who tries and tries and tries until finally it's right. And when we get the right answer; when, after long effort, our answer matches the teacher's, it is a moment of intense, immediate pleasure. There is no other area of endeavor which has the immediate reinforcement and reward that mathematics brings to the student who tries. But the timid student, wounded by misconceptions about how mistakes reflect on self-worth, will never get to the reward, will continually be punished by mistakes, and will hence give up. He never learns that mistakes are good, the fuel of learning and growing.

The cure for math anxiety, which has been intuitively practiced by good math teachers for centuries, is two-fold. First, one must remove the onus of blame from mistakes and, secondly, effort must be rewarded. The best teachers convey to their students the message that if a mistake is made, it's a positive sign, because it shows that the student is progressing and learning. In fact, a sensitive teacher can tailor a series of exercises of increasing complexity where the student would be challenged to a slightly more difficult task at each level mastered.

The only teaching necessary is in response to the student's mistakes. At the end the student can honestly say, "I did it on my own!" All that the student needs to bring to this task is courage. Mathematics is an activity. Teachers are like coaches. A swimming coach can't do anything with someone who won't jump into the water. Swimming around and showing how easy it is only discourages timid students who are quick to ascribe some magical ability to someone who can do something they are confident they cannot succeed at. The coach has to somehow coax the student into the water, urge him to try, give him pointers and make his mistakes into opportunities for learning. Mathematics is something you do, not something you watch, just like living. The most important job of the teacher is the subtle psychological task of removing the blameworthiness, the feeling of worthlessness, stupidity, or laziness usually associated with mistakes. When that burden is lifted, the student can finally jump in and begin to learn by trying.

The same cure works for "life anxiety," for it is the fear of making mistakes that paralyzes action. If mistakes are demystified and made less threatening, we will find the courage to dare to try, to act, to make commitments. In fact the same strategy that works in learning mathematics is applicable to life's problems: Mistakes are necessary steps in the living/learning process. But the analogy is not perfect. The reason why mistakes are not blameworthy in life is not that some celestial Teacher is guiding us through our errors, but that the fundamental factor we sometimes blame for making mistakes — the existence of uncertainty — is more abundant today. The implication here, simply put, is that the future is not predictable. People unnecessarily take responsibility and blame themselves for the consequences of actions; but often, if they examined the situation more closely, they would recognize that the outcome was primarily due to chance. To free ourselves from the blame for making a mistake we have to understand that some things are under our control and some things are not under our control, but are in the domain of Fortuna. We are only responsible and accountable for the former.

MISTAKES

- are not always our fault in a world of uncertainty
- should be seen as learning experiences

Some natural forces which are unchanging and which continually surround us are invisible. They have to be brought to our attention. The ancients did not feel themselves surrounded by the earth's atmosphere; medieval man did not feel the pull of gravity. Our psychic makeup is somehow adjusted to disregard whole realms of pervasive phenomena which do not strongly signal their existence to our perceptions by movement or change. Chance is like that. We've been taught to look for the logical and causal connections between things but we've rarely been encouraged to look for the presence of chance. It is difficult to focus on the pervasive fact that many ordinary events have no deterministic cause at all and happen just by accident. When the invisible world of Fortuna is brought to our attention (as through reading this book) it is easier to discover which consequences of our actions are and are not under our control. We discover that especially in situations involving a large degree of uncertainty, we can only be expected to influence rather than control events. Where planning is impossible, mistakes cannot be condemned.

Shy people especially have difficulties in social situations because they have an over-developed sense of responsibility. When they walk into a room, they fear that everyone is watching them, that the conversation will stop unless they contribute to it, and that the whole structure of the social space will shift and adjust itself in reaction to their presence. God forbid that they should make an awkward movement, say something foolish, or have something wrong with their clothing! Shy people plan all sorts of strategies for dealing with those situations whenever they cannot get out of them altogether. Their planning is futile: what happens in that room is usually too big and complex to be significantly affected by how they act or what they say. There is a complicated situation occurring before they enter the room. How it touches them at the moment they enter is an accident which is impossible to predict or control. If a shy person could bring himself to give up his plans for controlling the situation, he could then avoid making the mistakes he so fears. The mistakes shy people make are more in their heads than in their actions, for the only problem is that what happens does not happen the way they anticipated. Let it happen; do not try to over-control; allow the pieces to arrange themselves and then be prepared to react to them. This is the advice the Fortuna philosophy would give to shy people.

In terms of personal planning, when we enter into an active life in the world of chance, we should expect that nothing will succeed exactly as it is planned and, similarly, that the course of failure can seldom be apprehended in advance. To condemn ourselves for mistakes means that we could have known otherwise and chosen more wisely. But when we take a chance that something may work out, and it doesn't, that's not our fault. At each moment of our lives, we should consider all the available information, make the best possible assessment of the situation, and move forward actively, taking a chance that pleasure will result. In other words, we must step out of the safe, central domain, where most things are under our control, and enter the world of chance. If instead of the anticipated pleasure, something bad occurs, we just had bad luck. There is only one aspect of this process which is under our control — that's in choosing whether to be active and take that chance, or not to dare at all. The best advice we can give is to take that chance. A more regrettable mistake would have been made had we not stepped actively into the world of chance. Everything around us is changing rapidly, and we'd better change and grow with it.

A friend was berating herself for making a bad mistake. She recently had an opportunity to change jobs and she moved to South Carolina. Everything seemed fine, but after a few months her seven-year-old son began having a mysterious series of respiratory problems. He was in and out of hospitals for several months before doctors discovered the cause. Though he had never before shown any types of allergies, they found he had an extreme sensitivity to a type of flowering grass which is ubiquitous in South Carolina. "I feel so bad," she said. "If only we had stayed in Massachusetts, he would have been spared so much discomfort, not to mention losing almost a year of school. I'll never forgive myself. Now we have to move again but I'm afraid to choose. What if I make another mistake just as bad as this one?"

This friend is accepting responsibility for something that is really out of her control. An accident did happen; she thought that her family would be healthy and happy in South Carolina, and she did her best in choosing to move there in order to achieve that outcome. She was mistaken. But she's not to blame. If she had known that her son had a tendency to allergic sensitivities and hadn't consulted his doctor before the move about potential allergens in South Carolina, then she could have been blamed for carelessness. But the allergic reaction was unforeseen. The outcome was an accident; it was out of her control. It's not always possible to make the best choice when Fortuna is in the picture, but nothing is gained by blaming ourselves when things don't work out perfectly. We have to make our preparations and then, when we have to make a decision, make it.

Accidents like this happen all the time, whether we act or do not act. They can't be avoided and should not be used as an excuse for not acting. The ancients said, "Fortuna has the last word." Remember that the future along the unchosen path is also unknowable: had my friend stayed in Massachusetts, her son may have developed a sensitivity to an allergen there with even more serious consequences. He might have been run over by a truck or kidnaped! Maybe the choice she made really was the best for her son. She'll never know.

Blaming ourselves for these types of mistakes in life accomplishes nothing. It only results in making us passive. We flee from situations which are ripe with possibilities and we long for certainty. But maximum personal freedom is found when the future is unconstrained and abundant. If we avoid making choices for fear of making mistakes, we will drift aimlessly through life, completely out of control, reacting to things that happen to us but not acting and never learning.

Did you ever make a mistake? Think about it.
Ask yourself these questions:

- Are you really so certain that it would have turned out better in all respects had you chosen otherwise?
- Could you have known at the time that the other choice was preferable?
- Has the mistake made you passive and afraid to make future choices?
- Was it your fault or was it the work of factors beyond your control?

The Fortuna philosophy suggests:

WHY NOT LET FORTUNA SHARE THE RESPONSIBILITY FOR MISTAKES. IT WILL LIGHTEN YOUR BURDEN.

When we choose, we are the most free and alive. We step forward and influence our future. Accompanying us at that fork in the road we recognize the formerly invisible form of Fortuna. We make our choice (this is the expression of our freedom) but the outcome is determined jointly by our action and by chance.

One can castigate oneself for carelessness, stupidity, neglect or laziness, but not for being unable to perfectly predict the future. There is, however, only one mistake which can be regretted. Dante painted a vivid picture of souls in hell, tormented by visions of desired but lost opportunities — an invitation turned down, a friendship not pursued, a business opportunity not exploited. We perhaps make the biggest mistake of all when we turn our backs on life for fear of making mistakes. Of course, sometimes, when an opportunity which we do not want presents itself, the best action may be to reject it. But a student who wants to learn math can't learn if he gives up and doesn't even try the problem before him. To get what we want out of life, we have to trust ourselves and our preparations. We have to choose and act. Trusting in the benevolence, or at least the neutrality of Fortuna, we can take hold of opportunities and step off into the future. Mistakes are the tools we use in learning how to live. The realization that the future is uncertain not only provides us with a richer life consisting of many possibilities, but also frees us from some of the paralyzing fear of making mistakes. To cherish uncertainty, without fear of the mistakes that might accompany it, is to choose freedom.

THE MATRIX FOR CHAPTER 4

	A	B	C	D	E	F	G	H	I	J	K	L	M	N	O	P	Q	R	S	T	U	V	W	X	Y	Z
A	3	14	16	3	7	16	15	17	14	9	7	6	11	3	6	14	16	15	3	6	18	20	11	17	11	15
B	20	15	5	14	15	8	16	18	5	3	9	8	2	20	6	14	12	11	13	11	2	17	20	13	11	20
C	19	6	16	15	7	12	5	20	18	3	7	10	18	6	16	10	19	10	17	20	13	13	5	8	5	6
D	18	19	3	16	2	6	13	6	17	10	7	5	9	19	14	20	17	5	9	15	18	8	9	10	8	6
E	5	11	10	17	17	7	19	3	6	17	7	9	9	15	10	9	2	7	20	8	6	19	2	6	11	12
F	15	10	9	6	11	9	9	2	15	11	5	15	16	10	20	15	16	11	17	3	9	16	12	7	10	8
G	6	9	18	8	12	9	17	11	6	20	10	16	18	3	16	10	11	2	16	6	16	16	17	8	15	3
H	8	12	5	15	9	10	20	6	17	20	20	19	20	14	9	2	6	6	20	8	6	8	8	14	18	20
I	8	8	15	5	18	11	9	19	17	12	15	17	18	12	13	12	14	18	11	11	20	10	10	11	5	10
J	8	7	14	7	12	10	8	20	5	12	10	18	9	2	9	17	20	12	12	13	13	8	3	16	16	20
K	10	3	15	7	19	18	18	14	12	3	12	17	16	3	14	17	5	12	9	18	8	18	5	19	7	11
L	15	11	5	11	20	18	3	14	18	12	3	5	7	16	7	7	14	13	7	10	11	20	19	18	12	15
M	10	11	20	18	19	11	2	2	6	13	8	17	19	17	5	10	16	17	3	2	9	20	6	12	17	10
N	16	8	8	12	6	2	12	11	10	18	8	8	15	2	8	19	7	17	16	9	5	20	8	3	2	8
O	16	14	19	9	7	20	5	19	19	19	9	18	13	11	17	6	15	15	15	16	15	8	10	12	16	7
P	7	11	12	8	17	12	15	5	11	13	18	7	12	19	7	5	19	19	17	9	20	6	16	9	2	13
Q	6	6	10	6	16	16	15	11	19	11	10	18	16	15	16	18	16	2	19	18	10	6	7	8	9	18
R	3	18	17	5	5	16	15	10	10	11	13	5	12	9	3	20	20	3	11	3	17	12	13	5	20	5
S	16	10	15	15	20	9	10	11	5	8	7	2	15	20	16	8	19	17	14	18	7	3	15	3	20	18
T	14	6	20	12	15	13	12	16	6	15	19	11	15	20	8	5	16	10	17	15	15	8	12	19	13	5
U	15	2	7	20	6	17	3	19	15	20	18	15	7	8	8	19	7	8	7	5	5	5	5	5	13	20
V	15	9	5	10	8	15	7	7	13	2	16	7	20	14	18	15	19	11	3	5	19	19	19	14	14	11
W	13	9	7	10	14	18	12	5	17	6	20	16	9	6	14	2	17	17	9	10	10	18	7	5	9	11
X	20	20	14	15	14	16	14	16	15	5	9	20	20	12	13	5	20	7	19	12	10	8	19	2	6	6
Y	19	18	17	5	14	9	6	9	6	2	19	7	3	17	14	2	20	9	2	12	2	11	8	13	16	2
Z	12	18	20	18	5	10	9	16	5	8	2	8	16	13	2	8	12	12	8	16	15	8	18	2	11	20

On the chart, find the place where the initials you've chosen intersect. Read the chapter whose number appears at that intersection.

5

OPPORTUNITY

"In the field of opportunity it's plowing time again;
There ain't no way of telling where the seeds
will rise or when."

NEIL YOUNG,
© 1978 Silver Fiddle

Success in life depends, to a large extent, on the happy coordination of the right time, the right place, as well as the cooperation of other people and things. Whenever all these factors come together, we have a good, and sometimes a fantastic opportunity.

Happiness in life, however, depends on what we do when we are given a favorable opportunity. What we do, or whether we do anything at all, depends most of all on our own attitude towards opportunity. It is not enough just to be surrounded by good opportunities all the time. One has to learn how to identify them and, more importantly, one has to learn how to act as a fortunate individual when opportunities present themselves. What is an opportunity? How do we deal with it? Is it something to be feared? Is it proper to take advantage of opportunities? Is it all right to be called an opportunist?

When opportunity comes your way, remember:

- Fortuna is the Mother of opportunities
- this is a chance to act or not act
- uncertainty is not a threat, but an open door into the future
- opportunities are a natural phenomenon of life
- we are free to grasp or not to grasp them
- sometimes, it is better to do nothing; not to choose is to choose well
- Fortuna does not expect anything in return
- it is an invitation, not a command to act
- it is not possible to predict with certainty all the consequences of any action

---

Fortuna is known as the mother of opportunities. The word opportunity is related to the word Fortuna and refers to those things which the goddess brings. As Fortuna brings opportunities to humans, it is up to us to use them to our best advantage. Our attitude toward the idea of opportunity determines, to a large extent, the way we look at life and the way we live. An opportunity is a chance to act or not to act. The opportunity for action can only be brought by Fortuna. The reason so many people do not grasp opportunities when they occur is that they really do not believe that there is such a thing as chance. We will call such people "blocks," to distinguish them from those who follow Fortuna and her wheel — whom we will call round, or whole. These people are of two types: the religious blocks and the social blocks.

Religious blocks are the fatalistic types. They believe that our destinies have been decided for us in advance; that our future is already determined in the eyes of God or perhaps even written in the stars. Opportunities do not exist for these people for if it is written that they will be poor all their lives, then, it makes no sense to them to struggle in order to better their lot. As they see it, there is no chance in the world that they can strike it rich. Some blocks believe that we are born either saved or damned and there is nothing we can do to change this. Among these types of blocks, there are some who are more liberal and who believe that God does indeed place in front of us opportunities to do good. If we seize these opportunities, then, they claim, it means that we are among the chosen and thus will be saved. But as they see it, in the end, whether we choose to do something or not is not up to us but up to God.

The social blocks are the ones who say: "I don't belong there; that's not for me." Social blocks are legion among the poor. When they are urged to rise, or at least protest against the rich, they will respond: "What will happen to us poor souls without the rich? Who is going to care for us? Where is the money going to come from?" In the Public Television Series of *Upstairs, Downstairs,* the point that masters and servants are essentially different was made abundantly clear. One is born Upstairs to be a master or Downstairs to be a cook, a maid, or a butler. One cannot change his or her state in life. Only fools, or perhaps revolutionaries, believe otherwise and attempt to change the system.

It is not enough to claim that we are not fatalistic. We must also live our lives in ways that do not depend on fate. Even though many of us believe that we live in a classless society, we still deny ourselves numerous opportunities for social improvement. We say things like: "What's the use? You can't change the world. You can't fight City Hall." Social mobility is a gift of Fortuna. She encourages changes in social status. The daughter of a baker can become a judge. When presented with the opportunity, the son of a shoemaker can become a senator. We hear these things said daily, and yet, it appears that few people believe that this could really happen to them. They may even believe that there is something wrong about moving too high. They may be afraid of the disappointment of trying to change, and failing. It is not nice, after all, to be a social climber. It is even worse to be called an opportunist. So, people stay in their places, afraid to grasp opportunities. Parents who have never had the opportunity to go to college have mixed feelings about their sons and daughters going to college. On the one hand they feel very proud of the new social mobility of their children — "My son the doctor!" — but, on the other hand, they cannot avoid viewing with suspicion the whole world of education which allows for this very social mobility. Archie Bunker personifies this ambiguous attitude towards the whole realm of change, opportunity, and social mobility.

Religious and social blocks, people who believe that our place in heaven and our place in society have been decided for us at birth, espouse a world-view which has served as the ideological support of some specific types of social and political systems. Feudalism, a situation in which the aristocratic elite is allowed to rule without question, is a good example of both social and political stagnation. In our times, most dictatorships exist because both the rulers and the governed believe that it is their destiny to either rule or be ruled. They believe it is useless to try to change things. The rulers were born to rule and the rest of the people were born to follow orders and it will always remain that way. Dictatorships are not lands of opportunity. The dictator and his close circle of friends have imprisoned Fortuna and appropriated her opportunities. Opportunities, under a dictatorship, are for the very few, not for the bulk of the people.

The idea that even your child could one day become President of the United States is a revolutionary one. It belongs in the politics and philosophy of Fortuna. Destiny and Fortuna are mortal enemies in the religious, the social, and the political arenas. Belief in destiny means that everything is set in advance while a belief in Fortuna means that we are free to make what we want of our lives. Fortuna with her opportunities is the democratic entity par excellence and, in free democratic societies, she has full reign. Destiny, on the other hand, does not provide any opportunities. The word destiny itself has political overtones which place it at the far right of the political spectrum. Often, when you hear the word destiny, you may find some form of fascism behind it. Similarly, Communist Man is also destined. All totalitarian systems, fascist or communist, find their destiny in time; fascism looks toward the past, while communism looks toward the future.

FEAR OF SUCCESS

The world of Fortuna is the world of democracy and is filled with opportunities. As we go further and further into this present age of uncertainty, we will become more aware of the presence of Fortuna in world and human affairs. Uncertainty comes with Fortuna. Instead of perceiving uncertainty as a threat, we can see it as neutral open door into a future rich with opportunities. Uncertainty is a blessing for those who have begun to meaningfully answer the question, "What exactly is an opportunity?" People fail to succeed because they don't know very much about opportunities. It is too simplistic to say that they fail to succeed because they fear success. When they are said to fear success, it is probably because they simply do not know how to handle opportunities. Some do not even believe that there are such things as opportunities because to do so would put them in the position of having to admit that chance plays a major role in their world. Everything they have learned, at home, in church, and at school, has taught them that every effect has a cause and that things do not happen by chance. So, if they are presented with an opportunity they just won't believe it. Now, if you are given a raise or are promoted from lieutenant to captain, or from corporal to sergeant, there is almost no problem because these gradual changes are "in the line of things" and are, in a way, expected. An opportunity is, first of all, an unusual change, like a sergeant being promoted to the rank of officer, or a clerk being invited to become a manager. Secondly, an opportunity is a sudden change. Misunderstandings about these two facets of opportunity are common.

The current press is full of articles dealing with "fear of success." In a recent article on this subject (March 1983) by Bryce Nelson of the N.Y. Times Services, the general reader is given the current popular array of explanations for "fear of success." Bryce Nelson reports that a "debilitating fear of being successful, which some regarded in the 1970s as particularly prevalent among career-minded women, increasingly appears to be an abiding problem for members of both sexes. Indeed, at times, it seems to afflict almost everyone." One point is clear then, that both men and women fear success. The author also notes that "psychiatrists and psychologists say that they are still far from understanding all the reasons for fear of success."

As usual, as in most current literature on behavior for the general public, this journalist draws on Freudian theory to explain what he calls "this syndrome of self-sabotage." According to current theories about the mind, the person who is afraid is not you but a little person living inside of you who is, as they say, "rooted in the subconscious." Predictably, their little person fears other similarly fictitious little persons acting out their roles on a miniature puppet stage. The little person can be punished, cut off, or rejected by the other characters in this mental stage. Oedipus reigns supreme on this mental stage. It is as though people believe in the Oedipal triangle just as one may believe in the Holy Trinity.

In order to illustrate "fear of success" the journalist, Mr. Nelson, lists three examples of people who have sought psychiatric help for their "fear of success." In all three examples, the inhibiting force of the "daddy" appears prominently on the psychic stage. The "daddy" can be anybody: a principal, an officer, an actual father. Our Fortuna philosophy does not attempt to eliminate the role of these very important people in our lives. Instead, while recognizing that they do indeed play a significant role in determining our behavior, we also recognize that they contribute only one part of the many circumstances that control our behavior. The fortunate individual does not see the restrictive triangle of mommy, daddy, and me everywhere.

In the article's first example, "a talented, perfectionist teacher became extremely anxious after being made principal, the very job he wanted. The man's unconscious fears (the little person inside him, we would say) of the memory of his own angry father (here big daddy comes on stage) were somehow equated with the possibility of provoking that anger by taking on a job that would, in a sense, be competing with his father — the paternal role of principal."

Let us emphasize that we have no quarrel with the author of the article who did a beautiful reporting job on the psychological terrain of modern day America. Our quarrel is with the current and popular oedipal theory in which every situation, however diverse, is twisted and tormented until it can be reinterpreted in terms of the power struggles within the oedipal triangle. People are triangulated and forced to answer "daddy, mommy, me" to everything.

Under the Fortuna philosophy, the teacher would have been told that what he was facing in terms of becoming principal was an "opportunity." He would have been told that opportunities are a natural phenomenon of life. After discussing with him in detail what are opportunities, what is chance, and what does Fortuna stand for, he would have been told that grasping opportunities is all right. In essence, he should have been made to understand the fundamental fact that opportunities belong to Fortuna, not to daddy. He should have been made comfortable about refusing to continue as principal if that's what he wanted to do. It's all right to be just a teacher, a janitor, a cook, a nurse, a driver. All jobs have their own dignity, their own worth, their own bag of joys.

Conversely, while his psychic distress was alleviated by bowing to daddy, he could have been told that he also would have been happy as principal had he understood the nature of opportunity. Instead of being taught something about chance, a subject on which there is much ignorance in the world, the teacher was denied his opportunity, for, as the article states, "After he gave up the principal's spot and returned to the classroom, his disturbance disappeared."

The Fortuna philosophy teaches us that we are free to grasp or not to grasp opportunities when they are presented to us. Had our teacher understood the workings of chance in the affairs of men and women, he would have known that he could have become principal another time, under different circumstances, when he felt better disposed to become principal. However, under Freudian psychoanalysis, the poor triangulated teacher will no longer, in his life, want to be principal. He has been told that the principal is daddy. He has been indoctrinated into saying "daddy, mommy, me" to everything he sees or does. He has been taken; taken for a ride to the theater. To watch Oedipus.

The second example in the article previously mentioned deals with "the sergeant's syndrome." This is the fear of success demonstrated by noncommissioned officers when they are suddenly given a commission as an officer. Anybody who knows military life can appreciate that moving from sergeant to lieutenant is a very rare sort of promotion. One either goes to Officer Candidate School (OCS), or stays all his or her life as a sergeant. The difference between sergeants and officers is much like that between blue and white collar workers. Blue collar workers have their own career tracks and becoming foreman may, in some trades, represent one's highest achievement. Shifting to a desk job after twenty years in the shop is not something every worker looks forward to. People are often happier in environments which have proved rewarding through experience.

The type of promotion offered the sergeant fits the description of a typical opportunity. An opportunity is often a sudden and unexpected change. It is a change which can happen under special circumstances, like war for instance. It is a change which involves Fortuna. As the article says: "the sergeant often felt he had already achieved the limit of his aspiration and didn't want to be separated from the ordinary soldiers." What the sergeant was saying, if the World War II American psychiatrists who identified this syndrome in the Pacific theater had listened carefully, was that the sergeant felt that it seemed illogical, irrational, and almost illegal to shift from one imaginary "line of achievement" to another line. He saw his life as a linear progression in space with, "limits" at both ends of that imaginary line.

To become an officer, because of the circumstances of war, when officers are urgently needed, was for him a contradiction of the world as he saw it in his mind, a purely deterministic world where chance plays no role. People who have a deterministic view of life, a view where everything has to have a cause and where nothing is left to chance, these people have difficulty dealing with opportunities. There are two reasons for this: First, they don't trust opportunities because opportunities are like accidents and accidents have no place in the way they figure out the world. Second, they have little, if any, experience dealing with opportunities. They may even have in their minds some remnants of the old medieval wheel of Fortuna which taught humans for one thousand years (it's still in our language) that it was dangerous to seize opportunities; that it is evil to be opportunistic.

We are not trying to say that we must grab all opportunities. It's all right to let some opportunities slip by you. Sometimes it is better to do nothing. Not to make any choices is sometimes the best choice to make. The French essayist Montaigne said: "If there is nothing done, it means that I was in doubt whether I should make a choice because sometimes not to choose is to choose well, or that I may have decided finally not to choose at all." Montaigne puts it all in a few words which he borrowed from Cicero who in turn had borrowed the idea from the Greek philosopher Theophrastus: "Fortuna, not Reason, rules the life of humans."

Both the teacher and the sergeant in the above examples should be made to understand that Fortuna brings the opportunity but that she does not pressure us into accepting what she brings. It's all right to become a principal or an officer, and it's also all right to refuse. Nobody is going to get angry either way. Neither is particularly "meant to be."

That the problem has to do with a misunderstanding of Fortuna and not anything to do with daddy or mommy is very difficult to show because psychiatrists often quote patients who do indeed say "daddy and mommy." But patients speak like that because they have already been triangulated, rectangulated, or squared under the sign of Oedipus. Going back to our article, we read that one discontented ex-sergeant said "I'd rather be mother than father."

It seems that all psychoanalysts want to hear is "mommy, daddy, me." The psychoanalyst does not care about what a sergeant does. What interests these doctors is not what one does but what one is; not what happens but what comes out of it; not actions but objects and characters; not movement but still-pictures like photographs in a family album showing mommy, daddy, and you when you were five years old. Furthermore, psychoanalysis is offensive not only to sergeants but also to women for, according to the psychoanalysts, sergeants are mommies and officers are daddies (or bosses). The sergeant, as we recall, did say: "I'd rather be mother than father."

People work to receive rewards like money, working companions, etc. They do not go to work in order to play daddy and mommy. If we paid clerks as much as we pay managers, sergeants as much as captains, teachers as much as administrators, then "fear of success" would no longer be a problem to be dealt with by psychoanalysts and quite a few of them would be out of work. Indeed, the article reports that a certain psychoanalyst in Washington "has found that fear of success affects over half the patients he sees."

The Fortuna philosophy, on the other hand, views success and failure as having a lot to do with opportunities. Opportunities are created when Fortuna stirs up the environment. A philosophy of life which gives a larger role to chance (Fortuna) also gives a major role to the environment in cases of success or failure. People should not be made to feel bad if they fail, nor should they be overly praised when they succeed. The environment, with its circumstances and its opportunities, is the one to blame or to praise. People who are unemployed might not be lazy. Likewise, people who are rich may have inherited their wealth or Fortuna may have placed opportunities for success in their paths.

People do play a role in making their own happiness: They make choices, they seize opportunities. But the part the individual plays in running his or her life is only the smaller part. The larger portion of the success belongs to Fortuna. We can see now that the worst thing that happens to people when they are triangulated is that Fortuna is excluded. The most troublesome character in the trio of "daddy, mommy, me" is "Me." The "Me" character takes all the responsibility, all the guilt for everything that happens. The "Me" of psychoanalysis is alone in the world.

The article ends with another psychoanalyst's diagnosis of "a young man who had given up middle-class aspirations. 'I'm in bad shape if I win, and bad shape if I lose, so I'll drop out,' the youth said. The youth unconsciously fears not only earning his father's retaliation by succeeding, (because he would surpass his father), but also fears his father's criticism if he fails to succeed. 'Being afraid of both victory and defeat, the easiest thing is to do nothing,' the psychoanalyst says."

Again, our philosophy does not deny the role of our parents in explanations of why such things as "fear of success" happen. What we are saying is that "fear of success" is a much more complex matter than just "mommy, daddy, me" and that perhaps it involves more ignorance than fear. It involves a great deal of ignorance about the nature of an opportunity. People who understand opportunities are happier and more confident in both accepting and rejecting them.

Both the psychoanalytic method and our method guide and console patients who have turned down opportunities for success. However they differ in that ours goes beyond consolation and into encouragement. The psychoanalyst diagnoses the problem as "fear of success"; he then explains to the patient the source of the fear: He says "daddy" to his patients and sends them on their way. The patients leave his office with their fears neatly labeled and packaged. They may not have been encouraged to make any changes in their lives. On the other hand, our Fortuna philosophy actively encourages people to seize opportunities and it consoles them for missed opportunities. Fortuna brings opportunity and it is up to us to accept or reject whatever she brings. The fundamental difference between psychoanalysis and Fortuna is that daddy is possessive while Fortuna is generous. Better still, Fortuna doesn't care whether we seize her opportunities or not.

The philosophy of Fortuna goes way beyond mere consolation as it encourages us to change, to overcome fear, and never to fear in the first place. Fear of success originates in fear of uncertainty. As the patient begins to understand opportunities, he or she sees that the fear is not intrinsic to the situation but is only displaced fear of uncertainty. One of the things our philosophy can do is to help us make friends with uncertainty. More than being consoled, this philosophy encourages us to become successful.

We had to go into this development on psychoanalysis in order to free Fortuna from the clutches of all those who want to frame her inside a triangle or a square. We are now ready to continue on the marvelous adventure in search of the real nature of "opportunity." As we attempt to define what is an opportunity, we will always keep in sight the more important matter of trying to illustrate how one behaves in the presence of opportunity and how one can approach this mysterious world. It serves little purpose to know that something is a car if we do not know what to do with it. Our Fortuna philosophy has to do with events, with actions, and essentially with behavior. What interests us is not what is a car or who is the driver but how does the car work and what does a driver do.

CONSTRUCTIVE OPPORTUNISM

An opportunist is a person who knows how to deal with opportunities. The study of Fortuna advises us to pursue a variant of opportunism which is called "constructive opportunism." This is one of the most important lessons from the Fortuna philosophy. Opportunists are people who act according to circumstances and when faced with an opportunity are confident in their power to either accept or reject the possibility which is presented. They are aware that Fortuna rules the world and that opportunities are many and ready to be seized. Opportunities are the daughters of Fortuna.

Fortunate individuals practice constructive opportunism. We could say that a fortunate individual is also a constructive opportunist. Such a person is not afraid to create and take advantage of opportunities and he or she does it without harming other people. For instance, a constructive opportunist may be someone like Robert Rodale who pioneered the relationship between nutrition and health and who founded the successful magazine "Prevention." Since he honestly believed that information on nutrition would help millions of people find better health, he did not hesitate to merchandise his findings and to take a chance with his money. Constructive opportunists deserve every penny they can make. Health magazines are opportune as they are particularly fitting and suitable to our society today with its emphasis on physical fitness. Things that are opportune are seasonable, timely, and fit exactly the demands of the time or occasion.

However, nutrition advice can be either constructively or destructively opportune. The constructively opportune magazines actually help those who could benefit from their advice, by providing safe and tested information. The destructively opportune health books are those which are merely stylish and faddish. They take advantage of their readers and can perhaps do more harm than good.

There is nothing wrong then with being an opportunist as long as we act constructively. Popular ethics tells us that it is bad to be an opportunist. It's not polite to "grab" things. Fear of being labelled an opportunist prevents many of us from taking advantage of the many wonderful opportunities that Fortuna brings us. Instead of going along with this blanket disapproval of opportunism, we would like to invite our readers to consider the positive side of opportunism. Being an opportunist requires both courage and a willingness to work hard. Writing a good health magazine takes both. As Jimmy Cliff's song says: "You can get it if you really want, but you must try, try, and try."

SYMBOLS OF OPPORTUNITY

In order to become a constructive opportunist, we need to better understand the nature of opportunities. As we look at the history of the idea of opportunity, from the Middle Ages, through the Renaissance and into the modern Age of Uncertainty, we begin to have a much richer perspective on what this concept has meant to people throughout the ages and we, ourselves, will perhaps begin to see other alternatives for dealing with them. Symbols, such as the razor, the forelock, the wings, the sail, the wind, the sea, and the tides, were often attached to paintings, drawings, or statues of Fortuna and will be discussed in this chapter as they illustrate attributes of the concept of opportunity. Becoming familiar with them will teach us lessons in dealing with opportunities. Other familiar symbols associated with Fortuna, including the wheel, the cornucopia, the rudder, the clock, the blindfold, and the ball, are more thoroughly discussed elsewhere.

Symbols and meanings:

the razor	narrowness of time
the forelock	missed opportunity
the wings	opportunity is fleeting
the sail	events can be mastered
the wind	opportunity is free
the sea	opportunity is unstable
the tide	opportunities return
the wheel	opportunity is cyclical
the cornucopia	opportunities are abundant
the rudder	opportunity is controlled by Fortuna
the clock	opportunity is a chunk of time
the blindfold	opportunities are given without discrimination
the ball	opportunities are unstable

The future belongs to those fortunate individuals who are constructive opportunists and lovers of Fortuna. How does one become such an individual? We can start by examining closely what exactly an opportunity is. An opportunity is almost the same thing as an occasion or "a chunk of time during which something may or may not happen." If we see someone we would like to meet, at a conference, a party, a bus stop, or a bar, we have a limited amount of time to make our move. During that time interval, the opportunity is open to us. An opportunity, then, is first of all a piece of time. This is the definition given by Cicero some two thousand years ago. Now, this time, during which something may or may not happen, is brief. The symbol of the razor is used to remind us of the brevity of an opportunity.

During the Renaissance, people used cartoon-like images to illustrate ideas. These curious little drawings which they called "emblems" made it easier for people to remember things and to teach them to others. The emblems were a sort of illustrated shorthand for recording and recalling ideas. Thus, to record and recall the idea of chance, people would rely on pictures of a woman called Fortuna. The same picture of Fortuna was used to illustrate the notions of chance, occasion, and opportunity. Sometimes the Renaissance artists would write Fortuna under a picture of the goddess and other times they would write Occasion even though the pictures were of women who were virtually identical. At one time it seemed that the name Occasion was going to replace Fortuna as the name of the goddess. The names Fortuna and Occasion became interchangeable as both conveyed the ideas of chance and opportunity.

Fortuna was represented holding a razor in her hand. The razor stood for the narrowness of the slice of time and the brevity of the period in which we can decide whether or not to seize an opportunity.

So, when we want to remind ourselves or others that the edge of time between opportunity approaching and opportunity past is narrow, we simply picture with our mind's eye the image of a woman holding a razor in her hand. That chunk of time is an invitation to act; but only an invitation, not an imposition or a command.

An opportunity approaches, becomes available, and then passes us by. Renaissance thinkers stressed the point that an opportunity must be grasped or lost forever. In order to illustrate this, the artists who drew pictures of Fortuna some four hundred years ago drew a woman with a forelock, a wisp of hair streaming from the front of her head. With the exception of this forelock, her head was bald.

The woman with the forelock was Fortuna in her specific role as Lady Opportunity. Her forelock was a simple way to help us remember that we must grasp an opportunity as it approaches — grasping Lady Opportunity by her forelock — otherwise, once Opportunity has passed us by, we will be unable to grasp her, since the back of her head is bald. We can grasp her coming but not going! It's too late then. These old emblems encapsulated the wisdom of the ages. The first advice is that time to act, once given an opportunity, is very limited; secondly, that once we let an opportunity go by, it is irretrievably lost. The razor reminds us of the first aspect and the forelock of the second. Once we have made up our minds to act, we should remember to do so quickly. To symbolize this necessary haste, artists pictured Fortuna with wings on her back or at her feet suggesting that Fortuna is swift and fleeting.

This advice about opportunities is still useful today with minor but important modifications which must be made to them in order to adapt them to our times and circumstances. Faced with an opportunity, we must keep in mind two important precautions: First, we must act constructively. For instance, when oil companies act in the most socially responsible manner, they will seize an opportunity to dig for oil, while at the same time, taking necessary measures to avoid such harmful effects as oil spills. They can take advantage of opportunities while protecting and preserving the environment. This is constructive opportunism.

Secondly, we must act quickly but cautiously, or, as the United States Supreme Court put it in its 1954 Desegregation Decision, "with deliberate speed." This important advice concerning the need to act promptly and decisively but at the same time, slowly and cautiously, was symbolized by the painters of old in their illustrations of a young man rushing to grasp Fortuna by her forelock while another female figure representing Wisdom restrained the youth. This youth, pictured between Fortuna and Wisdom, stood for any one of us. We all require wisdom to deal effectively with the opportunities brought by Fortuna and to restrain ourselves from rushing too quickly and heedlessly after them.

THE CONTRAST WITH MACHIAVELLI

The lesson conveyed by the emblem of the youth being restrained, however gently, by Wisdom as he dashes impetuously to grasp Fortuna by the forelock, could be summarized as "with deliberate speed." As constructive opportunists, we should always be ready to grasp the opportunities that Fortuna presents us but should be cautious not to engage in reckless behavior. This contrasts with the advice which Machiavelli gave in the Renaissance to his contemporaries on dealing with opportunities. In *The Prince,* he recommended the sort of behavior which we might call reckless.

> *It is better to be impetuous than cautious, because Fortuna is a woman and it is necessary to cuff and maul her in order to keep her under. She lets herself be more often overcome by men using these ways than by men who proceed with calm; therefore, like a woman, she is always the friend of young men, because they are less cautious, more spirited, and they master her with more boldness.*

What we are advocating here in the Fortuna philosophy is not Machiavellian for we, on the contrary, do not place expediency and self-interest above morality. Our advice concerning opportunities is more suitable to modern times and modern attitudes toward women. Until recently, most philosophical systems were unable to deal with apparent contradictions. Everything had to be either black or white. The Fortuna philosophy, on the other hand, is quite at ease with contradictions. People and things can be both good and bad at the same time. The poets of the Renaissance exalted the delights of the "bittersweet." There are ways to be both impetuous and cautious. There are ways to win a race by maintaining a cautious rate of speed. There are ways to win a woman (or a man) by being both bold and courteous at the same time. Our actions can be bold and decisive and, at the same time cautious and gentle; gentle with people and with the environment. We must be gentle with Fortuna most of all, for she stands for the chance-like events and elements of the world around us, made up of people, animals, plants, and resources.

In the face of opportunity, act

- constructively
- quickly, but cautiously
- promptly, but with deliberate speed
- boldly, but gently
- decisively, but courteously

The Fortuna philosophy is at ease wth contradictions:

- hurry up slowly

If we are kind to Fortuna, she in turn will be kind and generous to us. The generosity of Fortuna is boundless as is evidenced by the cornucopia carried by the goddess in Renaissance emblems. The words "Machiavellian" and "Machiavellism" have acquired negative connotations in today's language. However, Machiavelli was not wrong for his times. Some aspects of his theories are just too extreme in terms of modern values. He was an expert on Fortuna, having dedicated many years of scholarly study on the subject. Much of his teachings on Fortuna, as well as his insights into the nature of chance, can be very relevant to our times. Some of his better advice can be seen in one passage of *The Prince,* wherein he compares Fortuna to a river which

> *when angry, turns the plains into lakes, throws down the trees and buildings, takes earth from one spot, puts it in another . . . Yet though such it is, we need not therefore conclude that when the weather is quiet, men cannot take precautions by building both embankments and dykes, so that when the waters rise, either they go off by a canal or their fury is neither so wild nor so damaging. The same things happen about Fortuna. She shows her power where strength and wisdom do not prepare to resist her, and directs her wrath where she knows that there are no embankments or dykes ready to stop her.*

There are two general types of opportunities: First, those that occur unexpectedly like a sudden discovery of a job vacancy for which we are qualified. Second, those that occur with some regularity, like floods. We discover from Machiavelli that Fortuna favors us when we are prepared to face both types of opportunities.

Will you know an opportunity when you see it?

- An opportunity is an unusual or sudden change.
- An opportunity is a chunk of time during which something may or may not happen.
- Opportunities are sometimes unexpected, sometimes periodic.

During the Renaissance, and even more so since then, individuals gained more and more confidence in their ability to take advantage of the forces in their environment. In order to make this very point, the artists of that period pictured Fortuna holding a sail. If the breeze signifies that which the environment provides, then, the sail, because it is man-made, signifies our mastery of events. When we wish to remember that we have a hold on things brought about by chance, like the wind, we can think of the sail held by Fortuna. In addition, we will be reminded by the sail (when we picture it with our mind's eye), that we are encouraged to take advantage of opportunities.

The sail was pictured in the hand of Fortuna, a beautiful young woman, against the background of the sea. The symbol of the sea leads us to one of the most important aspects of opportunity. You may recall that the forelock meant that an opportunity cannot be grasped once it is past. Now, the motif of the sea and that of the tide in particular modify in a positive and optimistic manner the message of the forelock. The trouble with the forelock alone is that it implies that an opportunity, once past, may be gone forever. The tide, on the other hand, tells us that some opportunities do return, that Fortuna is cyclical. This aspect of her nature was, of course, already apparent in the wheel of Fortuna, the wheel being the best illustration of her cyclicity.

The tide reminds us that the environment periodically brings favorable conditions to us. If we don't get our promotion this time, there'll always be another chance next time. We can be confident that opportunities will continue to present themselves to us. If we have just lost the love of our life, let us not despair; there are many others out there who can be a suitable match for us. Our chance will come again. So, the sea and the tide pictured behind Fortuna will help us remember not only the variability and mutability of Fortuna, but also, and more importantly, her accessibility and her favorable disposition towards the well-prepared, patient, fortunate individual who practices constructive opportunism.

NEW REMEDIES FOR REGRET

Fortuna's cyclicity is more at home in modern times than it has been in the past. Most people during the Renaissance were not as comfortable with Fortuna as it is possible for us to be today. The prevalent idea in those days was that of the flight of time. The passage of time was then, and still is for many of us today, a notion which fills people with fear and anxiety. We are often oppressed by the idea that it will be too late; that we will have missed a good opportunity. While people in the Renaissance believed optimistically that individuals were the makers of their own fortune, at the same time, they made themselves miserable by thinking that grasping Fortuna was an obligation. Not to grasp an opportunity would be a failure which would be their fault. This notion was most clearly expressed by the French Renaissance poet Gilles Corrozet who wrote these lines under an illustration picturing Fortuna holding a sail and standing on a wheel floating in the sea:

"Hurry and grasp the opportunity when it
approaches, for if you let it escape,
you will regret it."

Regret is foreign to the fortunate way of living. Fortunate individuals learn not to regret missed opportunities. What happens is past. We should forgive and forget. Renaissance literature and art is full of the anxiety-ridden notion of missed opportunities. Shakespeare in the Tempest suggests this most common of then-prevalent themes, that of "lost opportunities:"

"By accident most strange, bountiful Fortune
If now I court not, but omit, my fortunes
Will ever after droop."

We have to free ourselves from the regret of not having acted at the right time. Not having grasped an opportunity in the past was perhaps not a mistake, as it is impossible to predict with certainty all the consequences of any action. Our actions and decisions unlock only one gate at a time to many different paths into the future. Just as we should not be afraid to grasp opportunities today, we should also not make ourselves miserable for missed opportunities in the past.

The cyclicity of Fortuna represented by her wheel and by the tide is one of the most important aspects of our learning to live in the present Age of Uncertainty. Fortuna's cycles open to us the possibility of an ever-returning abundance of opportunities that we are free to seize or not to seize. The difficulty is that old ways of thinking about Fortuna and her opportunities may make it difficult to adjust to a quickly changing world. On the one hand, people may fear to grasp opportunities. This is due to what we may call the Middle Ages syndrome when people were taught not to climb on the wheel of Fortuna. On the other hand, people can make themselves miserable for missing opportunities. This is the Renaissance syndrome.

We believe that our new way of interacting with Fortuna goes along with a realistic up-to-date view of the world. During the Renaissance, both the ancient idea of Fate and the view of a punishing Fortuna who turns the squared wheel of the Middle Ages were updated. People began living more comfortably and thus came to regard Fortuna as less menacing. They also began viewing Fortuna as a divinity they could deal with, cajole, pray to, and bring over to their side. By glancing at the many pictures of Fortuna, we can see that, in the Renaissance, she became more casual and friendly. The artists of the Middle Ages had pictured her as a portly matron, fully clothed, and wearing a crown as she turned her wheel. In the Renaissance, by contrast, the artists drew her in the form of a young, attractive woman who was always pictured nude, a sign of evolving and more tolerant social mores.

The attitude toward Fortuna in the Renaissance was tainted with a certain element of machismo. Authors like Machiavelli believed that the individual could and must dominate Fortuna. While we agree with their advice about the need for readiness of response in dealing quickly and decisively with circumstances, we draw the line at the advice to aggressively pursue each and every opening. These authors insisted on the old adage that "Fortuna favors the bold." People were thus encouraged to be active and to grab Fortuna violently by the hair of her forelock. If you let her go, she will be gone forever, they said.

This view of opportunity was not very satisfactory since it tended to focus too strongly on lost opportunities. It was, in some ways, a worse solution than the one that had prevailed during the Middle Ages; instead of blaming Fortuna, people began now blaming themselves: "If only I had done this or that!" "I missed my chance." "It's my own fault." "I let that opportunity go." We must cure ourselves of the apparent obligation that if we do not seize opportunities, we will inevitably suffer from regret. In essence we must get rid of the forelock of Opportunity, or "un-lock" it. The forelock and the baldness must be discarded as old relics of backward ways for dealing with chance. Unlocking Opportunity (conceptualizing Opportunity without a forelock) is thus a liberalizing process in line with modern attitudes towards opportunity.

We advocate a new way of thinking about opportunities which is built on a synthesis of past foundations. We have learned from the mistakes as well as from the achievements of history. Running through the evolution of the idea of opportunity, we can see that the old ways of thinking about chance and opportunity are still among us. There are many people in the world today who use either the Ancient, the Medieval, or the Renaissance concepts of opportunity.

Our modern conception of Fortuna and her opportunities is based on the principle that chance events, accidents, everything that happens is not caused by Fortuna (the Middle Ages view), or the Individual alone (the Renaissance view), but rather by both the individual and Fortuna. She brings; we take or leave. We should cure ourselves of the delusion that merit and blame belong exclusively either to external Fortuna or to the inner individual. The fortunate individual answers: "I did my best." and "There'll be another chance." She or he feels that it is never too late. The success of Continuing Education programs which advocate life-long learning is an indication that people feel that chances and opportunities do come again. New beginnings are possible. While a world of rapid changes brings with it an increase in disruptions, new structures will continually be created. Alongside statistics which reflect the current high divorce rate, for example, there is also evidence of a parallel increase of remarriages.

Opportunities are essentially the building blocks of a configuration of reality which includes time as its main component. Life must be understood as a series of events led by Fortuna through the fields of time. Fortuna leads her daughters, Opportunities, together with their friends, the fortunate individuals, through the land of time and circumstance.

THE MATRIX FOR CHAPTER 5

	A	B	C	D	E	F	G	H	I	J	K	L	M	N	O	P	Q	R	S	T	U	V	W	X	Y	Z
A	17	10	19	6	12	4	12	4	13	6	9	12	17	10	3	20	18	19	10	3	19	14	16	16	7	20
B	12	6	9	16	11	15	9	11	13	2	2	19	9	14	4	16	10	10	15	7	19	13	11	7	15	4
C	11	4	3	18	13	6	17	9	17	2	8	7	8	14	6	11	14	14	20	19	12	11	18	20	19	13
D	16	12	4	13	3	17	9	20	2	11	9	15	16	3	17	10	13	10	19	18	10	10	10	15	6	19
E	6	18	12	13	18	13	13	20	15	14	4	13	6	3	18	17	19	17	11	7	17	6	7	9	19	3
F	9	2	11	4	20	12	16	12	16	18	6	13	11	16	12	20	17	7	11	16	4	13	4	18	11	11
G	11	18	16	7	20	4	20	2	8	14	7	6	11	6	19	14	10	19	20	11	14	8	15	19	7	11
H	13	15	10	8	15	4	12	14	13	4	6	16	18	8	19	6	17	17	3	3	12	2	6	11	10	18
I	11	17	10	19	13	2	3	17	2	6	3	14	19	20	9	15	11	12	19	4	3	18	9	19	2	12
J	14	4	13	20	2	15	11	15	12	17	9	13	4	12	20	11	2	18	13	3	6	12	11	8	13	16
K	15	16	12	3	17	11	3	19	6	2	17	4	20	11	6	8	10	3	12	13	11	4	13	9	10	13
L	3	8	9	15	13	8	10	15	7	6	14	9	20	7	17	12	8	3	8	12	3	12	17	19	2	11
M	9	12	9	4	3	20	13	20	13	7	16	13	7	9	12	8	2	7	14	19	19	15	13	6	6	2
N	18	6	17	16	18	12	7	13	6	20	3	14	20	12	3	9	20	6	12	20	2	16	7	4	8	11
O	6	10	17	14	2	2	18	14	14	8	16	6	20	20	4	11	7	10	12	8	4	2	11	16	3	6
P	6	4	2	3	19	3	11	7	3	2	9	3	8	6	20	12	10	13	12	6	7	15	6	17	15	8
Q	15	10	11	10	10	20	19	4	16	19	17	20	10	20	10	9	9	14	12	4	13	15	10	18	19	20
R	10	11	19	12	2	14	9	12	13	16	3	16	7	17	4	9	19	19	19	12	14	2	18	11	16	8
S	9	20	20	19	3	7	14	12	16	4	20	8	10	7	14	4	15	2	13	6	19	15	17	17	11	7
T	20	11	19	10	7	18	18	10	15	10	7	2	7	13	3	17	10	4	11	8	3	2	8	7	12	8
U	4	16	15	16	2	12	17	2	13	18	8	9	4	18	15	9	20	12	8	2	16	12	8	12	3	11
V	19	10	3	15	18	18	9	4	10	8	14	12	7	3	3	19	6	10	12	19	20	2	13	2	8	13
W	12	16	19	19	7	19	2	17	7	3	13	11	6	9	11	6	12	4	18	16	2	10	2	11	8	3
X	17	15	13	7	8	15	4	18	3	8	10	17	4	9	15	12	13	13	2	3	13	10	10	11	16	16
Y	11	20	4	20	2	19	17	2	20	7	4	10	7	12	15	7	10	3	11	18	4	13	18	6	19	3
Z	15	7	12	14	19	16	3	4	12	3	20	10	7	10	14	12	15	19	18	15	17	6	14	7	8	19

On the chart, find the place where the initials you've chosen intersect. Read the chapter whose number appears at that intersection.

6

COINCIDENCE

In 1950, *LIFE* magazine reported that on one day in March of that year, all fifteen members of a church choir in Beatrice, Nebraska were late for practice. The reasons each member of the choir gave were quite ordinary; the minister, his wife, and daughter were late because his wife waited until the last minute to iron her daughter's dress; one girl was finishing her homework; one had car trouble; two lingered to hear the end of an especially exciting radio program; one was napping, and so on. Altogether, there were ten different and quite unconnected reasons for the tardiness of the fifteen people. The time of practice was set for 7:20 PM. At 7:25 the church building was destroyed by an explosion. No one was in the church; no one was hurt.

Recently, television reported the story of twins who had been adopted at birth and raised by different families. They rediscovered one another as adults. They both had been named Jim, married women named Linda, were divorced, then married women named Betty. They both drove Chevrolets and lived in big, white Victorian houses, with well-stocked workshops in their basement, and an ornamental iron bench painted white girdled the large old trees in both their backyards. Also, they were both crazy about fishing.

Some friends were bicycling in upstate New York after visiting New York City to see one of their brothers off on an adventure — a boat trip up the Amazon. In a small town they stopped in at the combination general store/service station for some help with a flat tire. As they chatted with the manager, they discovered that his son had just left for the same adventure and would be travelling up the Amazon River in exactly the same boat.

On July 4, 1826, exactly fifty years after signing the Declaration of Independence, two former presidents and giants of the American Revolution, Thomas Jefferson and John Adams, died within hours of one another.

An acquaintance was travelling in the south of Spain. He knew his family originated from a small town up in the mountains, and had visited there, but now he was sampling the night life in the seaside resort of Torremolinos. After a flamenco show, striking up a conversation with a gypsy who had been singing, he mentioned that the next day he was planning to go to Marbella, fifty miles to the west. The gypsy insisted that, no, he should instead go east to the Caves of Nerja, which were an unforgettable sight. This was the first time he had even heard of these caves and he decided to visit them. The next day on the bus he asked the conductor for a ticket to the Caves of Nerja and was handed a ticket punched for the village of Maro where the caves were located. The name was faintly familiar. He knew his father had come from a place named Maro but had no idea where it might be located. He never expected that it might even be in this region. It turned out that the caves of Nerja were located in his ancestral village and that day was spent excitedly exploring the crumbling ruins of a family castle, peering into the gardens of a seaside villa whose beauty had been described by his mother, talking to a peasant who had been taught to read by his grandfather, and eating figs on a path down to the beach, as his father had described doing when he was a boy.

We all have our favorite stories of coincidences. In a public area of the railroad station in Geneva, Switzerland, one of the authors of this book, who was inquiring about timetables, met the chairperson of his department who was just passing through. Also, when he began his university teaching career, he inherited an office that had been previously occupied by a specialist on the Italian Renaissance. This professor had left behind several books. In browsing through one, our author discovered that it contained confirming evidence for a theory he had developed concerning how a famous 16th-century French masterpiece had been written. There is no way his researches could ever have logically led him to this book. The other author of this book has a friend in California. Regularly, perhaps every two months, they call one another. One night she picked up the phone to dial his number but didn't get a dial-tone, so she hesitated and didn't dial. The line sounded funny so she said "Hello." Her friend answered. He had just dialed her number and she had picked up her phone before it rang.

Coincidences like these are spooky. When they happen, we are tempted to think that they are caused by some force, be it natural or supernatural. In 1861 the German spectroscopist Kirchhoff was comparing sixty lines in the spectrum of iron with the same sixty lines in the spectrum of the sun and found many similarities. He calculated that "... the probability that this coincidence is a mere work of chance is ... considerably less than 1 over two raised to the 60th power ... and hence this coincidence must be produced by some cause ..." From this he correctly concluded that there must be some iron in the makeup of the sun. His type of reasoning seems to suggest that if we find a needle in a haystack it is so unlikely an occurrence that someone must have placed it in our path. When this type of reasoning is applied to coincidences like those which began this chapter, we attempt to deny the role of chance in creating the coincidence and search for some unknown cause to which it can be attributed. The minister in the first example believes the existence of God has been proven for He palpably showed His hand in the miracle of sparing the members of the church choir. The TV announcer, commenting on the case of the twins, began to speculate on just how extensive is the influence of our genes on the social details of our life. Our acquaintance who travelled in Spain had an eerie feeling that the gypsy had supernatural powers and that his ancestors were sending him a message to visit his ancestral home. Several minutes of a coast-to-coast long-distance phone call were spent discussing the possibility of mental telepathy. The search for reasons behind coincidences can sometimes lead to legitimate conclusions in science, but too often it can lead to unscientific, irrational explanations.

Some coincidences are pleasant and fruitful, leading perhaps to new discoveries. This is called serendipity. Some are worrisome and puzzling. But they are always interesting. Coincidences are events that have a small, extremely small, probability of occurrence. If an event has a probability of 1/1,000,000 (one in a million), that means that we might expect this thing to occur just once in a long series of one million happenings. In other words, it is a rare event. The smaller the probability, the more rare the event and the more unlikely it is to occur. But just because an event is rare, should we attach any significance to it? Must there be mysterious forces (other than chance) at work when an extremely rare event occurs? Should we perk up and be astonished? Is it even interesting?

Well, interest is a subjective state. Some people are interested in baseball; some won't even glance at the most outstanding and exciting plays. An objective index of interest, applicable to coincidences and other events of low probability, was developed by Professor Warren Weaver in 1948. He calls an event "surprising" if the probability of its happening is not only small, but also small when compared to the probability of other things which might also have happened. For example, if we were dealt a typical bridge hand consisting of A-K-J-6 of hearts, 10-2 of spades, A-Q-J-10-5 of clubs and 9-3 of diamonds, this is a very rare event. The probability of this particular hand is less than 1 in 635 billion. But while this is very rare, the hand is not very interesting or surprising. It is a very ordinary hand. The probability of any other specific hand occurring is exactly the same, 1 in 635 billion. We know that one hand or the other had to be dealt so the occurrence of any particular hand does not seem very exciting to us.

A somewhat different situation occurs when a coin is spun into the air and lands on a flat table. The probability of it landing precisely on its edge and staying there is, shall we say, one in a billion. Since the probabilities for all possible events must add up to one, the probability of landing on one side or the other is just under one-half. When this coin is spun, three things could happen, heads (probability about ½), tails (probability about ½), or edge (probability one in one billion). Either heads or tails is expected; this would be probable, uninteresting, and not rare. But if the coin lands on its edge, we would be in the presence of an outstanding event, both improbable, rare, and interesting. According to Dr. Weaver, seeing the coin on its edge is "surprising" even though it is 635 times more likely than the ordinary unsurprising bridge hand described above, because the probability of its happening is so small compared to the probabilities of any of the other possible outcomes. It's the relative size of the probabilities involved, not the absolute size, that draws our attention to coincidences. Our interest is not excited merely when some event which has an extremely low probability occurs, but when the probability of that event is much lower than the probabilities of other events which could occur.

An application of this principle explains why a bridge hand of all spades is so surprising. When it is dealt, play will often be interrupted, people will gather around to exclaim, and letters to the editor will be sent describing this remarkable event. If it happens at home, no one will believe you did not stack the deck! The all-spades hand has exactly the same probability of occurring as the nondescript hand described above, but people find it surprising. Why? The reason is this: we mentally divide the outcomes of shuffling and dealing into the categories of perfect hands (all of one suit) and imperfect hands (all others). The probability of the first outcome is very tiny, 4 in 635 billion, while the probability of the second is almost certainty. The relative difference in the sizes of the probabilities accounts for the surprising nature of the perfect hand. We ourselves divide events, even equally likely events, into a small class of unusual events and the much larger class of usual events. There are more events in the class of usual events so the probability of a usual event occurring is much higher than the probability of an unusual event. Hence when an unusual event occurs, it "surprises" us.

However, unusual and coincidental events can be seen in another light, the light of the variety of the natural world, and in this light the mystery surrounding the occurrence of even surprising and "interesting" coincidences is transformed into something much more natural, and indeed even expected.

Consider, for example the case of the all-spades hand. Under very modest assumptions about the size of the bridge playing population of the United States and the frequency of play, it can be predicted that a perfect hand can be expected to occur somewhere about once a year.

So even this surprising event becomes a relatively common newspaper story and everyone has heard about this "remarkable" coincidence. Coincidences do not have to be seen as arising from the actions of mysterious forces, such as Fate, God, or the supernatural world. They happen quite regularly and automatically whenever similar circumstances are repeated a large number of times. They are merely a consequence of the immense multiplicity of events which come into our lives by the workings of chance. They are the natural daughters of Fortuna.

The coincidences we encounter in ordinary life can be explained much like card hands. They are complex events randomly dealt out of a large deck of possible factors. Every event that occurs is a coincidence: each everyday event that occurs, even seemingly simple ones like drinking our morning cup of coffee, has a complicated and rare structure. It is not exactly like any other event. In order for this particular event to occur exactly the way it did, a large number of unrelated factors had to come together in an improbable manner. The probability of my drinking this cup of coffee at this time in this manner out of this cup is extremely small. But it is an ordinary event, so it does not seem surprising. On the other hand, some events, like those coincidences described at the beginning of this chapter, are like the all-spades hand. We sense that they have an unusual structure and hence place them in a special small class of events which are then relatively less likely to occur than other ordinary events. This accounts for our surprise when we encounter them. The probability of each and every one of our everyday events (like a particular card hand) is very low. But since there are so many events happening all the time (like the numerous card games), we should regularly expect to observe surprising coincidences (like the all-spades hand). These unusual life events which we call coincidences are, on the one hand, very surprising but, on the other hand, not uncommon.

Another way that variety and multiplicity account for coincidence is this: Consider the case of the twins who had so many traits in common. If we were to list all of their characteristics, including the names of their children, where they spend their vacations, the brand of beer they drink, the color of their cars — the list is endless! — there are many possible places where one of these traits could have matched the corresponding trait in the other twin. Even in totally unrelated people, if one tries long enough, one can find several accidental similarities. These coincidences are revealed all the time in cocktail party chatter. It's not surprising that the twins had some traits in common. It would have been even more surprising had an intensive search turned up no similarities at all between them.

This fact, that with a large number of possibilities one should expect some exact matches, is at the basis of the success of daily astrology columns. By casting a broad enough net, they trap us into finding correspondences between the subjects they mention and some event in our daily lives. Again, the traveler who met a colleague in Geneva had many acquaintances; in addition at every moment he has to be somewhere. It's not too surprising that at some place he met someone he knows. Coincidences like this happen regularly, every day, but when they happen in exotic places or under unusual circumstances they strike us as mysterious.

If one were to shuffle the deck of factors which go into the makeup of ordinary events and "deal" any event, that particular event would have a very low probability. But events are occurring all the time and are so numerous that we should regularly expect some events of low relative probability to occur. Often these events will have unusual structures, as those at the beginning of this chapter. But coincidences are not unusual and they happen all the time. Remember this when someone calculates that an event has an extremely low probability and therefore "must be produced by some cause." Events like this do happen regularly, but for no reason at all! The only mysterious force behind the stories with which we began this chapter is the abundance and variety of chance operating in our everyday lives.

Look around you. Examine your surroundings. Examine the events that you are passing through at this moment. Try to focus your attention on what is accidental in your present circumstances. Look for the coincidences, both small and large. Each time you do this, you will see the handiwork of Fortuna and become more aware and more responsive to the role of chance in your life.

The cornucopia of Fortuna represents this constant abundance and multiplicity of events which, by turn, results in the regular occurrence of coincidence. The fact that coincidence abounds and that each one of us has his or her particular story to tell is witness both to the frequency with which coincidences do happen, and to the power of chance as an active force in everyday lives. When we encounter a striking coincidence, there is no need to superstitiously imagine mysterious forces at work. Coincidences are signs of the presence of chance in the world and should be expected to occur.

The word coincidence comes from two Latin words, "co" meaning "together" and "incidere" meaning "to fall upon" or "to happen." Thus two things that fall together coincide. In geometry a coincidence occurs when two figures which are identical are placed so that one covers the other. Things may "fall together" either in time or space. Two people can meet if they happen to be in the same place at the same time, but love occurs only if they both "fall" in love. Mutual love at first sight is indeed one of the most marvelous coincidences in the universe, yet it happens all the time. Fortuna is in one of her most alluring guises as the entity who brings lovers together.

And yet, the fundamental coincidence which shows our eternal indebtedness to Fortuna has not yet been mentioned. This coincidence is essentially different from the coincidences of everyday life which are as common as being dealt an all-spades hand. It has the even more rare quality of surprise and uniqueness, like a coin landing on its edge. Billions of years ago there was no life on this planet. Scientists now believe that the purely accidental concatenation of primitive amino acids which accidentally fit together, in an environment consisting of the proper chemicals and energy, was responsible for the creation of all life. The probability of this not happening is as certain as the probability of the coin landing either heads or tails instead of on its rim. However the unexpected did happen; the almost absolute certainty that this would not happen still left the door of possibility open just enough to allow life to begin. It is as if the coin had landed on its edge and stayed there. If there is even the slightest chance that something can happen, we know that it must eventually happen. The power of Fortuna to realize extremely unlikely events cannot be disputed. We are living inside and are part of the most unusual coincidence of all. Fortuna's most fabulous gift to us is the gift of life.

Coincidences are happening all around us all the time. Whether we notice them or not is a measure of our sensitivity to the all-pervasive force of Fortuna. Each time we pull a box of breakfast cereal off the grocery store shelf, a part of our mind should stand in wonder at the marvelous web of accidental circumstances which put this particular box into our hands. It takes practice to see the world this way. We need only lift off the veils put over our eyes by the old-fashioned world-view of determinism. When unusual and interesting coincidences occur, these are gifts from Fortuna as she demonstrates vividly her presence and reminds us forcefully, "Don't ignore me!"

THE MATRIX FOR CHAPTER 6

	A	B	C	D	E	F	G	H	I	J	K	L	M	N	O	P	Q	R	S	T	U	V	W	X	Y	Z
A	14	15	13	9	17	12	10	19	15	11	10	18	16	15	11	8	14	20	17	16	15	11	15	4	15	16
B	18	7	11	17	8	17	7	14	15	17	8	9	3	9	12	10	3	14	8	20	18	19	8	10	9	10
C	20	9	20	10	19	18	18	15	13	18	4	9	3	11	13	17	20	13	15	13	2	20	20	7	8	10
D	10	15	19	14	13	8	8	19	13	16	11	2	3	18	2	16	5	17	13	5	19	11	12	5	3	17
E	17	14	13	11	15	8	20	10	11	16	9	11	19	20	7	8	18	15	2	19	11	4	16	7	14	13
F	18	15	18	15	5	4	15	15	8	17	3	19	3	11	9	7	20	13	10	12	16	5	19	15	14	7
G	20	13	8	14	4	12	11	9	18	2	19	19	12	12	14	13	19	12	10	8	4	11	5	2	13	13
H	17	13	12	3	19	14	13	18	2	15	10	3	14	15	2	8	19	14	18	16	10	15	3	7	16	10
I	13	11	16	2	10	7	8	2	4	17	7	7	8	11	3	3	2	5	17	2	12	19	3	13	7	18
J	7	19	17	2	15	13	9	18	19	19	14	4	16	14	13	15	19	10	7	9	19	19	7	10	15	12
K	13	17	8	4	9	13	11	20	17	5	9	16	3	19	9	14	19	18	4	10	12	2	11	13	18	12
L	2	16	19	13	10	9	11	9	9	15	10	16	18	18	14	16	17	12	5	11	8	7	16	13	4	20
M	4	19	8	7	15	9	16	16	7	18	13	18	3	3	18	14	17	13	2	17	15	13	3	4	3	8
N	10	12	19	13	8	16	16	8	3	8	2	4	8	11	7	4	14	18	2	18	17	5	2	5	7	13
O	10	12	11	7	14	16	3	9	9	9	2	12	12	15	5	20	17	14	5	11	9	15	8	13	7	8
P	9	13	10	4	9	2	4	10	16	9	5	11	16	7	11	15	13	20	13	8	11	18	20	8	3	15
Q	3	9	19	2	3	13	14	16	11	7	16	11	18	14	7	15	8	4	15	8	18	7	15	13	8	3
R	18	20	18	3	3	2	3	17	11	15	18	15	5	14	13	12	9	11	16	11	18	5	10	2	13	4
S	11	5	18	13	10	18	3	9	8	9	3	16	19	11	19	2	13	3	19	13	20	10	12	20	12	20
T	19	17	15	2	3	14	20	11	13	12	12	3	9	7	17	8	13	16	9	11	19	3	17	15	3	18
U	13	20	11	5	13	15	8	13	2	8	12	12	18	2	18	3	18	11	16	3	9	15	13	9	17	9
V	8	4	4	20	13	3	13	19	11	13	13	18	9	15	13	12	16	8	10	4	9	16	2	13	13	14
W	3	3	12	11	5	20	17	15	20	10	2	8	16	17	17	19	14	19	17	19	4	17	18	20	2	4
X	12	2	15	12	20	12	7	20	12	12	4	2	10	7	5	8	19	4	4	9	7	20	14	3	8	9
Y	17	19	11	15	9	14	19	7	12	19	8	14	9	10	3	11	19	13	15	3	3	8	4	17	3	5
Z	20	11	18	13	15	19	15	9	10	10	17	4	14	18	18	13	8	5	16	17	18	17	7	12	20	13

On the chart, find the place where the initials you've chosen intersect. Read the chapter whose number appears at that intersection.

7

TIME

How can we be effective in our lives? In times of uncertainty there are so many active forces which touch our lives that we feel out of control. One vote cannot affect the outcome of an election. Putting money in a savings account won't turn inflation around. A good and valuable worker could still lose his job. Extended families break up as people disperse all over the country for job opportunities. The random impacts of these forces in our lives are signs of Fortuna's increased activity these days, and there is no way to avoid it. But she is not a domineering matriarchal goddess who demands our submission. There is no need to fatalistically lie back and accept everything that happens to us as inevitable and fixed. There is a realm wherein we do have primary control and where we can significantly affect what happens in our lives. To perceive and exploit this opportunity we have to be sensitive about the nature of time and about its subdivisions into the past, the present, and the future.

Too much mental and emotional energy is wasted on the twin pursuits of planning and regret. To rely too much on planning is to live in the future. We try to change our lives by attempting to decide our future actions. To regret is to live in the past, wishing one had acted otherwise. These two activities, regretting and planning, are linked. If we count on the success of fixed plans for the future then, when the moment which was planned for passes and perhaps the plan does not work out, that loss becomes something to be regretted. Conversely, a past full of regrets encourages planning, because of our fear of making more mistakes which will turn into further regrets. And this cycle intensifies. For a person who regrets, every choice and opportunity will present itself as a chance for making mistakes which then lead to more regrets. Regretting and planning reinforce one another and together inhibit effective action. It's like trying to tune in a weak radio station. First we cast our mind into the future, planning, and then we cast our mind into the past, regretting. But we miss the station. The past and the future are not accessible to us. They cannot be touched or changed by efforts of planning and regretting.

Of course, it is wise to attempt to envision the future, and to anticipate events which might be on a collision course with our life. It is also wise to learn from the past. But the real locus of action is the present, the now. Now is the time we can act and react, the time we can change and choose. The malleable clay of human lives can only be touched and molded at one point, the present. Try it! Lift up your arm. An action as seemingly insignificant as this can show that we have freedom and power to change the shape of the present moment. But if we drift off station letting our mental efforts wander into the past or future, we become powerless.

The present holds within itself the complete
sum of existence, backwards and forwards,
that whole amplitude of time, which is eternity.

ALFRED NORTH WHITEHEAD

The present, the now, is not just a fleeting instant, here now and quickly past. This is a myth. One really lives in an eternal now. The past and the future are the fictions, having concrete reality only within the human mind. At every moment of one's life, the eternal present is continually available for action. It's all we have and we are constantly here in its presence.

The ancients viewed time as a series of natural cycles, called kairoses, which they thought of as a series of propitious moments. During each of these moments something very specific could be done: milking the goats, gathering olives, hunting, fishing, playing, singing, loving, etc. They were simple people, shepherds and farmers, who apparently lived happily with this notion of time. For these people, existence was ruled by the natural cycles of life: the seasons, the passage from birth to death, and the inevitable regeneration of flowers, of fruits, of lambs, and of babies. Fortuna was the bestower of all these goods. Chance is a palpable reality for people who live in close contact with nature and its cycles; and kairos, the Greek word for "occasion," is closely linked to Fortuna throughout history.

To every thing there is a season, and a time to every purpose under the heaven:
A time to be born, and a time to die; a time to plant and a time to pluck up that which is planted;
A time to kill, and a time to heal; a time to break down and a time to build up;
A time to weep, and a time to laugh; a time to mourn, and a time to dance;

ECCLESIASTES

At some point this concept of time changed. It was a gradual development over thousands of years that happened as people moved away from a close relationship with nature, living in small groups, to the more complexly structured societies of cities and states. The ultimate change, which fixed chronos as the dominant mode of perceiving time, occurred with the rise of modern science that began with Galileo. Applying the Renaissance idea, itself revived from antiquity, that God is a mathematician and that uncovering the mathematical structure of reality would reveal traces of His handiwork, Galileo began the measurement of the physical world. One day in church, observing the swinging lamps overhead while counting his pulse, he discovered the basic fact that the time it took a pendulum to complete one swing was not affected by how widely the pendulum was swinging, but only depended on its length. From this observation, he went on to discover a simple physical law which accounted for the regular oscillations of a pendulum as a function of time. From that time forth, Galileo and other scientists used measurable time as one of the fundamental tools for describing regularities in motion. Eventually Newton completed this line of development by discovering the three laws of motion which can be used to predict the motions of any object, ranging from a falling apple to the rotating moon.

Because of the successful consequences of this measurement of time, an abstract concept of time, called chronos, became firmly established in the world of science. Time was perceived as marching forward at an inexorable pace. It was likened to the measurable straight line of geometry, which could be broken into segments of arbitrary lengths and which is composed of an infinite number of infinitely tiny points. The unit of time became the moment which flashed by instantaneously instead of the extended moments of kairos, characterized by the same continuing activity.

<< . . . . (past) . . . . • . . . . . . (future) . . . . >>

NOW

Nowadays, we think of time in terms of this same linear metaphor. The idea is striking but, while it may be extremely valuable for scientific purposes, it distorts subjective time. The present is minimized by compressing it down to a point, while, on the other hand, the past and the future are relatively over-emphasized in that they are given a physical reality which seems immeasurably larger than the present.

In this modern image of time the past and the future stretch endlessly forward and backwards, apparently larger and more important than the now, which becomes reduced merely to the point of division between the past and the future. Since the past and the future are unchangeable by any direct measures, we come to feel powerless and helpless before those accidents which chance uses to shape our individual life experiences.

During the passage of mankind from a primitive closeness with nature into the state of culture, people became more distant from personal daily contacts with Fortuna. When people began separating themselves from concrete contacts with nature, they began thinking in more abstract terms and began conceiving of time as an abstract sequence, an imaginary line in space. So it was that in the late Hellenistic period of the Ancient Greeks, kairos first began to give way to chronos. The change was finally and firmly established by the time of the Renaissance with the invention of clocks and the rise of modern science.

While chronos is a more scientific way of dealing with the idea of time, it is also a less natural way. Chronos, because it is a line, can be cut up into smaller and smaller segments. People began arranging their lives according to these portions of time. We can see that the modern individual in the modern city lives according to his or her appointment book, cutting up the waking hours quite artificially into class hours, visiting hours, dating hours, and nine-to-five working days. This makes people live their days not according to the cycles of nature but according to the dictates of linear and segmented time: chronos. At nine o'clock, we go to work. At noon, regardless of our personal involvement in work activities, we break for lunch. Then, even though the kairos of lunch may be pleasurable and engrossing, still developing even, we check our watches and interrupt it to return to work at one o'clock. One event follows another inexorably on the imaginary straight line of chronos and unnaturally bumps and excludes its predecessor.

Try this. On your next free Saturday or on your next vacation, take off your watch and ignore chronos. Let each occasion, or kairos, unfold naturally; stay with it until it reaches a natural conclusion. Eat when you're hungry. Sleep when you're tired. Let each conversation persist until it's finished. Stay on the beach until you've had your full measure of sun and sand. It's bound to be a delightful experience!

With chronos, or linear time, people are thus obliged to find their pleasures not in independent bubbles of time but in the pursuit of a point in time which is forever being put off. Gratification is forever being deferred. People today do things in order to get pleasure later. This brings a feeling of unfulfillment; there is the distinct feeling that the results obtained from our efforts are constantly being put into question. Nothing seems to be completely over because of the constant fear of what tomorrow will bring. The expression "what tomorrow will bring" can, as we see it, be translated by "what Fortuna will bring" since Fortuna is "the one who brings" by definition. We fear the mysterious and the unknown. Because the chronos system of time tries to ignore chance, we therefore come to fear anything that happens outside of the straight line of predictable events. We seem, under chronos, to take our pleasure not in time arrested but in moving time; not in rest but in movement. Movement brings with it goals in the future toward which people strive — sometimes without ever reaching them.

Another adverse consequence of thinking of time in terms of chronos is that it tends to create a deceptive order in life. Thus, people who are completely drawn into a life of time schedules, of appointment books, of deadlines, view the idea of kairos as unstructured and disorderly. Living in terms of kairos, for them, would be living without goals, without purpose. It would mean living for the occasion at hand and not for tomorrow. It would mean living a life made of disconnected instances of living. Such a life for them would be full of irregularities. Chronos does not allow you to enjoy the present because it brings with it both the past and the future. On the other hand, kairos allows for living in the present moment, enjoying fully the moment at hand, without worrying about the past or the future.

A new and more fruitful image of time may be gained by combining these two images, kairos and chronos. Neither need be completely excluded. We have to magnify the dimensionless point of the present in order to see the eternal now. We need to discover in its detail the timeless loops of kairos:

This new model of time is more faithful to the way the human mind and memory really work. For example, when we reminisce, our memories are strings of bubbles, linked loops of time, each enjoying its own internal pace. Use your imagination to picture how we remember, think of a day at the office, the ride home, dinner with your family, an evening at the movies, a night spent asleep in your bed, a morning spent over coffee and the papers, preparations for a picnic, sun-bathing on the beach . . . And so it goes. Each loop is a self-contained happening with a beginning and an end. Sometimes a loop (like a picnic) is made up of smaller loops (setting the table, cooking, eating, cleaning up). These loops are the extended present moments which when linked make up the biological time in which we live: kairos. Even in busy lives, full of jobs, children, responsibilities, and obligations, it is possible to be aware of when we are in a pleasurable kairos, and then to relax and enjoy it.

Whatever the moment that an opportunity comes to us, when Fortuna presents us with a gift we can act within the present kairos.

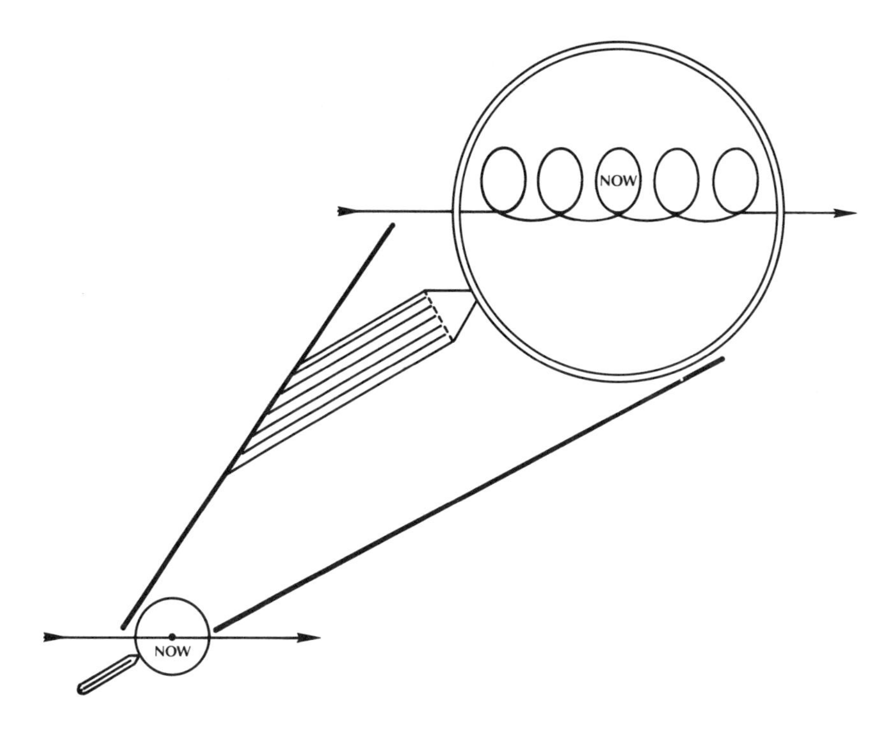

Because it is NOW, we can exert our power within this period of the tangible loop of kairos, and in doing so we can influence the next extended present moment. For example, when we sit down with a young child to read a book together, it is not the time to wistfully regret that our job has kept us away from the child all day (living in the past). Nor is it the time to plan about how we're going to teach the child to read and how pleasant that will be (living in the future). Now is the time to move, to act, to shape, to create. We read the story, speculate together about the pictures, point out words and letters. When the phone rings or when we're called to dinner, we're drawn on to other activities; the kairos is complete. But in this time period we've seized an opportunity to permanently change our future and the child's.

Activities like these are exactly what is meant by "seizing opportunities." In these extended present moments, these loops of kairos, chance presents to us many different opportunities for action. In them, we are free to act and change our lives, just as easily as we can lift our arms at will. But our sense of time, our sensitivity to the now, must be acute. The past cannot be changed and the future can only be touched indirectly by our actions in the present; we have to attune our attention to the NOW. If we can see time as a string of loops, if we can insert kairos into the straight line of chronos, the now wherein we can act expands from a point to an indefinite timeless region. This expansion of a point in time allows us to pause, look around, enjoy life, and consider the opportunities at hand. It is during such pauses, as we step off the train of chronos that carries us relentlessly forward into the unknown, that we can take hold of our existence. Unlocking time, we enter into this timeless NOW through an act of will. Once inside this loop of time we have ample opportunity to be effective in our lives, even in a world of uncertainty. We can make a difference.

THE MATRIX FOR CHAPTER 7

	A	B	C	D	E	F	G	H	I	J	K	L	M	N	O	P	Q	R	S	T	U	V	W	X	Y	Z
A	10	3	10	16	8	10	8	15	8	10	8	13	19	17	20	9	9	4	9	8	10	2	10	14	18	17
B	10	2	6	18	10	13	13	2	4	13	15	16	19	4	14	3	9	5	11	2	11	12	4	17	13	9
C	12	14	10	9	6	11	9	6	16	13	13	16	20	5	2	4	8	17	6	14	16	12	14	11	13	8
D	14	3	9	8	4	10	2	10	19	18	20	14	2	14	6	17	18	12	20	11	4	17	15	18	5	3
E	11	8	8	4	2	5	5	18	14	11	6	12	12	17	4	14	16	9	15	17	5	14	3	15	4	17
F	10	8	10	19	2	8	8	5	4	4	2	2	18	19	5	16	4	17	3	4	12	9	15	2	13	16
G	4	20	14	12	19	17	19	14	17	4	20	13	20	17	3	6	17	9	18	17	8	10	9	12	4	16
H	15	3	17	10	14	20	9	11	15	19	11	17	8	4	11	11	8	15	5	6	5	12	14	17	6	9
I	4	20	18	14	9	3	20	14	8	18	8	20	3	17	8	5	5	9	2	12	4	5	18	16	11	9
J	3	11	8	8	19	6	10	12	3	6	2	15	10	9	14	18	5	17	2	2	3	20	12	17	11	2
K	12	2	19	12	8	9	13	15	4	20	15	13	17	16	3	18	14	13	13	19	10	17	14	4	2	6
L	4	20	10	6	17	15	16	12	4	11	19	17	19	17	9	10	4	11	10	9	10	19	3	6	5	6
M	11	2	19	14	17	16	10	18	20	19	17	6	8	14	4	5	5	2	6	10	12	11	8	16	16	15
N	19	3	12	15	12	5	13	14	9	3	16	13	17	16	19	5	16	15	4	15	11	13	20	10	9	15
O	8	5	10	13	8	4	16	4	10	4	17	3	6	2	20	3	3	16	6	5	11	17	5	4	17	16
P	15	12	16	18	12	17	5	14	9	4	14	2	4	18	12	2	15	2	8	11	2	16	5	5	16	16
Q	19	8	18	5	12	6	3	5	20	5	4	12	3	19	12	5	15	19	11	15	20	16	2	19	17	2
R	15	2	5	6	11	18	11	4	16	5	9	11	16	15	11	15	8	4	14	9	9	15	19	4	6	6
S	12	17	16	11	16	2	6	4	9	2	18	6	2	2	18	9	6	19	16	5	10	20	14	12	9	14
T	2	16	10	6	8	11	9	5	12	3	4	10	10	10	18	9	17	18	6	13	14	15	9	20	20	12
U	18	3	8	3	5	9	4	5	9	16	11	17	19	4	2	15	10	15	13	6	11	17	18	15	19	18
V	20	17	13	4	15	19	18	18	16	6	9	20	8	8	5	14	11	13	13	17	15	20	17	18	18	5
W	20	11	3	13	11	14	3	20	6	19	6	5	3	20	3	10	13	10	5	12	9	8	14	3	13	15
X	16	19	8	14	13	19	12	10	14	3	6	16	18	20	18	2	9	15	5	2	18	18	12	5	17	4
Y	6	8	12	12	6	6	3	16	11	14	5	13	6	3	20	13	14	6	20	16	5	14	6	16	2	15
Z	9	12	14	6	11	8	12	20	20	4	16	3	4	16	16	18	10	14	15	20	16	3	15	11	10	4

On the chart, find the place where the initials you've chosen intersect. Read the chapter whose number appears at that intersection.

8

FORTUNA THE WOMAN

With more and more women like Sandra Day O'Connor and Geraldine Ferraro being considered for high-ranking, decision-making positions, many believe the time may be ripe for reconsidering the idea of God as a woman or the idea of a female divinity like Fortuna. Throughout the ages, Fortuna has been scorned and her existence challenged. Most people who know something about Fortuna believe, erroneously we think, that this is because the idea of chance is incompatible with the idea of God. These same people may be very surprised as we advance the theory that the reason why philosophers and theologians have tried to annihilate Fortuna is not because she is a deity but rather because she is a woman.

The question of accepting Fortuna the woman is more a political than a religious matter. Those who espouse fundamental or orthodox positions will reject her automatically while those who are more liberal in their religious beliefs will be more ready to accept the role of women in divine matters. For instance, fundamentalist Protestants have difficulty comprehending Catholics when they talk about the Virgin Mary, and traditional Catholics balk at the idea of female Protestant priests and ministers. Similarly, one can hardly imagine the Ayatollah bowing to any female. But the times are ripe for a rethinking of both the existence of chance in the universe and the place of womanhood in the realm of our religious beliefs.

THE FEMININITY OF FORTUNA

The fact that Fortuna is a woman, that chance is represented by a feminine symbol, has profound significance. The way we understand the world and the way we treat one another are intimately linked. If we understand the world in terms of chance, then we will be more tolerant of women and other minorities. Accepting that the world is ruled by chance and accepting that women can be anything they want, including priests, or even God, are two forms of reasoning that go together. We see in other parts of this book that Fortuna, as chance, is the key to freedom. We begin to see now that Fortuna, as woman, is also the key to freedom. We cannot be free as human beings as long as half of humanity remains in bondage. We will be free when we accept Fortuna not only as the personification of chance but also as woman. When adjectives like fickle are used to describe Fortuna, not only chance is being criticized, but womanhood itself.

We cannot enter into the twenty-first century with antiquated ideas about chance like those dating from the sixth century when the monk Boethius chased Fortuna out of his room and tied her up to a mechanical wheel. We cannot become civilized individuals when we continue characterizing Fortuna, and women, only as players of roles ranging along the limited spectrum from mother of God to whore. There is too much confusion in the way we generally think of chance and of women. We cannot enter the age of the fortunate individual when those ideas that Machiavelli spread throughout language and in the minds of men still persist. In Chapter 25 of *The Prince,* he wrote that because Fortuna is a woman, people should be encouraged to grab her by the hair, kick her, and rob her. Of course, he was talking metaphorically. He meant by that image that we should seize opportunities when they are presented to us. However, the language that he used is offensive to women. It is the barbarous language of rape. He also wrote, on that same point of "seizing occasions," that Fortuna likes to be treated roughly by young men for whom she has a special weakness. In other words, he depicted her as a stereotype of a jaded middle-aged woman who enjoys the company of tough enterprising young men. The place of women in the Renaissance was not too high, and the images Machiavelli presented for manipulating Fortuna reflect the way in which women were (and still are) manipulated and controlled. In modern times, new ways of dealing decently with women will lead to new legitimacy for Fortuna.

That the word Fortuna is feminine is an act of chance. Language contains masculine and feminine words. Except for animals which are either male or female, the gender of objects and ideas is arbitrary. The fact that we say "she" when referring to a ship in English is arbitrary. Also, the fact that what you are reading here is called a "book" and not a "buck," a "beck," or a "sook" is again, arbitrary. Although words are arbitrary in the manner by which they convey meaning, they do have their own individual histories. Fortuna is a woman because the word for chance was feminine in Latin. Chance, personified by the goddess Tyche, was also feminine in Greek. But, if one goes far enough back in time, there is no reason why chance could not have been represented by a male figure. Fortuna has another Latin name which is Occasion.

During the Renaissance, artists drew many pictures to illustrate chance and the same pictures were sometimes labeled Fortuna and sometimes labeled Occasion. Fortuna and Occasion became interchangeable words. However, the point we want to make is that Occasion, who was a woman in Latin, was a man in the Greek language. His name was Kairos. So we can see that the gender of ideas is arbitrary since the same idea (chance in this case) can be masculine in one language and feminine in another. For instance, the sun is masculine in French and Spanish while it is feminine in German. At the moment of their birth, Fortuna gives objects, animals, people, and all words their gender.

We could explain the difference between chronos (as defined in Chapter 7) and kairos by comparing them to trees and strawberries. The trunk of a tree, like an oak tree, inspires our ideas about unity. Trees give us our mental models of centralization, organizational charts, hierarchical forms of government, genealogies, reproduction, evolution, lineage, ascendence, descendence, transcendence, etc. Trees are masculine symbols par excellence. They represent the father, the king, the state, the law. Trees are also visible; their growth is predictable; the arrangement of the branches and the leaves gives us a model for order. The roots of a tree, even though they are hidden from view, are conceived as forming a mirror image of the visible tree. It's an upside down tree again. Roots are still part of the family tree. Alex Haley appropriately named his famous saga of an African family, *Roots*. The image of roots also gives us our model for the subconscious mind which we sometimes view as the roots, or "the other side" of our mind.

An entirely different model which we find in nature, more closely resembling kairos, is based on rhizomatic plants like strawberries. They grow in fairly unpredictable ways. They are not organized in units like the trees but constitute nomadic bands. They form pure multiplicities. They contain no readily visible center or hierarchical structure. With the tree, if you strike at the trunk, at the leader, at the father, you destroy the tree. With rhizomes you have to kill the whole colony, the whole tribe, otherwise a little part of the plant will procreate the whole tribe, the whole society again.

The difference that we are illustrating is not a botanical one; it is not about trees and strawberries but rather about politics. Rhizomes find their power in their multiplicity, in their diversity, in randomness, in letting the flows of growth, of experience, of desire, extend in all directions and sprout in unexpected places. Rhizomes, like occasion, like kairos, like Fortuna, are solutions which lead to freedom and happiness. However, throughout history, Fortuna has always presented a threat to law and order, a threat to the centralization of power, a threat to the tree trunk.

FORTUNA THE BRINGER

Fortuna means "the bringer." So originally, it seems that she brought things to humans. She brought all kinds of gifts: children, crops, husbands, wives, weather, wealth, etc. Howard Patch, the great historian of Fortuna, points to her origin as a moon-goddess, a sun-goddess, or a close relative of the goddess Isis. She was a protecting goddess, watching specifically over the welfare of women, presiding over childbirth, and providing humans with plentiful crops. She is often shown carrying a cornucopia, the horn of plenty, the contents of which she dispenses to humanity. There is a Roman statue of Fortuna nursing two infants who are believed to be Jupiter and Juno. Incidentally, these two babies were brother and sister before becoming husband and wife. The mother was known as Fortuna and also as Charity. Apparently, it was only much later in her history that Fortuna began to be viewed as capricious. She acquired the negative adjective, fickle, and was associated with uncertainty during periods of political and economic instability.

Fortuna became extremely popular in the Greek world during the life of Alexander the Great when war and imperial expansions made daily life extremely unstable and uncertain. She became even more powerful after the unexpected death of Alexander at the age of thirty-three. Alexander, whose name meant Defender of Man, died of a freak accidental fever. The shock of his death and other experiences in the daily lives of Greek citizens seemed to contradict the possibility of rational planning. The neat straight line of chronos was not making sense. People became increasingly skeptical about everything and this opened the way for a belief in Tyche (the Greek name of Fortuna). She was then a winged and capricious goddess standing on a ball. The wings symbolized the speed with which things could change, and the ball under her feet meant that she ruled over the world.

In Rome, Fortuna rose in popularity after the death of Caesar and the beginning of the Roman Empire. Servius Tullius introduced Fortuna to Rome and, subsequently, eighteen temples to the goddess were built. The affairs of men and of the world appeared to be infected by an element of caprice. One's life depended on the whims of moody emperors. That element of chance became personified in the minds of people and so, from meaning simply "the one who brings," Fortuna came to mean "the one who brings in a capricious way." Fortuna became institutionalized. There was the Fortuna of the Roman people and the Fortuna of the Emperor. *Fortuna Redux* was instituted in the year 19 A.D. to celebrate the return of the emperor Augustus from a journey to Greece and the Middle East. When one set off on a journey in ancient times, whether or not one would return was very unpredictable. This was particularly true when the journey was by sea. She was the Fortuna of the return of the emperor. She was the personification of all returns including her very own.

THE DENIAL OF FORTUNA

For Ancient Greeks and Romans, Tyche or Fortuna was the first-born daughter of the king of the gods, Zeus or Jupiter. As the daughter of the highest god in heaven and, occasionally, as his substitute, Fortuna was immensely powerful. She was perceived as a direct threat to both the religious and political establishments. Something had to be done to bring order in the house and to make people toe the line and bow to the inevitabilities of authority. The task was entrusted to playwrights who were actually priests in the employ of the state.

Greek tragedy was instrumental in casting down both woman and chance. Ancient playwrights created what we could call myths of mind control. People believed in these myths. This affected the way they thought and lived. The work of Freud and his followers has also been an attempt to make modern men and women believe in these old myths. The oedipal triangle has been advanced as an explanation of human behavior just as concrete as the laws of physics. We can free ourselves from the tyranny of these beliefs by viewing the whole of psychoanalysis as beautiful literature based on myths, a literature which is striving, with limited success, to paraphrase human behavior, and to establish itself as a science.

Freudian psychoanalysis is paternalistic; it robs men, and especially women, of their innate multiplicities, multiplicities of experiences, of Kairoses, of sexes. The myths surrounding Oedipus try to frighten us into staying away from the father's possessions and not touching anything that belongs to him: wives, daughters, concubines, servants, cattle, land. The modern interpreters of these myths said that males had phalluses and females had none. Now, phalluses are more than just male genitalia; they are symbols of power, like command staffs, swords, property stakes, war memorials, large obelisks, and pulpits. Women were, and still are, denied these symbols of power.

How did ancient playwrights try to limit or to eliminate the power of Fortuna? In the play *Oedipus Rex,* Jocasta, the mother and, subsequently, the unknowing wife of Oedipus, voices her belief in Fortuna. She unashamedly proclaims the reign of Fortuna and dares to deny, in public, the existence of Destiny. She believes, as any modern liberated woman might wish to think, that she is free to marry anyone she wants to. One of the lessons of the play is that she is not as free to choose her mate as she thinks she is. Jocasta was punished for saying on stage that she believed in and trusted Fortuna. Having found out that she had unknowingly married her own son, she hanged herself.

Sophocles thus succeeded not only in teaching women to be wary of Fortuna but he also succeeded in killing the goddess herself. When Jocasta hangs herself, it should be understood that it is Fortuna herself who dies because Oedipus, the son of Jocasta, had earlier claimed that he was the son of Fortuna. Oedipus had said in a previous scene that Fortuna was generous and that he was loved by her in a maternal way. He too, of course, is taught his lesson at the end of the play. These plays preach that women should let the church, the state, the family, arrange their lives for them. They should not go out and marry anyone they please, for that person could be their own son. The play does not attempt to answer such commonsense questions as why Jocasta must hang herself instead of adjusting to the situation, or simply getting a divorce. She becomes an instrument for a lesson about the powerlessness of women.

Another play which was also devised to enslave women's minds and at the same time deny the existence of chance is the sad story of Electra. Freudian analysis reduces the play to the family triangle made up of daddy, mommy, and child. Electra's daddy has gone to war, so her mother, tired of waiting, has taken another husband. When daddy returns from his war, Electra's mother and her new husband kill daddy. Killing daddy is wrong; he stands for the king, the state, law and order. People have to be told that if they kill daddy, the whole society will crumble just as when you attack the trunk, the whole tree will die, branches, leaves, and all.

In order to avenge the death of her father, Electra has to kill her own mother. She does this as a symbolic gesture to preserve the sanctity of the tree. The lesson of the play is that Fortuna is denied her existence. Nothing in this tragedy is left to chance. The power of Fortuna is denied in that the mother is not free to remarry. Also, the daughter is not free to refuse to kill her own mother as long as such essential moral (social and political) obligations demand avenging the death of the father. Why is the father so important? Is it not because he wrote the play, or at least, subsidized the staging of the play?

If the state, in the name of the father, supported these anti-Fortuna views, it is not because of any evil conspiracy. The defenders of law and order have the best intentions in mind for the good of society. People who are in power (both men and women) during times when others are enslaved know very well that a belief in Fortuna may lead the oppressed to wild dreams of freedom. Fortuna keeps the world in a constant state of change making people willing to take chances in an effort to improve their lot in life.

Once in power, it is always in the leaders' best interest to maintain the existing social and political structure and thereby, maintain their own power. Fortuna is closely related to things that flow like water and things that move with the wind. Tyrants see to it that people do not "make waves." The term "waves" is closely associated with the image of Fortuna sailing on the sea, propelled by the winds of change. Well-intentioned leaders invented the idea of Fate (a male servant) who decrees that your life has already been decided for you. They say to you that you have no choice, that Fortuna does not exist (she hanged herself), and that you should be content with your lot. This pre-Christian system, of course, made God inflexible and even cruel at times. The audience who came out after seeing these tragedies did not come out as free men and women but were, on the contrary, made to feel like rats trapped before being drowned in a cage held by the inflexible arm of Destiny. The course of events, as they saw it, was like the thin imaginary line of chronos which could not be altered.

THE RISE OF FORTUNA

Not all Greek writers robbed Fortuna of her rights and importance in the affairs of men and women. With the passage of time, people and ideas became more sophisticated. The playwright Euripides presents Fortuna on the stage as a force which rivals that of the other gods. Euripides, who was a religious man himself, was nonetheless open to the more modern scientific ideas of the Periclean age. Even though he lived 500 years before Christ, his ideas on the subject of chance in the world are very much like ours. Two centuries later, the Greek philosopher Lucian, again ahead of his times, proclaimed Fortuna as the real arbiter of human affairs.

Fortunate individuals, meaning people who are comfortable with the existence of Fortuna, whether in the personification of a goddess or simply as an abstraction, may espouse a wide variety of religious beliefs. Some may be atheists, others may be religious mystics like Saint Augustine. Lucian has been labeled an atheist because of his statements regarding Fortuna. Some have interpreted his defense of Fortuna as a skeptical statement denying the existence of God.

Many Christian writers, particularly at the beginning of the Christian era, retained both the Christian God and Fortuna, having reconciled the two ideas in order to explain human freedom. Fortuna is a divinity of transition. She arises at the time when one religious system is crumbling and a new one has not yet taken over. This curious phenomenon has occurred repeatedly in history and may even be happening today. For a long time following the assassination of Caesar, some forty years before the birth of Christ, Fortuna had been growing in power, gradually taking over the roles of the other gods, usurping their places to become the reigning female divinity of the universe. When Christianity came into power the ruling goddess was Fortuna. Thus the early Christians could easily accept the idea that power was shared between Fortuna and the new Christian God. "She was the last of the gods," wrote Patch, "and consequently retained most of their radiance, while the rest faded in twilight."

In the height of her former glory Fortuna had eighteen temples in Ancient Rome. Today, the traveler can still visit one of them. It is close to the river Tiber as you cross the Palatino bridge. In the year 872 A.D. this temple of Fortuna was converted into a Christian church named Santa Maria Egiziaca. At this temple, Fortuna was worshipped especially as the protecting deity of women. It is fascinating to realize that only one or two generations may have separated the women who came to ask Fortuna for a husband or for a child from the women who came to the same altar, upon which stood perhaps the same statue, in order to pray to the Virgin Mary, with similar fervor, and for practically the same things. This very prayer was forbidden to Jocasta who was living too soon for her own sake, and who was told that there was no woman divinity to address one's prayers to, there was only Fate.

Indeed, Christians need not fear Fortuna but instead may rehabilitate her in their hearts under her many forms as the beloved servant, daughter, or mother of God, performing His divine will. This provides a reasonable explanation for the undeniable existence of chance in the universe. In the times of Saint Augustine, fifteen centuries ago, Fortuna was still revered as the most popular goddess in heaven. She was represented in various ways among which *Fortuna Muliebris* (Fortuna of woman) was the best known. This tradition of Fortuna has lasted until today and her attributes are those of the weak, of women, and of minorities in general.

Paradoxes of feminine strength:

- the power of the weak
- the strength of the multiplicity of minorities
- victory through flight
- resiliency through bending
- growth through unpredictability
- constancy through capriciousness
- perseverance through motion
- change through passive resistance

There is today a new rising strength in minorities and women. This strength consists of the ability to escape from the spheres of totality and unity, in order to take full advantage of multiplicity unbound. The ability to change can be a powerful advantage in individuals and is definitely an asset in an actor or actress. The modern audience is becoming acutely sensitive to the fascinations provided by change. In a recent issue of *Time* magazine (Sept. 7, 1981), featuring actress Meryl Streep, we read: "What makes the viewer sit forward in his seat is that Streep is so thoroughly a creature of change. Her expression is shadowed by a dizzying mutability. There is no doubt that in an instant this woman could take flight toward any state of emotion or mind." No better description of Fortuna herself could be written. Words like "dizzying mutability" have been used to describe her throughout the ages and are still around.

Predictably, she has been called blind, although she sees sometimes; she is unsteady; she remains in no place for long; her face changes from joyful to bitter; she is envious; she can turn against you; she is stubborn; she goes her own way; she plays games, uses men and women, and laughs at them; she hurts men and women when she wants to and sometimes when they deserve it; she holds dialogues with men and women; she is a whore; she is frail; much depends on her smile, etc. Those who call her these names are, of course, poor losers. Only fortunate individuals who can be comfortable with her changeability can gain access to the dwelling of Fortuna which, traditionally, is a sumptuous and royal palace wherein she plays hostess to her subjects and attendants, and to all those who dwell with her. For these fortunate people, the gates of opportunity are forever unlocked. The gifts of Fortuna, which differ from the gifts of Nature, include honor, glory, fame, love, and, of course, the riches for which she is best known.

Only fools deny her existence and deprive themselves of her many gifts. There are those who hold desperately to obsolete notions of a rational and orderly universe and try to explain away chance by attributing everything that happens accidentally to hidden deterministic causes, giving Fortuna no real existence. Those who shy away from faith in Fortuna, and from faith of any kind, fail to realize that belief in the myth of a rational universe is itself an act of faith.

In Ancient Rome, Fortuna was sometimes represented in the figure of what was called Roman Charity. This was a statue of a beautiful woman, barebreasted and nursing a child on each knee. This figure symbolized the abundance of Fortuna's love for humanity. She represents the eternal mother. Her two babies represent humanity, male and female. Through history she has filled all possible female roles from mother of God to whore, running through the whole gamut including daughter, virgin, and queen. That she is the mother of mankind can be more clearly seen as we come to realize that the existence of life itself may be the result of a unique accident in the universe.

We will conclude, without pressing too hard, by drawing a parallel between Fortuna and the Blessed Virgin. Many art critics have noticed the similarity of some pictures of the Virgin by artists like the

Spanish painter Murillo to some drawings of Fortuna. Murillo's Virgin has a half moon at her feet. Critics suggest that as artists copied from earlier paintings, the ball upon which Ancient Fortuna stood became gradually transformed into the crescent under the Virgin. This ball, which signified both instability and dominion over the world, has been mistaken for the moon. Some artists see a moon, others see a ball or a wheel. Men and women of Ancient Rome thought of Fortuna sometimes as the daughter and, at other times, as the mother of Jupiter — the king of all gods — just as Christians revere her as the Mother of God and sometimes as His beloved daughter.

Whether ancient or modern, pagan or Christian, a female divinity is a welcome and appropriate idea for our times. This female figure, for all ages, has possessed a unique asset which is Charity. It is a divine virtue sometimes found among humans but best exemplified and represented by the woman, Fortuna.

THE MATRIX FOR CHAPTER 8

	A	B	C	D	E	F	G	H	I	J	K	L	M	N	O	P	Q	R	S	T	U	V	W	X	Y	Z
A	4	7	12	13	16	3	18	12	17	7	17	15	18	20	18	16	15	16	2	18	5	9	18	13	4	12
B	7	19	14	13	18	11	18	9	11	6	18	3	4	11	10	9	20	18	2	12	17	15	2	3	12	14
C	10	7	6	5	18	15	14	4	5	9	9	18	15	9	4	13	9	6	4	5	7	10	9	12	2	12
D	11	18	10	19	5	15	4	17	15	17	17	9	5	17	11	7	9	16	2	12	16	7	6	6	9	10
E	7	3	17	9	12	10	9	16	18	7	20	18	5	9	15	19	10	18	3	2	4	7	10	5	5	5
F	20	3	5	10	6	17	11	20	12	7	15	3	9	14	6	2	10	16	7	2	17	11	13	4	4	10
G	13	5	17	13	9	11	9	19	9	3	12	3	9	5	9	16	13	18	19	12	17	7	19	11	2	9
H	14	16	15	2	17	7	17	7	18	3	12	4	3	12	4	16	10	9	14	17	11	3	13	9	7	7
I	19	7	11	9	17	20	13	15	14	5	17	18	2	7	12	16	6	3	12	18	13	3	5	2	14	20
J	9	3	18	5	9	7	2	13	16	4	4	10	7	6	11	20	15	2	9	17	16	17	19	18	19	4
K	7	11	13	2	16	6	5	5	13	9	18	10	10	12	13	10	17	6	10	14	16	3	3	15	12	16
L	13	3	13	7	18	19	15	19	17	13	18	2	17	2	18	18	2	5	12	13	15	17	13	12	9	17
M	20	6	16	3	4	3	3	15	5	10	15	20	14	6	17	17	6	4	10	4	14	4	16	14	4	18
N	20	15	6	17	3	13	11	15	17	2	5	2	9	9	14	2	5	2	18	14	13	15	10	18	10	10
O	12	4	4	10	15	10	10	15	20	16	18	5	16	9	19	9	12	5	3	12	5	10	12	9	2	10
P	5	18	6	16	13	18	20	9	12	18	13	12	20	12	14	9	12	14	19	15	19	11	14	14	13	6
Q	4	2	16	13	18	9	6	12	4	17	12	19	20	2	2	4	14	20	20	3	19	11	14	6	5	14
R	19	17	3	11	14	9	6	13	20	4	2	2	11	11	5	16	13	5	7	7	20	11	6	9	18	3
S	7	2	17	3	4	3	4	19	10	6	5	19	6	15	2	16	14	10	10	17	17	11	5	10	4	15
T	11	3	11	11	12	17	10	18	18	18	13	14	16	3	20	3	18	2	18	10	18	14	11	4	4	17
U	7	15	17	9	18	16	19	4	4	2	20	5	14	12	20	18	15	19	19	15	18	2	10	17	12	19
V	3	7	19	13	3	17	2	6	15	7	17	11	16	11	6	4	3	5	15	9	14	18	16	6	9	2
W	7	13	11	15	9	4	18	13	2	4	18	15	18	11	13	18	20	2	6	15	3	9	16	6	14	20
X	13	14	2	18	18	9	10	15	16	15	13	15	9	19	4	17	14	11	17	16	9	7	13	12	15	11
Y	15	11	3	19	5	3	9	19	10	12	9	18	4	14	11	9	13	15	3	11	9	19	5	9	11	10
Z	5	14	4	12	2	20	6	11	9	14	3	2	20	7	5	10	9	3	7	4	6	5	13	16	18	6

On the chart, find the place where the initials you've chosen intersect. Read the chapter whose number appears at that intersection.

9

CONTINGENCY PLANNING

A special kind of preparation, called contingency planning, is needed in situations where the role of uncertainty is large. When one notices that the consequences of an action are much larger and more significant than the action itself (say when a decision about which woman to ask to dance could determine who will be our "significant other" for the next several years); this is a signal that we are a situation whose outcome is largely under Fortuna's control. Rigid planning, for example firmly setting our hopes on finding a blue-eyed, red-haired woman of Irish descent, is not appropriate in these kinds of circumstances. This particular wish will most likely not be fulfilled and we will be disappointed. In addition, it could get in the way of appreciating the opportunities that uncertainty does present to us, like the brown-eyed, black-haired, warm-hearted woman sitting next to us. Instead, contingency planning would be more appropriate. Contingency planning is a technique for maximizing our control and our rewards in situations where uncertainty is a major factor. We need to consciously acknowledge the role of uncertainty and take it explicitly into account. This technique cannot be used by those who would deny Fortuna her role in our lives or by those who believe that the human will can wrestle with the future and force it to comply with our plans. We need to cooperate with uncertainty, observe it and measure it, rather than fight it.

The future is contingent. The events that lie in our future are not necessary, they could be one way; they could be otherwise. It's possible that a future event might occur; possible that it might not. We are swimming in a great river of time. Events are the debris floating down the river towards us. There could be the branch of a tree, a piece of paper, an empty bottle; in life, a new friend, a trip, a winning lottery ticket. We have no control over the junk floating downriver, we can only see so far ahead, but whether we encounter one thing or another depends on what we do now. Our paddling around in the river has lined us up to meet some events, and to miss others.

In order to practice contingency planning we first need to know what we want in life. We need to clarify and quantify our values. Secondly, we need to know how likely it is that different situations will occur. The systematic consideration of these two factors and the interrelations between them form the heart of the method of planning called contingency planning.

What are our values, desires, priorities, opinions? Do we think it's important to have a lot of friends? A lot of money? Do we want a long-term committed love relationship or casual sexual thrills? Which is more important? The most critical foundation for decision making is found by looking within ourselves and knowing what we want. The Oracle of Delphi said, "Know thyself." The hardest part of this process is in comparing different values, like friends and money. Some people would say "It's like comparing apples and oranges." But most of us have no trouble deciding at any moment whether we would prefer to eat an apple or an orange. Life choices are only a bit more difficult. Which is more important, staying close to our family or attending a good college in another state? Lots of good friends here or a job in another city? These aren't easy decisions, so it's good practice to constantly quiz ourselves, getting into the habit of saying "If I had to make that decision today, what would I do?" Our questioning will lead us to better understand our values and priorities. In the situation of deciding whether to look for a job in a city which is far away from our home and friends, we may decide that our friends are more important than a new job. On the other hand, if a new job is more important than our particular present circle of friends, then maybe we will recognize the necessity of beginning to learn how to develop new friendships. At every moment we should be prepared to make decisions based on thought-out values. When we sight two chests filled with opportunities floating downriver, one on the left and one to the right, hesitation in deciding whether to swim left or right may result in losing both of them. And we will not get a chance to unlock either one of them.

The first part of contingency planning, as described above, involves looking inward, knowing our personal priorities; the second part involves looking outward, attempting to determine the probability of events. Some things are more likely to occur than others. A rare event may be very attractive and we may be tempted to pursue it. However, if there is some alternative event which is almost certain to occur, then, even if it were only to be a mild improvement over our present situation, this latter one might be a better choice because we're more likely to get it. It's not very realistic to situate ourselves at a place in the river where checks for $1,000,000 come floating down once in a century when there's another place where checks for $1000 come down once a month. On the other hand, if that check for $1,000,000 comes floating our way on the average of once a year, it may well be worthwhile to go gamble a few years of our lives and place ourselves in its path.

The language of probability is a way of talking about the frequencies of occurrence of events. This is what we need to know for this second part of decision making. Suppose an event has a probability of 1/100. That means that in 100 situations where it is possible that the event could happen, it will happen, on the average, just once. That the probability of a winning lottery ticket is 1/10,000 means that 10,000 people would have to purchase a ticket to produce one winner, or worse, we would have to buy 10,000 tickets (certainly at a cost that exceeds the prize money) in order to have a guaranteed chance of winning.

Probabilities are determined primarily by experience. We have to learn about life in order to know approximately how often certain things occur in real life situations. This includes studying history, paying close attention to current events, watching the stock market, acutely observing human behavior (including our own), reading realistic novels, and perhaps exploring other cultures to put our own into perspective. Curiosity, retention, and an avidity for wide-ranging personal experiences are all plusses. If all our information comes from TV soap operas or if we never leave the neighborhood of our youth, we won't have a clear perspective on how often our lives might be touched by experiences beyond this narrow circle. Even though movie producers do sometimes come into the corner cafe for a cup of coffee, an aspiring actress could spend years working behind the counter as a waitress before she ever set eyes on one. With a bit of research into the nature of the acting profession, she could have discovered that producers usually leave casting for bit parts up to specialized talent agencies and her probability of getting a screen test would have been greatly enhanced had she looked for one of these in the yellow pages and signed up. Education is advanced as one of the more certain roads to success because it provides us with an expanded domain of experience.

But even taking into account both factors, that is, if we know what we want and if we know how likely we are to encounter various situations, decision making is not easy. In everyday life, these two factors are often mixed in conflicting and confusing ways. The choices we have to make could be like that of choosing between one option, setting up a private mail-order business (high value for independence and potential wealth; low probability of stability), and a second option, a regular nine-to-five job (low value; high probability of stability). Or we may have to choose between marrying Joe (moderate value, he's a nice guy; probability certain because he proposed last night), and waiting for Steve (high value since you've been crazy about him since junior high school; probability low since he's attending an out-of-state college and you've heard he's dating another girl). In order to work out these more complicated situations we need contingency planning.

Contingency planning as practiced by large corporations is a branch of applied mathematics. It involves assigning a numerical value to priorities and probabilities and, following an arithmetical process, calculating a number which will indicate which choice among several is the most desirable. But even used informally, contingency planning will organize our thinking processes and help us see our future situations more clearly. It's like navigating on the river of time in a boat equipped with radar which can pierce the mists of the future for a short distance. Uncertainty cannot be banished, but our circle of informed control can be expanded.

Here's how contingency planning works. We start with a diagram which looks like a tree lying on its side, its branches opening to the right. Each branch represents a different possible path which is available in the future. The forks in the tree are either places where we can and must choose (represented by squares) or places where chance steps in (represented by circles). We progress along a branch from left to right. At the moment when we pass through a circular node, chance chooses for us the fork we will actually take and the possibilities of the future become transformed into realities.

Suppose, for illustration, that a young businessman is on the job market. He's had two interviews. The first was with Company A, a job which he thinks will probably be better than his present one, and the second with Company B, an opportunity he is really excited about. Company A has made him an offer which he much accept or reject within two weeks. Company B is incapable of committing itself for several weeks yet, but says that he is one of the four finalists for the position. The diagram below summarizes the situation in the form of a decision tree:

Each branch of the tree represents a particular possible future situation for the young man. For example, by moving along the top branch from left to right, we see the scenario where he decides to accept the offer from Company A and then it turns out that this job is more satisfactory than his present job. The numbers in the two right-hand columns (⅓, ⅔, ¼, ¾: 60, 50, 90, 50) are the young man's best judgment of the probabilities involved and the relative value of each of the four outcomes for him. Each individual would assess these values and probabilities differently and might come up with different numbers. That's what personalizes the decision. The only constraint is that the probabilities at each circular node most add up to one. There may be any number of branches out of each node. It's even

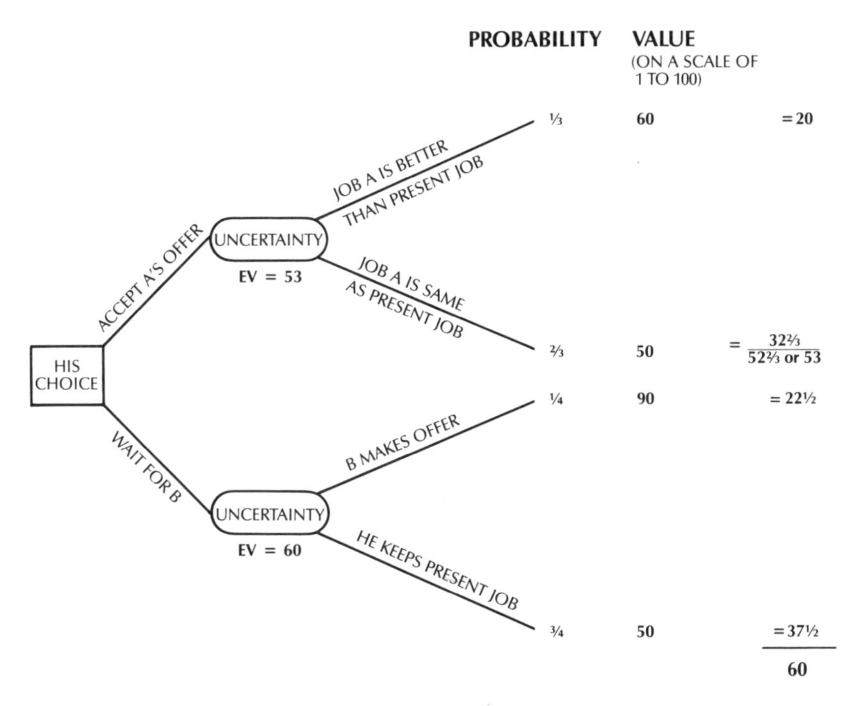

possible to construct decision trees which have many levels and which are much more complicated than this one. Before we proceed, it is recommended that you go back and carefully examine this diagram in order to make certain that the numbers seem reasonable to you and that they appear to accurately describe the young man's situation. Trace down each of the four branches and try to visualize the four possible future scenarios.

For each circular node, a number is calculated and contingency planning recommends that one make the choice which will lead to the circular node of highest value. This number is called the expected value (E.V.) and represents, on the average, the value we can expect to receive if we decide to progress down the path to that node. It is simple to compute. For each one of the branches coming out of a circular node of uncertainty, multiply probability times value and add the results together, as we've done in the column farthest to the right. The E.V. for the first circular node in the diagram above (accepting A's offer) is 53 (⅓ × 60 + ⅔ × 50). The E.V. for the second circular node (waiting for B's offer) is 60 (¼ × 90 + ¾ × 50). (Even if you don't understand these computations fully, the idea will become clearer as we proceed.) Hence, since 60 is larger than 53, the young businessman would be wisest to wait for B's offer. In general, when we stand on a square node and look toward the future in contingency planning, we should decide to proceed down the path which leads to the circular node with the highest calculated expected value. In other words, we should proceed towards that circular node, that uncertain future situation, which would, on the average, be most valuable to us.

One of the valuable consequences of contingency planning is that it forces us to be utterly honest about our values. Using it encourages us to constantly reexamine them. When an analysis is done, like the preceding one, the decision need not be fixed and final. It is not uncommon for the young man to respond "Hey! That can't be right. Here I have a pretty nice job offered to me which, if I work at it probably *will* be a nice improvement over my present job after all. Should I throw this away for a one-in-four chance at B's job?" What he is doing is looking closer at the branches arising from the topmost circular node and reexamining the numbers he placed there. His words suggest that the numbers on the new partial diagram shown below more closely reflect his feelings after greater thought.

EV = 65

	PROBABILITY	VALUE	
JOB A IS BETTER THAN PRESENT JOB	¾	70	52½
JOB A IS SAME AS PRESENT JOB	¼	50	12½

= 65

Note the changes from the earlier assignment of values and probabilities. Now that he is seriously considering rejecting A's offer, he begins to realize how appealing this job would be, and assigns it a value of 70. Since he would be willing to work hard to achieve success there, the probability that it would be better than his present job is now assigned ¾. The recomputed expected value for this node is now 65 ($\frac{3}{4} \times 70 + \frac{1}{4} \times 50$) and under these assumptions, he should accept the offer from Company A because 65 is larger than the earlier calculated value of 60 assigned to B's offer. There is a powerful cyclical effect going on here. If we are clear enough about our values, and if we are knowledgeable about the probability or likelihood of possible events, then contingency planning can help us choose. Our calculations and the choices they indicate we should make, in turn, help us to refine our values and alert us to the probabilities which are most important to know.

In addition, contingency planning gives us practice in visualizing the future as being determined by two types of bifurcations — first, there are places where we can and must choose; secondly, there are places where the outcome is out of our control, determined by Fortuna. At the first kind of fork, it is appropriate to act; at the others, it is appropriate to accept what happens. Practice in contingency planning encourages the wisdom, first articulated by the Stoics of ancient Greece, of knowing both what is and what is not under our control. A beautiful and rich world of opportunity lies ahead. The key is in our hand. It is our choice as to how we move into that future.

Only certain people can apply this type of planning in their lives. To be that type of person, we have to keep our eyes open and recognize the innumerable moments when the river of time presents opportunities for our choice. That means we can't be looking wistfully downstream, regretting something that has passed, or dreamily peering far upstream, waiting for that special event we've planned for. If we are alert to exactly where we are now, in terms of values and realistic appraisals of our place in life, we'll be able to assess which event is closer and whether to turn left or right. If, in addition, we are self-accepting and trust ourselves to do well, we will be prepared for split-second decision-making. Recognizing that these are uncertain times, that we are paddling around in this river of time regardless and that some things are bound to hit us unexpectedly in the head, no matter what we do, will give us the courage to at least try; we might as well paddle over in the direction of something we want instead of just treading water here. These personal attitudes are needed to maximize happiness and success in times of uncertainty and are a necessary foundation for successful contingency planning. (These recommended personal attitudes, and others, are more fully discussed in Chapter 18, The Good Life.)

An early example of contingency planning, though not formalized in a diagram, was given in the seventeenth century by the French philosopher and mathematician, Blaise Pascal, one of the founders of probability theory. In attempting a scientific justification for the belief in a Supreme Being, he argued that even the skeptic would agree that it is not impossible for God to exist. There is some probability of His existence, say one in a thousand. And since He promises eternal life if we believe in Him (high value) and eternal damnation (low value) if we do not, the prudent gambler will agree to believe in God and live the Christian life. This argument, traditionally called "Pascal's wager," is summarized in the diagram below.

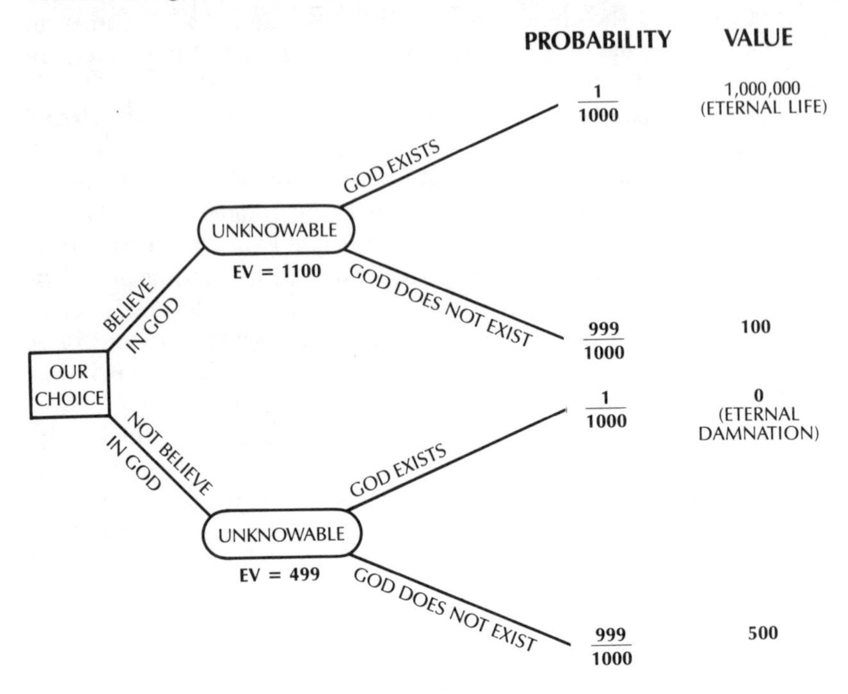

The second and fourth values given above (the 100 and the 500 values) reflect the fact that living a wild life, gambling and partying all night long, is generally conceded, even by some good Christians, to be more fun than going to church every Sunday and leading an exemplary life. The expected value (E.V.) for believing in God is 1100 (which is $1/1000 \times 1{,}000{,}000 + 999/1000 \times 100$) while the E.V. for not believing in God is 499 (which is $1/1000 \times 0 + 999/1000 \times 500$), illustrating Pascal's conclusion that the scientific gambler will choose to believe in God.

This argument not only shows the long history and versatility of contingency planning, but also it might easily be modified to help us decide whether or not, as citizens of the twenty-first century, we would be wiser to acknowledge Fortuna and take her power into account in our preparations for the future. It is in this spirit that we invite you to make a diagram for choosing to believe or not in the existence of Fortuna. Assign your own values and probabilities, calculate the expected values (E.V.), and draw your own conclusion!

THE MATRIX FOR CHAPTER 9

	A	B	C	D	E	F	G	H	I	J	K	L	M	N	O	P	Q	R	S	T	U	V	W	X	Y	Z
A	20	16	8	20	13	2	5	8	7	13	18	2	5	2	17	2	20	13	5	12	14	4	6	12	8	4
B	3	10	17	20	14	5	8	16	19	12	17	17	17	12	7	5	13	8	12	17	3	3	13	2	7	12
C	15	8	4	11	11	13	11	8	19	7	19	17	17	10	15	16	6	8	11	8	3	18	16	16	12	20
D	17	10	11	5	11	7	20	7	3	2	19	3	7	11	18	15	16	13	17	7	3	2	14	8	10	11
E	15	20	14	6	6	11	7	7	17	4	17	10	11	2	8	20	4	14	5	18	8	2	6	13	10	19
F	8	14	17	13	17	16	5	14	6	3	16	11	14	8	17	8	3	19	13	15	3	20	14	3	18	18
G	16	19	7	18	10	16	18	3	7	5	18	18	19	19	6	11	12	4	3	3	6	15	10	10	18	7
H	16	8	19	12	2	17	19	19	12	13	4	11	17	11	18	4	16	7	12	13	19	17	19	16	3	3
I	10	5	6	10	11	4	7	6	16	8	5	15	11	16	20	17	12	2	5	16	16	2	11	10	20	19
J	11	17	5	18	14	20	19	16	15	3	19	17	11	3	6	6	3	3	17	10	4	3	14	3	4	8
K	4	6	3	13	7	17	19	13	3	4	13	12	6	10	8	5	3	10	5	15	5	10	4	17	15	4
L	18	5	8	14	12	20	2	13	16	3	15	6	6	20	5	8	10	15	13	15	19	4	7	3	3	3
M	19	17	4	12	14	13	12	13	14	17	4	7	20	4	8	18	11	6	5	15	17	17	15	8	10	13
N	6	14	2	10	15	3	18	16	16	11	17	16	13	6	18	15	8	10	3	17	19	10	6	16	16	7
O	17	11	13	8	20	14	6	12	18	5	19	19	8	4	11	13	11	12	20	18	12	7	2	7	12	19
P	16	17	3	6	3	4	2	12	19	5	2	18	15	17	18	17	4	6	11	2	6	10	17	6	18	18
Q	12	14	2	12	2	14	5	13	12	12	2	5	19	7	18	14	19	11	6	10	17	8	5	17	10	5
R	14	13	6	8	13	3	2	16	4	2	10	7	13	3	19	6	2	12	2	2	16	14	3	10	10	11
S	15	19	10	20	18	14	16	8	12	10	6	11	16	12	12	6	3	20	6	15	3	6	16	6	8	13
T	7	19	5	7	4	5	3	12	4	6	17	6	18	17	14	12	20	17	2	7	5	13	18	14	18	6
U	11	5	20	10	16	19	20	20	11	10	16	14	20	7	6	11	6	6	20	12	4	16	3	10	15	17
V	13	14	17	3	7	10	15	12	2	10	3	19	18	10	8	13	8	16	4	2	16	4	15	3	2	8
W	15	20	17	7	4	16	13	19	3	18	12	2	14	4	12	15	5	18	7	6	6	15	10	18	16	13
X	15	7	19	8	15	13	11	6	5	4	20	8	17	4	10	13	3	6	8	5	4	14	11	20	18	18
Y	14	6	14	18	18	20	11	15	8	8	14	3	15	8	18	14	4	12	17	8	7	15	12	12	12	6
Z	8	2	15	5	17	11	20	2	6	13	19	15	5	14	12	14	4	10	20	2	13	15	12	18	16	17

On the chart, find the place where the initials you've chosen intersect. Read the chapter whose number appears at that intersection.

10

LUCK

It was often said in the Renaissance that Fortuna favors the young. The young do seem to have everything going their way — adventure, opportunities, new experiences, young love. When we're young, things just seem to automatically turn out right. We're naturally lucky. Middle age and our golden years often seem to be periods of shrinking horizons, lost opportunities, as we learn to settle for less and less. But the domain of luck is not solely for the young. It's not the chronological age of the downy-cheeked youth or that slip of a girl that makes them lucky. It's their outlook on life and their attitudes. Seeing all the years of their lives stretching before them and not yet having experienced too many disappointments, they are prepared to plunge into life, boldly seeking new adventures. They are curious and eager, and willing to start anew. Fortuna favors them because they are bold enough to court her favors. So even if we will never see eighteen again, we too can cultivate some of youth's traits. We can go even further and enhance our chances in life by applying some of the wisdom which is usually only available later in life, until we become as lucky as we can possibly be.

What does it mean to be lucky? It commonly means someone who gets something valuable without really trying: someone who inherits one million dollars unexpectedly, someone who buys a winning lottery ticket, someone who is in the right place at the right time. The bright, young attorney who happens to catch the boss's eye just when a top vacancy in the legal department has to be filled; someone who discovers a map showing buried treasure in a trunk in the attic, or a lost Rembrandt; or someone who finds a twenty dollar bill blowing in the supermarket parking lot; the workers and their families who sold everything and left Detroit in 1959 during a slump in the auto industry, who made up caravans to travel to Alaska over rough and primitive roads, and who were in on the ground floor when that state began rolling in oil money — these are lucky people.

In the most general sense, "being lucky " means meeting up with a fortuitous unexpected event. Since we have no control over the "when" and the "where" of these events, we can't make them happen to us. The only way to influence our luck is to master ourselves; to be open to all possibilities. The first rule is to seek variety. Seek out new experiences. Encouraging diversity will result in a richer life with more opportunities. The more varied our life is and the more different strands there are running through it, the more unexpected combinations there will be of occasions which occur, giving us the opportunity to grab hold of one of these strands and improve our situation. Our lucky break won't come to us sitting at home watching television! Modern evolutionary theory teaches us this lesson, and it applies to individuals as well as to species: The best evolutionary strategy in changing and unpredictable times is to maximize variability. In this way we become more adaptable. A fixed style of life could become a dead-end if the circumstances favoring it change and its ecological niche vanishes.

To bring luck into your life, bring Fortuna into your life.

- Seek variety
- Relish uncertainty
- Be courageous
- Be active
- Be accepting
- Step off into the future with confidence

LET IT HAPPEN!

When we are searching for something, like a lost pair of glasses, it doesn't make sense to always follow the same pattern of search. If we always start in the basement and systematically work our way through the house, we may waste time repeating mistakes of the past. Instead we should learn from the past. Each time we misplace the glasses, we should start our search at the place where we last found them. It only makes sense to constantly vary our search pattern in order to incorporate past successes. Searching for happiness is like that. Be flexible! Learn from your mistakes. Try lots of different possibilities.

It's impossible to run after something at the same time that we are running away from it. We can't seek variety at the same time that we are running away from uncertainty, trying to protect ourselves. We have to really love Fortuna, welcome her influence on our lives, and accept her abundance. We have to like surprises. We've all heard people say "I hope nothing happens!" Well, to be on Fortuna's good side, to really become lucky, we have to say "Let it happen!" The more things happening, the more likely that events will occur which we can construe as positive. We must abandon ourselves into the arms of Fortuna, not just tolerate her. Let us relish uncertainty, for happiness lies in that realm.

Variety is necessary for happiness. No matter how rich our lives may seem, if they only consist of expected events and repetition, boredom creeps in. Fairy tales are full of bored princesses and jaded sultans, whose enviable opulence sinks into a dull background of repetition. The modern mind is not substantially different from the mind of the primitive hunter, searching the forest for tiny signs of movement, ignoring the still trees around him, and thrilling to the slightest whisper of an animal moving through the leaves. We find pleasure in the unexpected and surprising. Obligatory birthday presents do not move us, but we can be strangely touched by unexpected small gestures of generosity or affection. Chance makes the difference. Saying "yes" to uncertainty adds a youthful zest to life and contributes to our luck. And it can belong to anyone.

It's not always easy to do this. Another trait which is characteristic of youth, which seems to spring sometimes more from lack of knowledge and prudence than from anything else, is courage. They're not afraid to act. They love adventure. That something bad could happen to them is the last thing on their minds. Taken to extremes, we see joy-riding while drinking, experimentation with hard drugs, and young girls hitch-hiking alone as illustrations of this mindless courage. Somehow their luck usually carries them through and most teenagers survive to become cautious adults. It's a lot harder for older people to be daring and courageous. We know more about what could happen to us. We've got more to lose. It seems easier to use our mature strength to build barriers, to protect ourselves from uncertainty. We wear seat belts and only drive when sober. We buy life insurance, household insurance, and automobile insurance. We work hard in our jobs and put money away for a rainy day. But it really doesn't work. All this prudence can't guarantee safety. We can't protect ourselves from uncertainty. Another driver could cause us to have an accident, our house could burn down, inflation could wipe out our savings, or recession could take away our job. If we were living in more certain times, we could build a brick house on solid ground and protect ourselves. If we build this house on the sands by the sea of uncertainty, it will only topple. We have to water-ski over the waves of the sea of uncertainty, hitting both the highs and the lows, or else we'll sink.

Action to bring variability into our environment is necessary in order to experience growth and a richer, freer life. Without flexibility, we court disaster. In a storm, a stout linen sail which is tied securely to the mast may be tattered and torn while even a fragile bird can ride out the fierce winds. We had better find the courage to fly and stop trying to hold on to certainty. But fear of the unknown tends to make us passive in the face of uncertainty; fear and passivity breed withdrawal from life. How can we find the courage to act, the courage of the young? How does one break away from the passivity of fear?

It's not that hard. We only have to do it just once. Each one of us should find one action that will increase variety: ask an acquaintance to lunch, subscribe to a new magazine, take a different route to work, sign up for a night-school course, plan a party. Do just this one act. There will certainly be some positive consequences. Focus on them. This positive reinforcement, together with the pleasure of sensing our power in exercising our free will, should give us the courage for the next act. Acting in the face of uncertainty builds our courage and confidence while hiding only makes the unknown appear more fearful. Action itself will free us from the fear of action. Once we realize this, there's no choice left but to act. We just have to start. This is what courage is.

Have you been putting off a decision because of uncertainties? Today, weigh the pros and cons and make it! Trust your decision. Trust your ability to make the best of whatever the result of that decision entails. Move forward, actively, to the next stage in your life and meet those uncertainties with courage and acceptance.

Encouraging Fortuna's role in our lives, acting with courage to seek out variety, is a lesson we can all learn from youth. This lesson once learned will result in our sharing their luck. But there are other lessons too. Acceptance is another key element in the attitude with which we should approach the idea of luck. By this we do not mean passive acceptance. Acceptance must always be closely linked with an active life in order to clearly differentiate it from fatalism. We are not supposed to accept our fate, passively following a narrow path into the future that has somehow been absolutely determined to be our lot. Instead, what we recommend is accepting who we are and where we are in our life story, thereby acknowledging that the past is fixed. This is the best foundation for living in the present and stepping off into the future. Fate and Fortuna are different entities. Fate is associated with limitations, constraints, and powerlessness; Fortuna brings freedom, possibilities, and abundance.

Human beings are always in a state of becoming, creating themselves at every instant. According to the psychologist Carl Rogers, in his classic work *On Becoming a Person,* the good life is a process. A healthy human organism will provide automatically for itself what Rogers believes is the most important healing tonic a therapist could give to a troubled personality: unconditional acceptance. Recognizing and accepting that contradictions, diversity, and ambivalence are inevitable parts of what we are in every moment, the individual comes to realize that he need no longer fear what experience may bring, but can welcome it as part of his changing and developing self. The individual participates in life rather than attempting to control it. As self-knowledge and acceptance grow, the individual experiences an increasing trust that his organism has the ability to function successfully in all its complexity and that it will select that behavior, from the multitude of possibilities presented to it, which at any given moment of time will be most generally and genuinely satisfying.

We cannot change the past. Therefore we are at this present moment exactly as good and perfect as we can possibly be. We could not be otherwise. Accepting ourselves exactly as we are at this present moment provides the courage to move forward. Since we are the best person we can be, the choices we make at this moment, by openly expressing our wishes and desires, are the best choices that can be made. Believing this and knowing that this acceptant attitude will continue in the future provides us with the motivation to move forward. Believing that all our choices in the past were the best possible ones we could have made at that time frees us from regret and reinforces our belief that we are as good and perfect as we can be at this present moment. This feeling cycles around and around, reinforcing itself. The best preparation for the future is self-acceptance in the now. Self-acceptance and trust in your organism are the foundations of confidence and courage.

Some of us might fear that our personalities are rotten, full of impulses to dangerous or improper actions. We feel we need to have the controls of rigid planning in order to prevent our impulses from leading us into disaster. We do not accept ourselves. But if we try to lock these desires in a cage and hide them from ourselves, they will become even more dangerous like unknown, unpredictable forces waiting in ambush. We should trust that our personalities are strong enough to integrate their dangerous components, if only they are allowed the freedom to acknowledge and work on them. Let the beasts out of their cages, make friends with them, tame them, allow them some say in decision-making. As a result, our integrated personality will be stronger, more diverse, and more capable of making decisions in the future. And we might even have more fun.

Self-acceptance, courage, and action don't guarantee good luck. They guarantee only a richer and fuller life with more opportunities for unexpected events that can enrich our lives. But not all the events that come our way are desirable. Fortuna never grants unmixed favors. The frightening thing about opening ourselves to the world of uncertainty, and the reason why so many people turn away from it, is that bad things can just as easily and unexpectedly happen to us as good things. Is it worth it?

In the Middle Ages, Fortuna was traditionally depicted with a half ugly, half beautiful face, representing the fact that she brings bad fortune (losses and ruin) as well as good fortune (treasure and success).

To avoid the pain of bad fortune, people were advised to turn away from her completely, to reject the search after earthly rewards, and to seek consolation by devotion to spiritual endeavors. This may have been appropriate advice in the static Dark Ages but it's not sufficient for today's uncertain times. The Fortuna of antiquity, which is a better image for today, did not have two faces. She only brought the event; every person made his or her own happiness. A remnant of this outlook survives in the folk wisdom that says "Look on the good side of things," or "look for the silver lining in every dark cloud." In every event there is a mixture of good and bad; we are free to concentrate our attention on either aspect. If we allow it, a scratched fender can ruin an otherwise perfect outing on a beautiful summer day. But we admire, and should emulate, the attitude of the handicapped individual who manages to live a normal life, who is full of cheer to share with others, while constantly beset by difficulties and irritations that would bring gloom and despair to the rest of us. Since we cannot control events, we must begin by managing ourselves. Our attitudes can be under our control. We should actively place ourselves in the path of events, attuned and expectant, ready to receive the favors of Fortuna. When good things come our way, we should be ready to savor them. And enjoyment of the moment should not be poisoned by dwelling on the fact that the pleasure will pass. Change is a natural state and we need to be able to "let go." When painful events are sent to us, we suffer. But without despair. Every event has some positive features. We must look for them and build on them. Bad luck should not be allowed to discourage us and make us falter from our involvement in life. We heal quickly and must return to the center of action, ready to accept whatever next comes our way.

Life offers us a banquet of possibilities, some good, some painful, but all inextricably linked. To enjoy the good and pleasurable things in life we have to open ourselves to the possibility of the bad and the harmful. If we can stand the buffeting of painful events, only then may we taste the pleasure of really living. If we live a full life, we should expect to live intimately with feelings of pain, for growth and change are never easy; but we will also be able to experience more vividly feelings of ecstasy. The young man who asks out every woman who attracts him may receive a few painful rebuffs (which he will learn to handle, eventually, much better than if he had only feared, but never experienced, rejection) but he will also have a lot of interesting dates! Willie Nelson summed it all up in the title of a song, "The Goin' Up Is Worth The Comin' Down."

Of course there is no guarantee. One could cultivate all these attributes we recommend here and still be involved in a terrible automobile accident. The most negative, rigid, timid person may win the Irish Sweepstakes. If the gifts of Fortuna could be turned on and off by our actions, she would be powerless. Determinism would reign supreme and we could completely control our destinies. But she cannot be controlled or predicted. She is totally impartial. Randomness is a natural force like the wind, the rain, or volcanoes. We must adapt ourselves by boldly stepping out into the gale of change and unpredictability. The pursuit of happiness is not easy for the faint-hearted. It requires courage. It means accepting that we ourselves will change, moment by moment, in response to the accidents chance brings into our lives. We do not control that change but only experience it. Yet, because of the presence of chance, we are free to act. Our future is not determined by the stars; we help make it.

One who lives this way, following the Fortuna philosphy, will be a lucky person. And not only lucky in the sense of receiving many gifts from Fortuna but lucky in becoming happy too. As uncertainty increases in the world around us and Fortuna's power over our lives is intensified, we can no longer rigidly fight to hold on to what we have. It's time to come to terms with the forces of chance and uncertainty. It's time to make friends with Fortuna.

THE MATRIX FOR CHAPTER 10

	A	B	C	D	E	F	G	H	I	J	K	L	M	N	O	P	Q	R	S	T	U	V	W	X	Y	Z
A	2	13	6	14	14	14	19	3	18	14	2	4	9	19	12	18	6	3	19	7	2	16	5	2	12	2
B	19	3	2	5	17	7	6	17	6	20	3	14	13	3	17	18	15	20	16	5	20	11	15	4	20	2
C	4	20	15	17	3	16	16	14	20	12	18	5	19	17	12	6	16	3	7	9	9	17	7	15	14	16
D	15	11	2	3	19	3	5	2	6	13	6	18	17	15	15	9	12	20	7	13	7	4	16	3	13	20
E	12	9	2	2	13	14	12	14	9	12	13	19	3	4	14	3	13	12	7	9	20	15	20	12	2	11
F	13	6	13	17	7	2	12	9	18	5	8	7	2	6	3	4	7	20	16	8	11	2	20	6	2	15
G	18	14	2	9	18	13	14	15	20	17	9	20	16	7	4	18	18	7	13	15	15	13	4	6	3	20
H	19	14	3	17	18	18	3	5	19	8	8	8	6	6	15	14	3	11	16	15	3	18	2	2	12	15
I	20	4	7	15	20	18	11	20	15	7	13	8	20	3	6	11	17	20	13	3	8	11	12	17	17	11
J	19	9	11	4	8	9	4	19	8	20	5	20	18	16	2	2	11	19	8	20	14	13	5	9	3	14
K	8	18	11	18	14	20	9	7	18	15	14	18	11	14	15	6	16	8	6	4	3	15	18	11	4	2
L	12	18	6	5	3	3	20	8	19	4	11	13	15	3	20	19	7	16	15	19	6	13	11	20	7	2
M	17	16	2	19	5	15	20	7	2	16	2	5	17	8	2	19	3	5	4	18	7	8	18	19	12	17
N	2	20	20	5	7	19	9	5	11	14	12	6	14	7	4	13	18	14	15	2	4	12	19	19	19	14
O	20	19	6	12	12	9	20	18	12	20	4	9	18	8	16	8	20	13	9	7	7	16	13	8	5	11
P	11	15	17	5	14	20	8	16	8	11	11	13	7	16	9	18	8	11	15	19	14	12	13	4	7	4
Q	17	4	5	4	13	8	18	17	17	2	11	14	15	17	13	11	2	17	3	12	3	9	3	12	14	6
R	16	15	9	15	16	12	19	3	7	7	8	9	6	2	15	17	16	18	20	16	13	19	12	19	5	15
S	2	16	4	12	19	8	17	6	2	12	2	14	8	16	11	20	18	12	11	8	14	5	2	5	2	16
T	5	9	13	8	16	4	14	9	2	19	3	5	12	16	13	4	9	13	13	2	2	9	20	12	7	3
U	14	13	14	6	19	2	15	12	5	14	19	8	17	6	14	6	3	13	4	17	19	11	7	20	8	15
V	11	16	16	9	4	6	8	15	8	3	6	13	11	12	4	17	4	12	14	13	8	6	8	11	17	16
W	11	6	15	18	19	11	7	18	16	7	17	7	5	8	7	20	2	5	14	7	16	11	15	4	6	8
X	6	8	9	20	5	7	16	5	6	11	14	3	19	11	16	20	5	16	13	14	14	12	2	13	14	17
Y	8	9	20	14	11	5	7	8	18	5	7	9	8	18	2	12	17	4	13	6	17	2	13	5	20	7
Z	13	5	5	17	20	6	14	17	4	20	9	17	17	2	11	17	6	4	3	14	2	19	20	15	17	3

On the chart, find the place where the initials you've chosen intersect. Read the chapter whose number appears at that intersection.

11

THE WHEEL OF FORTUNA

In front of the abbey at Fecamp, France, a monk in the twelfth century built a wooden wheel. It was a rather large contraption which was activated by a moving mechanism. A crowd of curious folk would gather around the wheel and our monk would start his lecture which was really a nice piece of propaganda designed for social control. This wheel must have looked very much like a smaller version of our modern Ferris wheel. However, it was not used to give young people pleasure but rather to frighten them. The monk nailed a dummy to the rim of the wheel and, as he activated the crank that moved the wheel with one hand, he would use his other hand to point at the dummy with a stick. This must have been one of the oldest mechanized teaching props on record. As the monk made the wheel turn, the crowd of faithful gathered there could watch how the dummy was going up on the wheel and, as everybody could clearly see, the dummy would inevitably fall head down in the mud as the wheel kept turning. The dummy would sometimes be made to look like a king and as the wheel turned, the king would be driven on the wheel first upward then downward so that his face would hit the dirt or mud to the great amazement of these simple people. The audience, which consisted mostly of illiterate peasants and serfs, would experience a curious feeling of fear mixed with pity not unlike the one experienced by the ancient spectators of a Greek tragedy. Their fear was further enhanced by their sense of awe toward princes and kings.

SOCIAL IMMOBILITY

The social lesson taught by this wheel was like the one conveyed by *Oedipus Rex:* that people should be content with their lot in life and not attempt to change it. They should not attempt to rise on the social ladder. As a matter of fact, there was not even such a thing as a social ladder in the language or in the minds of people at that time. Social mobility was unknown because it had been forbidden for so long. One theory which is said to account for this is that, during the period of the decline of the Roman Empire, the Roman tax collectors thought that it would be easier to collect taxes year after year if they did not have to change their records. They forbade people from changing their occupations, so the son of a baker had to become a baker and continue paying taxes under the same name. Be that as it may, change was discouraged.

So, as the monk turned his wheel, he would demonstrate that anyone who climbs on the wheel will, without fail, be cast down. The lesson for hundreds of years was clear: "Do not aspire to high places because you will inevitably be cast down." This lesson had two consequences: First, it contributed to social immobility as people gave up trying to better themselves. Second, because people were taught not to climb and challenge high positions in society, it allowed those in power, the kings, queens, princes, and the members of the high clergy to remain safely in place. The monks who taught these lessons were not evil men. It may be viewed as beneficial for both the individual and society to take refuge in stability during periods of excessive instability. The same can be said for the ancient playwright-priest as for the modern commissar or psychoanalyst: they all act under the best of intentions.

Fortunate individuals will follow the general advice given here on how to live at peace with chance, uncertainty, diversity, variability, and plain change. They will find in the wheel of Fortuna a mysterious symbol for lessons in fortunate living which open the doors to happiness. This very ancient symbol of chance is still important for life in the information age and in our daily lives. Familiarity with the workings of the wheel can help us solve the problems that Fortuna herself brings us at every moment.

Remembering the history of the wheel, the fortunate individual will:

- be tolerant and love humanity
- seek social mobility
- avoid prejudice
- enjoy falling as well as rising
- avoid machismo
- question authority
- view events as neutral; rule himself
- adapt to disorder and unpredictability
- realize that escape is always possible
- see the possibility of renewal
- respect the physical and social environment

THE SQUARE WHEEL AND THE ROUND WHEEL

The medieval wheel may be called a square wheel with its four determined positions: rising, being on top, falling, fallen. In contrast to this oppressive square wheel, the beauty and richness of the round wheel of Fortuna, which we are trying to rehabilitate, can be illustrated by means of a very simple mathematical exercise. Let us take a triangle. Suppose that we cut one triangle out of cardboard. Let's make a hole at the center of the triangle and attach a pointer that spins around. The pointer, spun in the triangle's center, would, when at rest, indicate one of the three sides. There are only three places where the pointer can land. We can say that, from the view of the pointer, the triangle contains three different opportunities. It can land on only one of the three sides. The pointer can be said to have only three chances.

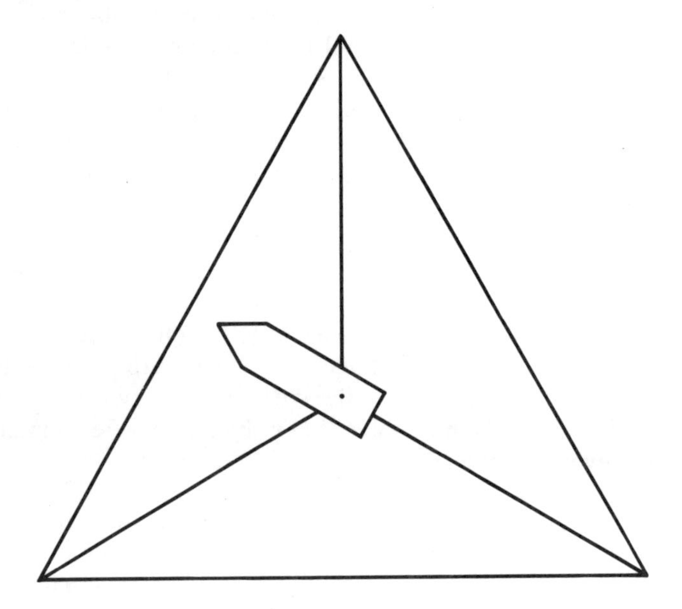

Now, consider a square also made out of cardboard with a pointer pinned at its center. We can say that since it has only four sides, the pointer, when spun at its center, will also have four chances. Another way of seeing it is that each of the sides of the square has one chance in four of getting the pointer to rest there at the end of a spin. Let us take now figures with more and more sides, like pentagons, hexagons, etc. The more sides a figure has, the more chances it contains. If the sides of the triangle were of three different colors and if each of the eight sides of an octagon were of eight different colors, we could say that the octagon was more colorful, more diversified, more varied, more like the world of Fortuna.

We notice that as we add more and more sides to our cardboard figure, it begins to look more like a circle or a wheel. It can be said that the circle contains millions upon millions and even an infinite number of little sides or chances. The figure of the wheel contains the largest number of opportunities, the most chance, and is, therefore, an appropriate symbol of Fortuna. The Ancient Greeks believed the circle to be the perfect geometric figure, comparable to God. The French Renaissance poet Pierre de Ronsard wrote that nothing in this world is perfect unless it is round. Roundness and perfection go together. The circle, however, is too abstract a symbol; over time, the everyday wheel, a very practical human tool, has come to stand as a symbol of Fortuna. We will use it as a positive symbol for the Fortuna philosphy and way of life.

UP AND DOWN

As we have seen, the wheel of Fortuna has not always been an image of optimism and hope in life. On the contrary, it was viewed for ages as an image full of portentous threats. But changes are coming. As the wheel becomes associated with the positive attributes of Fortuna — chance, uncertainty, opportunity — it will be rehabiliated as a symbol. In order to make this association, we have to abandon our deep-seated notion that up is good and down is bad. We have to free ourselves from simple prejudices based on metaphors which are no longer applicable in the modern world. We accept too often the notion that being on top or above is better than being below or under. However, we can think of countless examples in modern life where the distinctions between up and down do not work anymore in the traditional way and where it is indeed better to be under than on top. If we ever get a taste of a nuclear war, it will indeed be preferable to put the most important offices of a corporation building deep in the ground. The office of the chairman of the board would then be located in the lowest basement while the mail clerks would work on the top floors.

In some creative business enterprises, organizational charts are now being redrawn in a more sensible manner, making the structure of the organization independent of the basic opposition between up and down. In the family, the father is gradually losing, or perhaps gladly giving up his burdensome place at the top of the family heap. This may be for the good of all members of society. Oedipus may finally be released from his fixed position on a vertex of the family triangle with its limited number of chances: mommy, daddy, and me. In human relationships, wherever power is involved such as in work, love, and sex, macho man is gradually being replaced by that fortunate individual who is more democratic and loving. We must insist on disestablishing the rule of up and down because of the way that the square wheel has been exploited in the past to scare people out of their wits and to turn them into submissive serfs.

Too often, we label events as good or bad when, in reality, events are actually neutral. We are ourselves the culprits when we attach preconceived notions of good and bad to random sets of circumstances. Also, we make ourselves miserable by having fixed ideas about what we like and dislike. We carry our own hell with us. We accept blindly as fact that rising is good and that falling is bad in the face of many exceptions such as for members of sky-diving clubs who must love the thrills of free-falling. For mountain skiers most of the fun, it seems, is in the going down. Going up, confined to their lift-chairs, without freedom to move, is not nearly as much fun as going down. They pay money in order to be free to slide down at their own pace taking their chances and playing with Fortuna.

THE HISTORY OF THE SYMBOL

The notion of up being positive and down being something to avoid was most widespread during the Middle Ages. Cathedrals and churches were built to soar upward towards the Good. Base, worldly goods like money, comfort, and pleasure were to be avoided in favor of eternal salvation in the world above. Good Christians, especially learned ones, will find this simplistic separation between up and down to be, in fact, heretical since they know that God is everywhere, and that, just like in the circumference of the circle, there are no privileged points, all points on the circumference being equally distant from the center (God). The wheel of Fortuna that we wish to rehabilitate is the round one (the whole wheel), not the wheel which perniciously divides the world into good and bad things, or good and bad people.

During the Dark Ages, the wheel was used to teach people the benefits of submitting to established authority. The world below, or life on earth, was divided into high and low, up and down. In those times, to ascend the wheel was a euphemism for the ultimately vain struggle for worldly goods. There was a tendency in the minds of people during the Middle Ages to dwell on the unexpected, sudden, and rapid changes which were common in human lives. The world was full of danger; life was cheap; human existence was essentially precarious. The teachers of the time, who were for the most part monks, put the wheel to use in order to console the faithful. They would conduct their indoctrination in the cathedrals and in royal abbeys which also contained glass, wood, or stone representations of the wheel of Fortuna. The wheel was depicted in the negative "square" way for one thousand years; from the sixth century when Boethius wrote his book titled *The Consolation of Philosophy* until the sixteenth century during the height of the Renaissance.

The monk Boethius, not unlike many people today, supposed that more order and regularity existed in the world than was actually revealed in day to day experience. He had great difficulty admitting accidental coincidences and the existence of chance in life, so he rationalized everything including the wheel. The most obvious way of rationalizing the wheel is to break it into a finite number of manageable possibilities such as three, four, or five, to triangulate it or square it in order to rob it of its disquieting unpredictability. The wheel was divided into four positions and no more. In the drawings that have been found from the fourteenth, fifteenth, and parts of the sixteenth centuries, the wheel is pictured with four dummies nailed to its rim. One of these dummies, made to look like a king, with a crown on his head, is sitting on the top of the wheel with the inscription "I reign" written at his feet. Another figure is shown attached to the right (sometimes the left) of the wheel with the inscription saying "I will reign." Across from him there is another figure of the same king, nailed to the wheel upside down, with the inscription "I did reign," and the fourth figure is laying under the wheel, crushed by it in some

drawings, and with the inscription "I am without reign." Next to the wheel, the artists have drawn the picture of a lady with both hands on a handle cranking the wheel. She is the Fortuna of the Middle Ages. She is definitely not the one we wish to bring back to our present world.

Our Fortuna, the Fortuna of the fortunate individual, is the Ancient Fortuna who was usually shown standing on a ball which signified instability but also dominion over the world. That Ancient Fortuna is the same, for our purposes, as the one who reappeared during the Renaissance. During that glorious period of our history, some four hundred years ago, the goddess was reborn.

From the Renaissance to the present, people have been learning to adjust, to adapt, to escape, to make themselves free. The squared wheel should not frighten anybody any longer, either consciously or subconsciously. New attitudes were born during the Renaissance to counter the perverted wheel of the Middle Ages. The French essayist Michel de Montaigne pointed the way to that liberation. He helped mankind to free itself from one thousand years of fear of falling off the wheel: "When in danger," he wrote, "I do not think so much how I shall escape, as how little it matters that I escape. Even if I should fall, what would it matter? Not being able to rule events, I rule myself and adapt myself to them if they do not adapt themselves to me." In other words, Montaigne does not care whether he is on top or under the wheel. All positions on the wheel are equally suitable to him since he can adapt to them. More importantly, he does not limit himself to four positions on the wheel but allows himself a wider range of possibilities. All points of the circumference are good as they are equally distant from the center.

The medieval wheel was morbid — the person in the fourth position under the wheel is a dead one. Such a wheel symbolized an infernal machinery from which there was no escape because of the fatality of its rotation. Just like Oedipus in the Greek play, the lives of the poor souls who climbed on the medieval wheel were determined by Fate. Fate imprisons the mind while Fortuna frees it. The squared wheel has only four chances while the rounded wheel of possibilities has as many chances on its rim as there are points on the circumference of a circle. The squared wheel of the Middle Ages is like Fate while the total wheel of the Renaissance and of modern times is like Fortuna. The medieval wheel excluded the possibility of alternatives; it excluded accidents and events coming from outside that could disrupt the mechanism, bringing it to a halt, making it go in the opposite direction, or simply breaking down. Rejecting external events was perhaps necessary for the first steps humans took along the path of scientific rationality. However, rejection of the event, and rejection of the legitimacy of accident brought by chance, as vital aspects of this world-view, led to stagnation. Pure chance, that which causes events and accidents, was seen as the domain of risk, the fearful reign of the unknown, and was hence forbidden. But the Renaissance conquistadors and navigators broke that circle of fear.

THE METAPHYSICS OF CHANCE

Under the apparently simple opposition between what we call the square wheel and the round wheel of possibilities lies a fundamental philosophical question which we must point out as briefly and clearly as possible. The two positions that are at odds here are the metaphysics of determinism and the metaphysics of chance. The metaphysics of determinism refuses to accept that life on earth may be just an accident. It incorporates human life into an idealistic rationalization proceeding inevitably from the inferior to the superior. Just like the medieval wheel, determinism turns, grinds, and progresses towards a definite goal. There are no surprises on that wheel, just as there should not be any surprises for Marxists in their striving for Communist Man and for other deluded dreamers under the banner of teleonomy, the flag of all those who believe in the fictions of ultimate goals and ends.

Much different is the metaphysics of chance, the Fortuna philosphy we advocate here, which views life as a very rare event in a play of encounters ruled by both chance and necessity. In such a world-view, we recognize that most mechanical rationalizations are after-the-fact fables produced by our brains. The squared wheel of our monk was not only a fable but also a fraud, for not all dummies who rise on the wheel will inevitably fall. Some rulers and people who have made it to the top have lived long and happy lives. Notice also that on the drawings of the medieval wheel of Fortuna, the goddess keeps both her hands on the handle of the cranking mechanism. This suggests that she has been made a prisoner of her own wheel. Her hands are tied to the infernal machine. She is made part of the machine, a victim of Fate. Much more natural, appealing, and exciting is the Renaissance Fortuna who, no longer submitting to it, has discarded the squared wheel of old and adopted new accoutrements such as the sail, the knife, the hourglass, the forelock, and the cornucopia. The liberating significance of these new attributes is described in Chapter 5.

By excluding the event, the medieval wheel is the direct ancestor of modern Hegelian idealism and Marxist materialism, two systems that give the illusion of working by themselves as if they were self-generated and as if accidents did not happen. These theorists chase Fortuna out of their systems just like Boethius, in the sixth century, chased Fortuna out of his cell and invited in Lady Reason. (He was in jail when he wrote his famous book, *The Consolation of Philsophy.*) This book turned out to be a bestseller and was required reading in the schools of Europe for one thousand years. Even though he is not talked about much these days, the way we think today, in particular about chance, is still very much influenced by what he wrote. Many books today contain echoes of the ideas Boethius spread about chance. Sweeping away these antiquated ideas will make us freer. There are essentially two ways of perceiving the world around us. One acknowledges rule, law, and order in everything; the other recognizes accidents, events, the improbable, the uncertain, the singular, the individual, and a certain dose of disorder in life. Both views are valid. One represents chance, the other necessity. The solution lies in bringing together these two apparently contradictory postulates into a complementary synthesis. While the medieval wheel was the instrument of necessity, the new wheel of Fortuna symbolizes the union of both chance and necessity.

THE WHEEL OF LIFE

Furthermore, the wheel must be reinterpreted not as a closed system like the medieval wheel but as open to the environment. Fortuna has been made to rhyme with Luna by the poets but, unlike the moon which does not require any energy from the outside in order to accomplish its revolutions, the new Fortuna wheel must be patterned along the lines of living organisms in order to represent human life. Our wheel needs the environment, the ecosystem, to get its nourishment from its chance-like surroundings. Our wheel then becomes a self-organizing system just like Lake Erie, a university, or a brain, all of which maintain a constant relationship with their ecosystems. Chance occurs, or Fortuna exists, at the surface of contact between a system and its ecosystem; between a human being and his or her environment. The wheel must be reinterpreted along these lines.

The medieval wheel represented only one aspect of time: the time of inexorable repetition, the time of duplication with its synchronous movement. The movements of this synchronous time are sterile and never-changing, like the inexorable rotations of the water-wheel or like the moon turning endlessly around the Earth. The new wheel adds to time the notions of renewal, of change, and of novelty. This is the diachronic sense of time. The old wheel was based on the principle of forcing order to emerge from disorder; it took the social disorder of the times, the suffering by men and women in the face of dire instability and uncertainty, and created order. But this order was an illusion as it did not reflect the way life really was, and still is:

chance-like and unpredictable. Medieval philosophers created the synchronous wheel that spun in what the modern French philosopher Edgar Morin calls "the little time" with its cyclic and clock-like repetitions. The new wheel follows the principal stated by Heinz von Foerster of "order from noise" where order is achieved not by exluding chance and accidents but by allowing "noise" and "error" to work by themselves to create chance and novelty. A clock with all its spinning wheels does not produce anything new, while a living cell, because it is in contact with the chance-like nature of the outside environment, produces something other, and sometimes different, than itself. Self-organizing systems, like humans or the new wheel which represents more faithfully the turns of life as well as of human societies, turn and evolve in what Morin calls "the great time, the diachronic time of disorganizations, of ruptures, of transformations, of creations." What Morin called "morbid rationalism" which we applied in our previous example to the mentality of the monk and his wheel, is the desperate attempt "to reduce the great time to the little time, to eliminate diachronic time, and to want a closed world." By showing a wheel which was actually a closed world, a sort of prison — no matter how comfortable or even joyful that prison might have been — the monk was unwittingly imprisoning the imagination and the will of his audience in spite of his intention to liberate them from secular values.

The wheel of Fortuna is the ultimate representation of the idea of chance. It stands for diversity, variety, opportunity, occasion, new vistas, new horizons, and, essentially, for liberty. The wheel, like the circle with its countless sides, symbolizes the richness of life's experience and the multiplicity of chances that can come our way. We should not fear the wheel as people did in the Middle Ages but, on the contrary, we should learn to love it and thereby learn to live a richer and fuller life.

The wheel of Fortuna has been used as a decorative and artistic motif throughout the centuries. Once we learn where to look, we can see wheels of Fortuna all over, around us. In almost every town in America there are churches which have wheel-like rose-windows on the front and sides of the buildings. Art critic Emile Mâle was one of the first to link the rose-windows in cathedrals and churches to wheels of Fortuna. The cathedrals and churches built in the Middle Ages in Europe contain many wheels of Fortuna sculpted in stone. According to Mâle, certain of these wheels have been traced to the major medieval literary work on Fortuna, Boethius' *Consolation of Philosophy.* In England, these wheels can be seen in Rochester; in Italy, there is a famous one in the cathedral of St. Zeno in Verona; another can be seen in Basel, Switzerland; and in France, in the cathedral of Amiens. One need not go to those places, however, to see wheels of Fortuna since churches throughout the world have rose-windows built with hubs and spikes based on the wheel. It is interesting to speculate that perhaps these wheels do not go back only to the sixth century influence of Boethius, but may go all the way back to the eighteen temples of the goddess Fortuna in Ancient Rome. The Romans associated the wheel with Fortuna. Specifically, Cicero mentions that Fortuna's wheel turns without stopping and causes sudden falls from power. These temples, as we know, were converted to Christian churches at the beginning of the Christian era and their wheel-like decorative ornaments may have influenced later builders of churches.

THE WHEEL, THE RING, AND THE CROSS

In architecture, a rose-window is also called a wheel-window and sometimes a Catherine-wheel-window, in memory of Saint Catherine (fourth century), who as the legend goes, escaped from martyrdom. She narrowly escaped being tortured and put to death on a spiked wheel, the shape of which is known today as a Catherine's wheel. Since the wheel was an instrument of torture and execution, how can we be asked to cherish such an object? Well, the cross was also an instrument of torture and execution and yet it is today one of the most cherished and revered symbols in existence. The wheel need not be feared and may even be cherished as the symbol of freedom and of love for humanity. The wheel stands for trust and confidence in the present, just as the cross is the symbol of hope in the future. Other objects and artifacts which have had pain and suffering at their origin are now cherished and revered, for example: the cross, the wheel, and the ring.

The rings that we wear on our fingers, and particularly engagement rings with precious stones, take their origin in the suffering of Prometheus, a mythical giant, half human, half god, who stole fire from the gods and gave it to humans. Once humans had fire, they became almost as powerful as the gods. Fire, of course, stands for knowledge and scientific knowledge in particular. As most people know, Jupiter, the king of the gods, was angry at Prometheus for having stolen fire from the heavens and giving it to humans down below. Jupiter (or Zeus as the Greeks called him), punished Prometheus for this theft and breach of trust by having him chained to a huge rock on a mountain where an eagle gnawed on his liver. This was Jupiter's own pet eagle and it fed on Prometheus' liver which grew back again each time. This awful torment lasted for many years.

Jupiter finally forgave him and Prometheus was unbound. Upon gaining his freedom, he took with him a piece of the rock on which he had been bound and upon which he had known so much suffering. He set the stone that he had gathered from the mountain on a ring that another god forged for him. Prometheus put the ring on his finger and wore it all his life in order to remind himself that he must forever be faithful to his master and not break his trust. Rings with stones are thus today beautiful symbols of fidelity. Men and women wear them today to signify their fidelity to an institution like a high school or a college. They are exchanged as symbols of fidelity and are traditionally used as betrothal symbols.

Thus the cross with the sacrifice of Jesus, the ring with the suffering of Prometheus, and the wheel with the near death of St. Catherine, have all come to represent that which is best among humans: hope, trust, and freedom. Love, the supreme human value, is present in all of the three symbols. Love of God is symbolized in the cross; love for another person or for an institution is symbolized by the ring; love for humanity is symbolized by the wheel. Hope, trust, and freedom are shared by these three symbols in different degrees. On the rim of a Catherine's wheel there are spikes. These spikes can be thought of as symbolizing the idea of escape by analogy with the escapement mechanism of a clock, those spiked, toothed, or ratchet wheels which allow the energy of the spring to escape one click at a time. Unlike the medieval wheel which provided no escape once you climbed on it, our modern Fortuna wheel allows for escape. St. Catherine did in fact escape torture and death, and Prometheus was finally allowed to escape from his tormentor, the eagle. Christ exemplified escape of the most exalted kind through resurrection.

And yet, accepting the wheel as a friendly symbol is not easy. The reasons for this are historical. First, for a thousand years of our historical past, the squared medieval wheel was used as a tool to control people, beat them into submission, and keep them from aspiring to a better life in this world. Second, the word "wheel" by itself, connotes torture. For a very long time, and until only a few hundred years ago, torture and execution were carried out in public on actual cartwheels. The victim was stretched flat on a cartwheel while his legs and arms were tied to the rim. The executioner would then proceed to break the arms and legs of the victim with an iron bar. Then the poor victim would be left to die slowly in the middle of a public square for everyone to see and, most importantly, to remember not only to obey the laws, but also by association, to fear the wheel.

The wheel has had a continuing influence on the planning of many of the major cities of the world, the most famous being Rome. And Paris has its Place de l'Etoile, Madrid its Puerta del Sol, London its Picadilly Circus, and Washington its Obelisk (shaped like the pointer on an ancient sundial), all with avenues and streets radiating from a central hub. However, modern cities more often resemble, particularly when viewed at night from a plane, a vast rectangular lighted grid like the circuitry of a computer.

However, there are many rich associations between the idea of the wheel of Fortuna and modern computers. They are both capable of dealing with randomness. They both utilize fundamentally the element of chance. The novel aspect of computer games is that each time a game is played, it can be entirely different. The element of surprise, of the unexpected, is what fascinates people when playing such computer games as "Dungeons and Dragons." The player at the console is, in a way, interacting with a contingent reality in a fantasy world ruled by the necessities of the game — for there are some rules. But that reality is also ruled by chance. The player is thus playing with Fortuna. This Fortuna is not the matronly, stern woman who cranked her wheel during the Middle Ages. She is a friendly and playful woman. We might say that she has come a long way.

Every period in history has its particular technology. Just as we have our computers today, the Middle Ages had the water wheel and the Renaissance had the clock. The morbid Middle Age wheel of Fortuna was based on the water wheel, the most familiar mechanical device of the times. That wheel would turn endlessly. People would see it with their mind's eye as wearing and grinding unfortunate human beings under it. By the fourteenth century the clock, a more modern and complex machine came into being and gave people a better model for interpreting life in the world of chance. Its advanced mechanism consisted of many wheels, all of different sizes. Familiarity with this new piece of machinery allowed people to imagine the possibility of variety and multiplicity in human affairs. There was no longer only one wheel, one fixed date, but many wheels, and thus many possibilities.

THE WHEELS OF MACHIAVELLI

This was an essential Renaissance view, and Machiavelli in particular held it when he wrote of several wheels of Fortuna turning in opposite directions. According to him, people must learn to jump from wheel to wheel. They must jump off a descending wheel and jump on a rising one at the most opportune moment. The Renaissance conceptualization of the wheel is not perfect but it was a significant step in freeing people from the medieval way of looking at chance in life. The philosophy of Machiavelli, with whom, we hasten to say, we are not in complete sympathy, is treated more extensively in Chapters 5 and 8. Nevertheless, a few remarks will be made here as pertains to our subject, the wheel of Fortuna.

Machiavelli has acquired an unsavory reputation because historians have failed to convey the circumstances and the historical context of his theories. His teachings may be viewed as an essential guide for survival in the places and times he lived. Machiavellian actions have come to mean actions, no matter how lawless or unscrupulous, which may be employed to maintain order and to gain advantage. His name has come to mean cunning and deceitful behavior. Our Fortuna philosophy parallels his in that it encourages the fortunate individual to jump from wheel to wheel. However, there are substantial differences. We should be encouraged to take our chances with proper preparation, of course, and we should seize occasions and opportunities when they are presented to us but, at the same time, we must temper our actions with a strong ingredient of fair-play and respect for others. The Fortuna philosophy advocates benign and fruitful interactions with our environment, which includes the people we come in contact with. It is founded on a respect for the physical and social environment we live in and interact with. It is a humane set of principles which, in the end, is more likely to lead to success than the crueler philosophy expounded by Machiavelli during the Renaissance.

Machiavelli viewed individuals as autonomous beings, wholly responsible for their actions. This was a significant improvement over the view during the Middle Ages when people were captives of fate and were locked onto the single square wheel. Not only were there more wheels, chances, and opportunities during the Renaissance, but also the notion became widespread that it was our own fault if we suffered. Conversely, we deserved praise if we succeeded. The individual, a newly discovered concept, was considered to be a unit independent of its environment. An individual was something divorced from the world it inhabited. All the glory as well as all the blame went to the individual.

THE WHEEL AS A METAPHOR OF TOLERANCE

The individual of the Renaissance was entirely responsible for his or her own fate. Individuals were thought to be wholly responsible for choosing whether they would get on this or that wheel or any wheel at all. In that period, there was little sympathy for the underdog. The usual road to success was over the broken backs of one's failed competitors. The difference between this Renaissance view and the one we are advocating is that we now view the individual as being a place where events occur. The most fundamental of these events are chemical and occur inside our cells where strands of molecules float, collide, and mix according to the rules of both chance and necessity, but events occur at the social level also. Since we should cultivate openness to events, to variety, to diversity — all attributes of Fortuna — and since we should love, or adapt to, all things that Fortuna brings, we should therefore also treat kindly all humans because they are the most precious events that Fortuna can bring.

We recommend then a modified Machiavellian philosphy involving altruism. If you smile on Fortuna, Fortuna will smile upon you. As we jump from wheel to wheel, bettering ourselves, it is important not to trample on other people. We live in a social world. Harming others is just another way of closing ourselves off to the possibilities and opportunities that interaction with others can provide. Even from a purely practical point of view, we are better off, in the long run, with friends than with enemies. Our friends can form the basis of our success. We can also help them as they help us. Machiavellism leads to lonely success. Without the adjustments that we must bring to the philosophy of Machiavelli, we may wind up being powerful but alone, a serious handicap for a happy life in today's world.

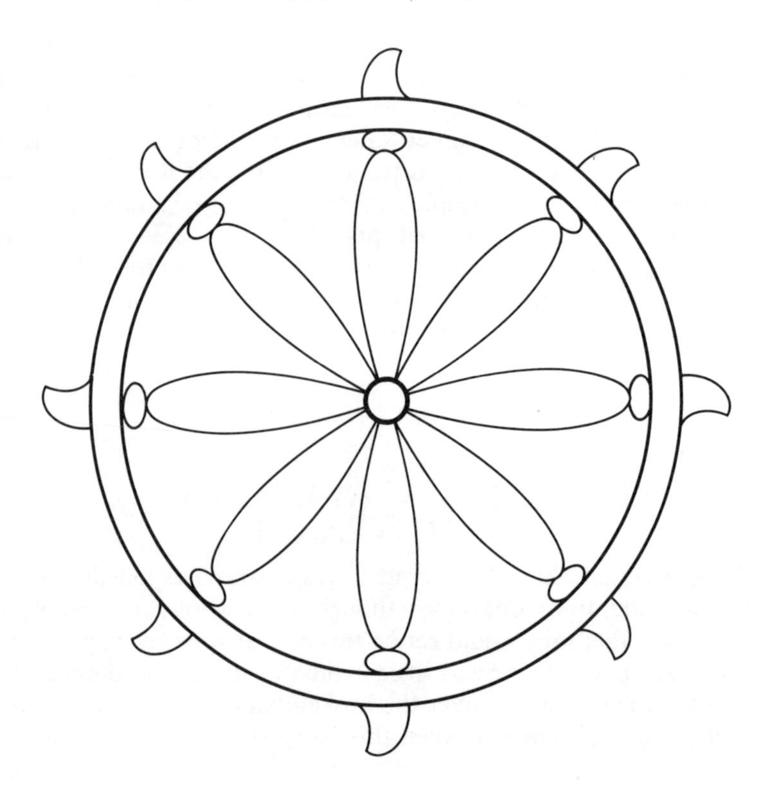

Finally, our modern wheel of Fortuna, symbolized most appropriately perhaps by a Catherine's wheel, with many little spikes on its rim, may serve to turn us into tolerant individuals. Just as the spikes are equally distant from the center of the wheel, all humans are equally loved by God and should be treated by us as our own brothers and sisters. Similarly, the spikes signify different points of view, different life styles, different modes of self-realization, all equally distant from the center, all worthy of acceptance, all equally deserving of love and understanding.

THE MATRIX FOR CHAPTER 11

	A	B	C	D	E	F	G	H	I	J	K	L	M	N	O	P	Q	R	S	T	U	V	W	X	Y	Z
A	15	2	15	12	6	18	13	16	12	19	3	3	15	4	14	13	3	7	6	10	12	10	12	8	10	7
B	15	14	3	2	13	9	12	12	14	18	6	4	12	6	8	20	19	6	14	9	13	8	17	6	2	19
C	9	2	9	3	16	9	13	17	9	15	17	4	7	15	20	2	2	16	12	2	6	19	19	4	10	7
D	5	16	17	12	6	20	19	15	4	6	18	10	13	8	13	5	8	6	16	2	15	18	19	4	14	12
E	10	19	4	7	14	3	3	17	19	6	14	3	13	7	17	2	9	4	6	16	10	9	12	3	9	2
F	5	9	6	8	15	13	18	6	17	10	17	4	13	20	14	9	13	5	2	19	19	3	9	19	20	13
G	2	2	12	5	5	7	13	13	10	13	2	4	3	14	8	20	3	16	9	7	9	19	6	7	17	12
H	18	20	9	4	6	6	7	2	5	7	18	10	15	13	12	18	9	2	17	20	9	19	9	12	13	6
I	2	15	9	20	8	13	6	3	9	13	14	12	16	8	2	4	9	14	6	8	5	13	6	12	3	7
J	15	16	3	10	6	4	20	10	13	10	18	5	8	19	17	9	17	8	3	5	7	14	8	19	18	10
K	19	4	5	10	18	8	17	4	10	8	7	6	12	18	17	19	15	19	3	9	17	16	2	14	14	10
L	8	12	2	3	19	17	4	2	20	2	12	8	9	15	3	15	20	19	19	16	17	6	6	8	15	16
M	12	10	13	16	16	19	5	5	19	3	20	15	5	18	9	16	15	16	13	12	13	12	4	2	8	7
N	14	17	18	3	5	17	15	20	15	6	20	17	5	10	15	16	10	19	9	6	15	17	5	15	12	6
O	3	18	5	16	5	18	7	2	2	7	10	10	9	12	13	17	13	2	10	10	2	9	3	10	4	4
P	14	16	19	14	8	5	13	20	14	17	19	9	6	4	5	14	18	12	3	18	17	9	4	3	10	2
Q	16	15	3	7	20	12	4	9	2	18	15	17	5	8	3	20	17	5	18	14	16	4	18	9	2	17
R	7	9	14	13	17	7	13	6	8	12	19	20	20	16	16	18	3	16	5	10	5	9	15	17	3	14
S	10	8	9	9	5	4	9	2	4	5	15	3	7	4	13	5	12	9	17	12	18	19	3	14	10	2
T	17	14	3	16	20	6	16	8	9	4	2	8	3	15	16	13	15	8	3	5	16	12	3	10	10	15
U	8	19	13	12	3	18	18	9	3	7	14	18	8	20	19	13	12	20	15	13	13	19	9	7	16	10
V	18	18	9	7	14	14	6	13	4	19	20	6	19	20	19	5	13	19	19	18	13	12	9	4	12	6
W	18	8	16	5	18	12	14	16	14	9	9	4	7	15	16	13	8	6	2	2	19	12	3	9	5	17
X	7	12	5	17	12	5	15	14	18	19	7	4	13	8	8	3	8	2	6	8	20	2	8	6	19	20
Y	18	15	15	16	7	2	15	20	19	13	15	8	5	15	16	4	7	10	12	4	14	6	9	14	18	4
Z	3	9	13	4	14	7	19	18	8	7	5	14	6	9	13	2	20	18	9	7	12	2	3	19	19	2

On the chart, find the place where the initials you've chosen intersect. Read the chapter whose number appears at that intersection.

12

THE MYSTERY OF LIFE

Imagine a clear beaker of warm water. A hand enters the picture and places a sugar cube in the beaker. Lights! Let the cameras roll! Speeding up the resulting picture, we see the corners of the cube grow rounded, the edges blur. It slumps into a mound of sugar, grows smaller and more translucent, and finally disappears, dissolved into the surrounding water. This natural process we've just observed is entropy at work. Random, chance-like interactions between the molecules of the sugar cube and the water, over time, result in a state where there are no longer any differences between the cube and the water, but only a beaker full of uniform sugar water in equilibrium. The second law of thermodynamics, the law of entropy, asserts this, that all matter and energy seek an equilibrium. Over time, due to the actions of chance, differences of state, like the difference between the sugar cube and the water, tend to be eliminated and everything becomes the same. That force which creates the sugared water is the same one, chance, which can transform jagged mountains into uniform grains of sand. Scientists say that eventually even the stars will wink out. At the end of time there will be no heat or cold, the universe will everywhere have the same temperature, and nothing will ever change again. This is the consequence of the workings of entropy.

Now we set the projector on reverse. We see a clear beaker of sugary water. Eventually a pile forms at one spot on the bottom. It grows, begins to form a distinctive cubical shape and finally pokes out sharp, pointed corners. This is mysterious! If we were to observe this happening in real life, we would exclaim, "Oh, how strange! I wonder what made that happen?" The growth of a sugar cube out of undifferentiated sugary water is anti-entropic and our intuition tells us that this process is unnatural. Something must have caused it to happen.

But this is really not an unfamiliar sort of observation. Picture this similar situation: two tiny cells meet in a warm place, full of nourishment, and in nine months there grows a human infant, with ten fingers and toes, eyelashes and fingernails, heart and kidneys, eyes and ears. The fingernails of an infant are more astonishing and unexpected than the corners appearing on a cube of sugar. It seems that something mysterious is happening here, something is happening for a purpose, something which is beyond accident and chance. Consider also that several billion years ago the earth was bare of life. Now there are whales that live under the sea, goats that clamber on hooves over rocky mountain ridges, bees living in hives, and people living inside elaborately complex cities, surrounded by the twistings and turnings of water pipes, electric wires, roads, electromagnetic radiation, and more.

Life is an anti-entropic phenomenon. From a physical point of view, the growth of complexity from simplicity is an unnatural phenomenon because it reverses the arrow of time and violates the law of entropy. Life gives the appearance of being endowed with a purpose, a drive, that impels it to ever higher and higher complexity. Just as the embyro must necessarily form itself into a human child, the endpoint and goal of all past evolution seems to be the perfection of its ultimate creation, the human species. This teleonomic or end-oriented force which drives the change has had many interpretations, ranging from God, the Creator, to the irresistible Marxist forces of history. But it is not necessary to assume that there is an intelligent purpose driving the evolution of complexity. It is possible for complexity to emerge, anti-entropically, all by itself, just by the workings of chance.

Here are a couple of thought experiments to illustrate this idea: Imagine a large number of small wooden cubes. Place them neatly in rows in a box and shake the box several times. When you open the box, there is a jumbled pile of little cubes. All the minute accidental bumpings together of the cubes just resulted in disorder. In this situation, chance plays a role in breaking down order, bringing destruction. This is the way people ordinarily think of the workings of chance and one of the reasons why chance is feared. We fear that if we allow the disorderly chaos of chance to touch our lives, we will be destroyed.

For the second experiment, imagine that we embed strong magnets into each of the six faces of each cube. Half of the magnets will be sunk into the wood so that their north pole is pointing outwards, the others with their south poles pointed outwards. The magnets are hammered into the wood so that the faces of the cube are again flush and smooth. Since north and south poles are attracted to one another, and similar poles repulse one another, it turns out that each face on one of these cubes will be attracted to exactly half the faces on all the other cubes and repulsed by the other half. Let's also suppose that the magnetic attractive force is strong enough so that the sides will remain stuck together even if slightly jostled. If we take a handful of these magnetized cubes, place them in a box and shake lightly, what will we see when we open the box? According to H. vonFoerster, the scientist who first proposed this thought experiment to illustrate his theories on the evolution of order from noise, "you may not believe your eyes, but an incredibly ordered structure will emerge, which, I fancy, may pass the grade to be displayed as an exhibition of surrealistic art."

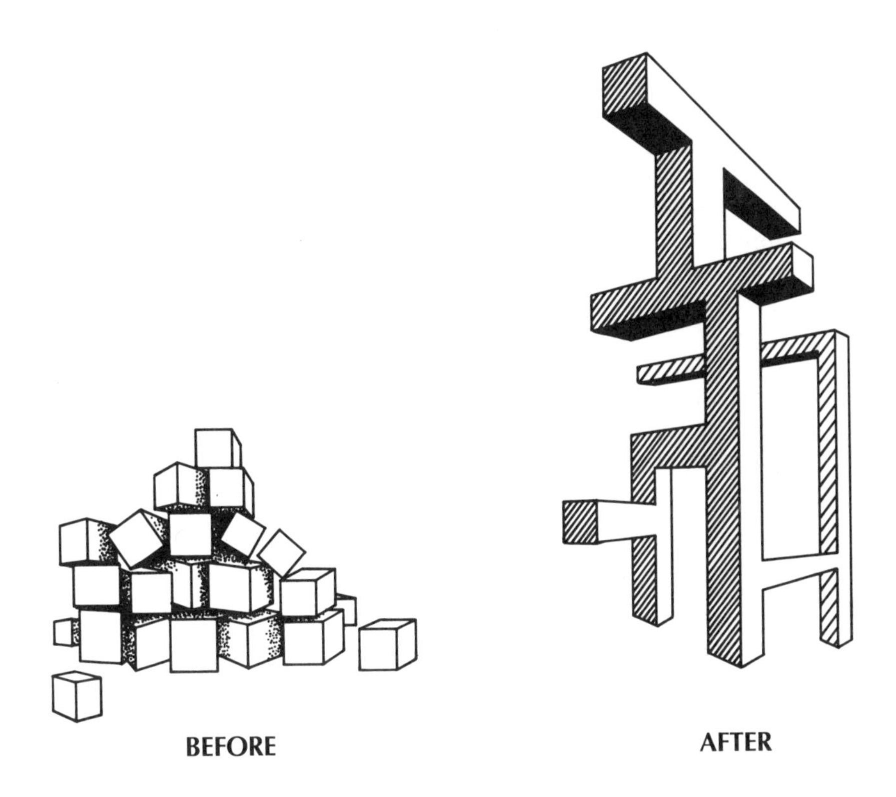

Anyone who sees this final structure of cubes, who happens to be unaware of how it came about, could not be criticized for assuming that some intelligence had constructed it for some aesthetic or practical purpose. But it came about just by the shaking of the box, just out of noise and randomness. The energy of shaking the box led to accidental touchings of pairs of faces and magnetism preserved these chance encounters. The final result could not have been predicted because the major influence on its shape was chance. Each time this experiment is performed, radically different structures will arise. The physical laws of magnetism make it necessary that some structure will arise but these laws could not be used to predict what it would look like.

When people are first shown this experiment, one of the most natural questions which arises is, "Where's the chance here? If the box were shaken exactly the same way again, wouldn't the same structure arise?" This intuitive belief that situations can be repeated and predicted is based on the outmoded scientific doctrine of determinism. Even Einstein spent the last years of his life unsuccessfully attempting to discover the underlying laws and regularities which would allow us to predict the outcomes of situations like these. But since his time, even in our most precise science of physics, the rule of uncertainty has prevailed. There are two fundamental reasons why the outcome of events are in principle unpredictable. First, precise measurements of motions and forces is an abstract ideal in science which can be approached but never ultimately attained physically. We can measure to the nearest hundredth of an inch, to the nearest millionth, but still we can never measure exactly. There are always errors or uncertainties in our measurements. So the shaking of the box can never be precisely duplicated. Secondly, even if we could duplicate the situation, then, at the atomic level where the atoms of one face of one cube brush against another, quantum mechanics tells us that the outcome of each interaction is entirely unpredictable. One time, one thing could happen; another time, another. These minute quantum irregularities could add up to give different outcomes even if we could achieve the exact same circumstances. And the smaller and more numerous the little cubes are (as molecules in biological organisms), the more likely it is that the outcome will be different.

This construction of a complicated, apparently purposeful, structure of cubes out of randomness illustrates the beneficial action of chance as a bringer of life. The force behind the anti-entropic movement of life from simplicity to complexity is chance. There is no need to posit a purposeful agent who causes life to evolve. It happens by itself. The theory of evolution gives an explanation of how apparently purposeful change, over time, happens by itself through the coordinated interactions of the natural forces of chance, invariance, and selection. We will discuss the role of each of these factors in evolution, and each is essential, but the primary force is chance.

The first major mechanism of evolution is invariance. It provides for permanence of structure. In every cell, the DNA molecule directs the building of proteins, faithfully following its encoded instructions. It never deviates and some species, like snails, have been able to reproduce without modification for hundreds of millions of years. Of course individuals vary slightly, one from the other. Each individual has slightly different genetic material and in every generation the genetic material of parents is shuffled by chance and recombined differently in their offspring. Also sometimes, by chance, changes occur in the DNA of an individual. These are called mutations. Either through external randomly encountered forces or just an accumulation of minute perturbations, a discrete modification of the DNA code sequence may occur in an individual. Differences in genetic material, resulting either from individual variation or mutations, will be automatically repeated in the genes of all the descendants of this individual, thanks to the blind fidelity of the duplication process. The fact that DNA has the property of invariance explains how changes are preserved over the course of evolution, just as magnetism explains how the little cubes are held together in the resulting structure. Chance determines which changes occur, and which are thus subsequently preserved, just as it determines which cubes touch which other cubes.

All the enormous variability of the biosphere can be accounted for by these minute perturbations of microscopic cellular entities. We must not underestimate the fruitfulness of chance. According to the Nobel prize-winning French biologist, Jacques Monod, in the human population of approximately three billion persons, there occur with each new generation some hundred billion to a thousand billion mutations. Indeed, in view of this abundance, we perhaps should marvel more at the stability of the human species, rather than at changes in its nature brought about by evolution.

The second major mechanism of evolution is natural selection. Mutations are acted on by the strong pressure of natural selection. For a highly evolved animal, with intricately linked biochemical reactions, changing a protein is usually like throwing sand into a well-tuned engine. Most mutations are slightly negative or sometimes neutral to the functioning of the organism. Very few contribute to the progressing evolution of the species as measured by increased differential reproduction. When a minor change in an organism results in that organism and its descendants having more offspring than other organisms, and when that group of organisms consequently becomes more numerous, we say that the mutation has been "selected for." The chance-like interactions of an organism with its environment of plants and other animals determines which animals will have more offspring. Some mutations could be advantageous in one environment, yet disastrous in another. Thus the workings of chance are also fundamental in determining which traits are selected for. Those random changes in the DNA which are selectively advantageous and lead to the reproductive success of groups of organisms are the source of all innovation and creation in the biosphere.

With inorganic material, minor random perturbations usually lead only to erosion and decay, but it is when random mutations are caught on the wing, when certain traits are selected for, and then preserved and reproduced by the machinery of invariance, that evolution occurs in living entities. Thus we see that the coordinated action of the three forces, chance, invariance, and selection, allows life to change anti-entropically. Nature's way of meeting future contingencies is to provide a very large number of creatures with small differences, due to mutations and individual variation, and to turn them loose so that selection might choose among them.

Just as magnetism, in the experiment with little cubes, holds together those faces that accidently come close enough together, invariance is the mechanism that preserves those variations which are selectively advantageous. Because of this, there is a movement in the direction of more complexity as changes are preserved and more and more information is stored in the structure of the organism. The law of entropy is a statistical law. This means that it is true in a global, or overall sense, but it does not always have to hold. Entropy can be turned about and reversed for a brief moment of time. In living beings it is precisely these minute anti-entropic changes, these increases in complexity, which are snapped up and reproduced by the replicative mechanism of the DNA. They are sometimes amplified when natural selection provides for that individual's enhanced reproductive success. In this sense, selection, operating on an immense reservoir of microscopic variation provided by the actions of chance and uncertainty, gives life the impression of a mechanism moving purposefully backwards in time, against the arrow of entropy. And the force which provides the material upon which selection works is pure randomness, chance, which we have chosen to call Fortuna.

We would like to think of ourselves, human beings, as necessary, inevitable, ordained from all eternity. We would like to think that there is a kind of perfection in an animal which walks upright, with two arms and two legs, and speaks — the ultimate end product of an upwardly progressing spiral of evolution. But just as any number of combinations of magnetic cubes is possible, the structure of our biological universe could easily have been otherwise. Fortuna played, and is still playing, a major role in the contingent shape of the universe. The details we find in nature are not absolutely determined. They are the way they are because of the accidents that happened as the present moment swept along the course of time. The accumulation of accidents over time, caused by chance, determines the final result. There is no way that the shape of any individual animal or species could have been predicted from first principles anymore than the particular configuration of atoms in a pebble we hold in our hand could have been predicted by any scientific theory. Scientific theories cannot deal with particular life stories of individual animals or with the details of the evolution of species. These are all unique, accidental events. When speaking about the final form of an animal, say the eight legs of a spider, it is enough to say that the actual existing object is compatible, or consistent, with physical laws and theory. It is possible for the spider to have eight legs because having eight legs countervenes no physical prohibition about matter, but the spider is under no obligation to be so constructed. In other words, the Earth's biosphere is contingent; it need not have been this way; it could have been otherwise. It was shaped by chance; it happened by itself.

The general evolutionary model, consisting of chance, invariance, and natural selection, as described above, is extremely fruitful for trying to understand how things change, but it cannot explain why things are the way they are. It explains flux rather than shape. It's a step forward in our comprehension of the world around us as we attempt to include, in our explanations of how things change, the fourth dimension of time as well as the three spatial dimensions. By isolating the three factors, chance, invariance, and selection, in any process wherein there is a movement towards complexity over time, we can better understand the contingent nature of the final stages of the process and gain a clear understanding of the major role played by Fortuna in determining what is.

The evolutionary description of change does not necessarily dethrone God, the Creator. It only makes His touch more subtle. The ancients placed Jupiter above Fortuna, because his power was superior to hers. The Creator of the physical universe determines what is possible. By determining the properties of matter and the laws of nature, and by creating the energy that sets the universe in motion, He decrees that some events are possible while some are impossible. In this way He provides the framework of potentiality within which chance, together with human free will, determines the contingent outcome. Necessity presents a banquet of possibilities; God the Creator is generous. He leaves us free to interact with Fortuna, to choose among possibilities, and to determine what will actually happen. Evolution only describes the process of change; it cannot predict its outcome.

We can apply the evolutionary model of change in other than biological areas. In other words, we can come to understand situations involving change by analyzing them in terms of chance, invariance, and natural selection. This analysis proceeds by asking the questions, "Where does chance enter into the picture?", "How are changes preserved?", and "What function results in the fact that some changes become more numerous or more successful than others?" The answers to these questions can help us to visualize the major impact chance has in areas of human life where we have not before suspected her presence.

Try to imagine how the general evolutionary model applies in your life. Picture in your mind one of your long-term friendships or a business relationship:

- What chance-like events have shaped this relationship?
- How have changes in the relationship been preserved?
- Have certain types of interactions and activities become more numerous? Have others been extinguished? How did this happen?

For example, consider the evolution of ideas. Ideas evolve and human culture changes over time, becoming increasingly complex and subtle. The locus of culture is the human mind. The mechanism of invariance is language. New ideas occur in individual minds through the chance interactions of the individual with his or her environment or sometimes through the interactions of the conscious and the subconscious minds. Human culture was born on that day when creative combinations of ideas — new associations achieved by one person — no longer had to perish with their creator because they could be transmitted to others via language.

In biology, a mutation in an organism must wait until the individual reaches sexual maturity to have the success of the mutation measured by whether the individual has fewer or more children than average. If one animal has a favorable mutation, say a longer tail on a monkey, one needs to wait until she reaches sexual maturity to find out the consequences of this mutation. If having a longer tail is advantageous, perhaps in getting more food, then she may have more children than other monkeys with shorter tails, and her children will also have longer tails. Eventually, but over very long time periods, it may happen that all the monkeys of that species will have longer tails. This is a slow process.

The pace of cultural evolution is much faster. As ideas are created by chance, like mutations, they are continually being transmitted from individual to individual. They also compete for the limited memory space within each individual brain. Within each mind, ideas are tested for plausibility, usefulness, and consistency with other ideas. Some are adopted and some are rejected, sometimes for good reasons, and sometimes just by chance. This is the selection process. The success of an idea is measured by the number of minds it currently inhabits. The idea that the earth is flat is almost extinct, while the idea that Vitamin C helps prevent the common cold is gradually becoming more successful. With the invention of printed books the fertility of potent ideas has been greatly increased, allowing one individual's creative thought to permeate millions of minds in a single generation. With modern communications turning the world into a global village, an idea can instantaneously circle the globe. Almost every individual in the human race is carrying the idea that man has been able to fly to the moon and back. We can only hope that some genius will accidently discover and transmit to all of us the secret that will allow us to continue living on this sphere without destroying ourselves.

The analogy of evolution is creeping into many new descriptions of reality, as it is recognized that the nature of change and the nature of "becoming" need to be explained. Biology, culture, behavior, the human creative process, and other changes in the direction of complexity can all be understood by uncovering mechanisms which provide for chance, invariance, and selection.

The fundamental fuel for change and growth is chance. Chance does not have to be threatening. It can be seen instead as a maternal force which provides the basis for life. Just as a screen door can blow back and forth in a light breeze until at some indeterminable moment, a sufficiently strong gust might push the door hard enough to latch it, randomness and accident provide the small anti-entropic changes which, when selectively advantageous, are captured and preserved by mechanisms of invariance. The progress of change over time is founded in the fruitfulness of Fortuna; its path is totally unpredictable and accidental. The complexity of the world we live in is only one of the many possibilities that happened to happen. Each outcome, even though beautiful and satisfying, is not necessary. It could have been otherwise.

Chance can work in two basic directions: It can contribute to the building of complexity and life, in cooperation with necessary physical laws or, in the other direction, it can bring death or destruction (like an unsuccessful mutation, a fatal accident, or, in accordance with the laws of entropy, the end of the universe). Chance can be a creative or a destructive force. Fortuna stands at the crossroads of life, like the Sphinx, asking passing humanity riddle-like questions about the mystery of life. We, in turn, at each crossroad of our daily lives, must answer these riddles and make the right choices. By our choices and actions we can invoke either the creative or destructive aspect of Fortuna. Our actions can trigger the cameras and the projection equipment, earlier described, and make them roll either backwards or forwards. We can either see the cube of sugar dissolve into nothingness or watch the cube come to life under our very own eyes. The paradoxical creative and destructive roles of Fortuna and the consequences of this for human freedom constitute the fundamental mystery of life.

THE MATRIX FOR CHAPTER 12

	A	B	C	D	E	F	G	H	I	J	K	L	M	N	O	P	Q	R	S	T	U	V	W	X	Y	Z
A	19	5	18	15	11	13	17	14	4	17	15	17	13	5	19	17	13	17	14	15	13	6	19	11	2	11
B	14	20	10	19	6	14	15	3	7	5	7	18	15	18	3	2	8	13	19	15	15	5	16.	18	14	3
C	16	19	8	7	5	14	6	10	3	5	11	15	4	8	9	14	15	11	14	10	17	2	3	14	18	9
D	2	4	5	4	16	11	15	9	10	15	16	11	19	20	10	18	15	9	10	16	17	14	2	17	20	4
E	20	5	16	15	16	19	14	8	10	15	18	14	15	18	16	16	14	8	14	4	13	10	14	11	3	8
F	19	19	3	7	14	14	7	8	19	8	14	16	20	15	15	14	5	8	4	20	13	6	8	14	6	2
G	14	15	19	2	14	15	4	6	19	15	16	7	14	4	10	4	7	8	4	13	18	5	3	17	16	17
H	6	17	8	18	13	9	11	10	6	10	2	6	2	19	17	9	18	4	10	2	16	16	18	20	17	14
I	14	19	2	7	5	10	19	4	13	16	11	6	5	18	15	9	16	4	16	17	14	6	17	8	13	4
J	10	5	9	16	18	19	17	5	17	15	15	8	17	17	5	13	14	9	11	16	20	6	10	14	10	15
K	6	8	7	19	10	10	4	11	9	14	16	3	14	20	18	13	18	17	16	2	2	19	7	5	5	15
L	9	13	11	4	16	13	5	5	13	8	9	11	13	9	4	9	11	17	16	4	2	9	10	2	11	4
M	14	3	7	15	2	8	15	11	11	6	7	8	11	7	14	2	18	14	16	13	16	18	10	9	7	3
N	5	10	4	14	4	8	14	4	4	15	11	10	18	20	17	6	11	11	8	19	14	2	15	6	17	17
O	9	7	9	18	6	11	8	3	3	10	13	15	5	6	6	16	2	3	17	20	14	18	9	5	6	9
P	10	5	20	2	15	16	7	19	13	19	6	14	18	5	8	8	20	5	14	5	3	20	18	19	11	19
Q	18	5	4	17	11	18	17	2	10	8	7	13	6	18	9	8	6	8	14	11	5	10	16	14	13	11
R	11	5	13	7	4	5	4	19	15	19	6	8	8	7	8	8	18	2	17	15	19	6	11	6	15	2
S	6	13	11	7	15	5	19	7	15	13	19	9	18	19	5	10	9	15	2	20	4	4	8	9	18	17
T	10	5	18	19	14	15	8	4	14	8	20	9	14	6	2	10	7	19	20	9	8	5	14	18	16	10
U	9	6	16	4	20	20	6	18	16	4	4	11	10	16	10	4	9	9	14	7	17	7	20	11	14	7
V	14	20	7	16	9	9	11	16	17	9	19	2	2	4	17	2	18	15	11	3	7	3	4	19	4	3
W	9	7	14	6	15	8	20	4	9	8	16	19	19	3	20	8	4	14	20	18	8	13	8	14	15	19
X	3	9	7	2	7	14	19	9	2	20	3	10	15	15	3	18	17	18	7	10	19	11	15	19	20	13
Y	16	10	16	17	3	10	2	10	13	4	2	19	18	13	4	19	5	18	18	19	13	4	2	10	17	20
Z	7	19	19	20	10	4	2	15	14	5	14	19	10	17	4	19	5	16	19	18	5	11	19	10	13	8

On the chart, find the place where the initials you've chosen intersect. Read the chapter whose number appears at that intersection.

13

RANDOMNESS AND SOCIAL MACHINES

Walking through a crowd of people, one is struck by the immense variability of the human form. We don't know if the next person we see will be short or tall, heavy or skinny, red-headed or blond. Some people have big heads, some small; some heads are hairy, some bald. Voices range from rumbling bass to lilting soprano. Indirectly, through various life experiences, we are also aware that other factors, which cannot be seen, like IQ, speed of reflexes, immunity to diseases, etc., vary greatly from person to person. No two people are exactly alike. When there is a great deal of variation, caused by chance, and where it's impossible to predict what attributes the next individual you see will have, scientists call the situation random. Physical attributes, such as height, weight, and IQ are said to be randomly distributed among all the people of the world. Randomness is associated with uncertainty, unpredictability, disorder, and lack of pattern.

But strangely enough, underlying the random display of physical traits some of the most beautiful mathematical regularities lie hidden. To see these regularities, all it takes is a change of perspective. When concentrating on individuals, prediction is impossible. Chance rules the lives of individuals. But from the point of view of the entire population, as we will see, these irregularities add up to an overall pattern of regularity. Essentially, the action of chance at the micro-level results in predictability at the macro-level. Like having a road map in a strange country, the person who can look at the broader picture and see beyond individual situations can better understand the jumbled chaos of physical reality, sort out what is happening from what is not happening, what is and is not important, and hence cope with their surroundings more effectively. A few illustrations may make this clearer.

For example, take a look at people's heights. How tall people are doesn't seem to follow any readily apparent pattern. But if you were to approach the next 200 adults who pass by you in a public place and ask to measure their heights, you would find that some are tall, some short, some average. Unless you are standing outside the dressing room of a basketball team, this should be a random sample. Find the average height by adding these measurements and dividing by 200. This number is called the mean height. Let's suppose that we discover that the mean height is 66″. (That means that, on the average, people are about 5 foot 6 inches tall.) Then find, on the average, how much each of these individual measurements differ from 66 inches. In other words, one person may be 5 inches taller than the mean, another may be 2 inches shorter, and yet another may be ½ inch taller. We average all the differences together (a slightly complex process that need not be detailed here) and the resulting number is called the standard deviation. Suppose in our case, the resulting standard deviation is 2″. That means that the height of a typical person deviates approximately two inches from the mean. So far the mean (66 inches) and the standard deviation (2 inches) we have just calculated only pertain to those 200 people whose heights we measured. But these computed numbers can accurately describe the entire population of all the people who could have been, but were not, measured. In more detail, we can use the mean and standard deviation of this group of 200 people to precisely describe the pattern of how human heights are distributed in general. Most heights in the whole population will be fairly close to the mean of 66 inches; in fact, if we take the mean figure plus or minus the standard deviation (that is from 64″ to 68″) the heights of exactly 68% of the population will be in this range. Very few people differ greatly from the mean; if we add three standard deviations to the mean (66+6 = 72), it is known that less than one-tenth of one percent of the population will be taller than 72 inches. It can be shown that any question about what portion of people are of a certain height can be answered by referring to the mathematical curve, called the normal curve,

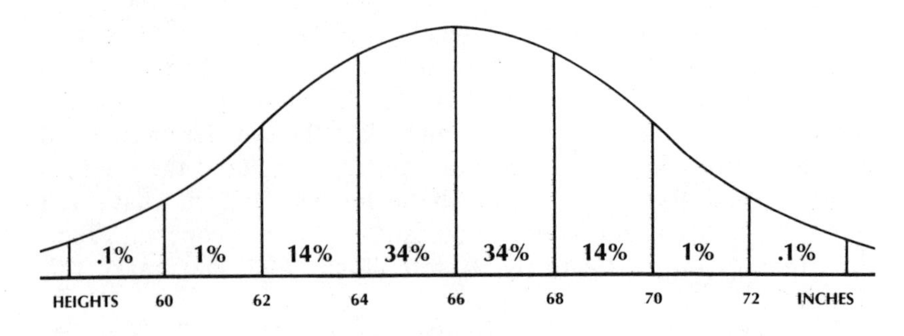

$$Y = \frac{e^{-\frac{x^2}{2}}}{\sqrt{2\pi}}$$

and calculating areas of regions determined by this curve. The details of this process are unimportant; what is important is the following: even when there is complete uncertainty regarding which individual has what attributes, it turns out that when the situation is regarded from the point of view of the entire population, the distribution of the attribute will be summarized by the regular mathematical picture above. Chance and accident at the level of the individual are consistent with, and in fact result in, regularities as seen from the global point of view.

Perhaps it is not so striking that scientists and mathematicians have found certain regularities in the distribution of human heights. After all, it is the job of science to study and discover regularities. But what is astonishing is that exactly the same pattern occurs in other situations which are completely unrelated to human heights. Consider, for example, a marksman aiming and shooting 200 arrows at a bull's eye target. If we measure how far off he is from the center each time, find the average distance off each time, and then find the standard deviation for these 200 shots, precisely the same pattern will occur. It's impossible to know whether his next shot will be 2 inches or 1/10 of an inch away from the center, but overall, if he were to continue shooting in the same manner, we could be confident that 68% of these shots would be within one standard deviation of the center and that fewer than one-tenth of one percent would be further than three standard deviations from the center — exactly the same percentages as in the description of human heights. Again the normal curve and its associated percentages completely describe the pattern of the shots he has taken today and all the shots he could take in the future.

And it's not only in these two situations, but in innumerable others that this situation occurs. If one measures weights, skin color variation, number of hairs on the head, speed of reflexes, or almost any physical or mental characteristic whose distribution throughout the population seems to be accidental and patternless, this hidden regularity, or a minor variation of it, will occur. Beneath the variability of our apparently chaotic universe is that beautiful form, called the normal curve, which is described mathematically by the formula above.

When scientists first noticed the ubiquitous nature of this normal distribution, they were puzzled. Some, interestingly enough, speculated that God was like a marksman, aiming to create the perfect man in His image, but because He was working with imperfect mortal clay, the individuals He created all differed from that perfect form in the same regular pattern that can be used to describe how the arrows missed the bull's eye. However, later mathematicians discovered that there is no need to assume that some force is causing this regularity. It happens by itself. It can be shown that whenever there are a very large number of independent random processes interacting (as in the numerous genetic and environmental factors which result in a physical characteristic such as height) the outcome of their combined effect is automatically lawful and predictable, and, further, that the law which is followed is the law of distribution described by the normal curve. A beautiful illustration of this idea is shown by using a flat box, raised at the back, which contains slots at the bottom and pegs near the top. If you were to drop one ball into the opening, it's impossible to predict where it would end up. The ways it can bounce off one peg and then another, to the left or to the right, are uncountable. One ball could end up anywhere. But 10,000 balls? If you drop them through the opening, one by one, each one pursuing its individual unpredictable path, the result, created by the totality of the balls, will be an accurate depiction of the normal curve. And the more balls, the more slots, the more pegs that we have — in other words, the more chance that we introduce into the situation — the more closely the resulting pile of balls approximates a normal curve. Chance causes the regularity to occur, and hence the picture of the normal curve is the modern mathematical image of the abstract idea of chance, which has been personified as Fortuna.

By adjusting the level of our perspective from the unpredictability of the individual to regularities of the whole, we are able to get a handle on predicting what will happen in otherwise unpredictable areas. For example, it is impossible to predict whether John Smith will take

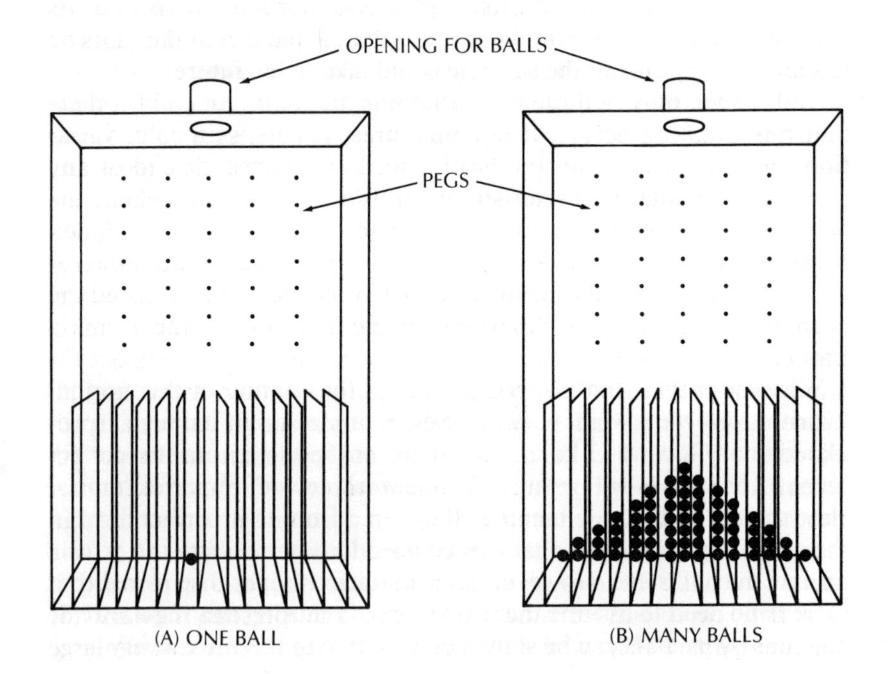

the bus to work this Monday, what he will eat for lunch, or what he will watch on TV that evening. But, from the viewpoint of an entire city, we can predict quite accurately how many people will ride the bus, how many pounds of fish or beef will be consumed that day, and how many people will watch the CBS News. There is no way to avoid chance in our individual lives: each day will be full of unexpected twists and turns, and choices which must be made in the face of uncertainty. But it's somewhat comforting to know that this meaninglessness is a part of an overall pattern and regularity.

SOCIAL MACHINES

Our social world is also full of uncertainties and chances. Very often we are ineffective in dealing with the world of people and organizations in which we find ourselves. The immense variability, complexity, and unpredictability of social situations make it sometimes difficult to cope with the stresses and strains of our lives. But a large part of the problem is that in certain essential ways we misunderstand the nature of the social soup in which we are swimming. We try, unsuccessfully, to find simple regularities in what is happening while we neglect the underlying pattern and meaning which could be provided by choosing a different perspective through which to look at our social sphere. Our resulting frustration in trying to get what we want out of life is like that of a man who wants to travel to another town and who climbs on a bicycle and tries to whip it into a gallop. Because he misunderstands the nature of where he is and what's around him, he is unable to achieve his goal.

Let's try to understand this social space. Let's start with common sense ideas. How do we ordinarily look at the world around us and describe it? Sometimes the hardest things to see and understand are right before our eyes. They're too close to see.

Human beings are social animals. Every individual is enmeshed in numerous, complicated social structures. Follow a man on his way to work. He eats breakfast, chatting with his wife and children, leaves and catches a bus, where he reads the morning paper, stares out the window or chats with other regulars about the weather. Arriving at his office, he greets his fellow employees, pours a cup of coffee, and sits down to begin work at his desk. In each of these environments, a different style of language and different topics of conversation are deemed appropriate or inappropriate. In each one he presents a different aspect of his personality, and indeed his personality can be said merely to consist of the sum of all these various aspects he presents. It is a trite complaint of modern life that our personalities are too fragmented and that we are required to play too many disconnected roles. There is no question that every individual is constantly involved in many of these structures. Even young children understand the differences between "at home," "with friends," "at the zoo," or "Sunday School," and recognize that appropriate physical and verbal behavior is defined by the rules of the particular structure.

However, let's stretch the concept of social structure further, concentrating on the idea that such a structure is defined as a circumstance in which a person is regularly immersed and which involves a correspondingly appropriate language (in the broadest sense of the word) and behavior. Granted this use of the word, a writer together with typewriter, a pilot with the plane's controls, or a swimmer and the sea are as much involved in a social structure as two lovers. Indeed most social structures are a combination of human beings and other material objects which help to define the environment. Examples of these are a group of workers on an assembly line, or all the people talking at one moment over a telephone network, or a government, consisting of but not limited to, people, land, dollar bills, buildings, and military equipment.

Let's call these generalized structures social machines, for they are constantly in motion and are productive. Social machines extend over time. Some are continuous, some periodic. Families, factories, religions, and hobbies, even daydreaming, are all examples of this kind of machine. At every moment, each individual is involved in one or several machines. If we look around us, each individual's social space is replete with these ubiquitous machines and our personality is fragmented into the various aspects we present as each machine demands its fractional role.

Living our roles in these social machines is what gives meaning to life. Being a mother, an accountant, a jogger, or a member of the PTA defines us and helps us find our way through life. Who am I? What do I do next? All these questions are answered, indeed temporarily suspended, when we are attached to the machines of jogging, reading, working, or conversing with friends, or to the traditional, long-standing social machines such as the family, the church, or the community. Our short term pleasures are often derived from immersing ourselves in temporary machines — an evening at a concert, conversations with friends, an engrossing novel, television. Machines play important functional roles in society. Parents deliver their children to Little League teams, expecting them to return "socialized," in the same way a farmer deposits his grain at the mill, expecting to pick up flour in return. We enjoy these machines. Sometimes, we die in wars to preserve certain of these machines.

What's the most frightening thing about social uncertainty? Why are social transformations threatening? Why do people look apprehensively to the future, talk about "bad times around the corner," tsk-tsk inflation, and impotent government? It's because we see some of our cherished social machines threatened, and hence the possibility of losing our meaning and pleasure in life. Change means, we fear, that our ways of life will be destroyed. If someone believes that the family structure is the backbone of a strong society, imparting important principles across the generations, and if they had happy childhoods and find enormous pleasure and comfort in their own homes and families, then reports of soaring divorce rates and mounting numbers of single-parent households will be alarming. They will be saddened both by the apparent disintegration of society and by the feeling that many people are missing out on one of life's greatest joys. And worried too, that perhaps their own marriages or those of their children may not survive societal influences that work against their preservation. If someone loves books, then the knowledge that this generation is turning away from books and searching for knowledge, adventure, and ideas in television and movies will touch them with a gnawing sense of discomfort and worry. Will books in which they find pleasure continue to be written and published? These fears, worries, anxieties, and uncertainties plague us today, as change seems to move at an ever-mounting pace. How can we slow down or stop change? What can we do to preserve our cherished social machines and recapture the enjoyment of life?

Wait a minute! We may be on the wrong track. Even asking these questions in this form presupposes a fundamental error in understanding what our social space is really like. We have misdiagnosed the source of our worry and anxiety. We are missing the unseen regularities. We can't stop change. Even if we could, the last thing one should want to do is to preserve existing social machines exactly as they are. Why? There is a misunderstanding here about the nature of social machines and hence about the source of our pleasure in them. And this misunderstanding can only be cleared up by a better understanding of the role of chance in social machines.

Social machines do not stand still, but possess a dynamic stability. That means that they are constantly changing, yet constantly the same, like a forest which persists through times even though individual trees and animals are born and die. The enjoyment we find through our roles in these machines is derived from the fact that within each changing machine our own individual growth and change is so effortlessly guided as to become imperceptible and anxiety-free. They mold us and cushion us from the trauma of change. The stresses of aging are not too difficult in the bosom of a family where everyone is growing older with roles and structures gradually being transformed. It is a delusion to imagine that we would be safer if change were stopped. A static environment is not a hospitable place for changing organic entities like human beings. Although the changes these machines go through are random, and therefore unpredictable and apparently threatening, there is a simple but hidden form to the role chance plays which, when uncovered, reveals these changes to be not only non-threatening, but even desirable. Social machines, too, are organic, living entities. They do grow, they do change. They only stop changing when they die.

To illustrate this, take a look at one of our most important social machines, the educational system. By this we mean that giant multi-tentacled organism consisting primarily of schoolrooms, teachers, and students, but which is not seen in its entirety unless you include parents teaching their pre-schoolers the ABCs, educational lobbyists in Washington D.C., scholarly journals of educational theory, teachers' unions, a family sitting down to watch public TV, and a Saturday afternoon college football game. It is a multitude of people and things involved in the activity of transmitting cultural information to those who do not yet have it. A specialized language has evolved, which is sometimes derided by outsiders as "educational jargon," but the more an individual is involved in this machine, the less strange and ridiculous its usage comes to appear. This language turns out to be the most efficient, appropriate means for people involved in this machine to talk to one another about common goals and processes.

How does this machine change and evolve? What role does chance play? Some people think that there are educational leaders in Washington who articulate a "goal for the eighties" and then the machine, like an automobile, turns and responds to their command. On the contrary, the educational leaders are usually just reporting on what is happening, or bemoaning what isn't happening, but their statements about what should happen are just a small part of the varied stimuli to which the organism is responding. The process which is really going on is more organic, and quite similar to the way in which a species evolves in response to environmental variation. External events impinge randomly on the educational machine: the Russians send up the first orbiting satellite, Spanish-speaking children arrive in a wave of immigration, computer technology evolves, inflation hits, taxpayers revolt. Because of its complexity, this machine is immersed in an unpredictable, random, unstructured, unpatterned sea of variety. As problems of adjustment arise, the question of how to deal with these new situations is raised and discussed by various people who are in daily contact with different aspects of the problems. Some answers are better than others, or rather, some convince more people than others. The ideas spread. People begin to respond. They develop and elaborate possible solutions. The more perspectives there are on a problem, and the more people there are working on various aspects of the problem, then the more probable it is that a good solution will be found. As teachers speak to students, book publishers speak to professors of education, lobbyists speak to legislators, and children speak to parents who vote — out of the raw mass of variety — solutions are carved out by the free competition of ideas. Sometimes one idea is pushed to the top; often several good ideas are held to be best by different groups of people, leading to "schools of thought" on the subject. In either case, the institution of education is changed and modified by the presence of individuals going about their day-by-day roles, guided by principles which have been generated out of the sea of chance and which have won their ascendency in the arena of competing ideas. The social machine responds and, in each response, changes its nature. Or, more precisely, a change in its nature is its response.

This illustration can help us understand what chance means to social machines. The variety and randomness of the environment is not something that should provoke anxiety. It is a necessity for the life of the machine, not a threat to it. As each component in a social machine, be it human or material, is involved in occasions where an individual response is elicited, that component changes. Out of the immense variety of accidental, unpatterned responses, the organism of the social machine will change and grow. Chance impinges on the body of the social machine and is incorporated into the machine through the actions or responses of individual components. Out of this randomness, the organism automatically, unselfconsciously, and by itself, builds its new and changing structure. This is the same process whether it is a horse building bone and blood cells out of the hay it has eaten, or a writer building a novel out of his jotted notes and life experiences, or the educational machine building the Head Start program out of the interaction of its goals and purposes within the existing economic stratification of the American society. The random chunks of structure, which are brought to them by chance, are food to these living systems.

To illustrate this in a new context, let's consider friendship. Friendships are social machines. There is a general language of friendship and specific forms of discourse which are developed between longstanding friends. Friendships are born out of the surrounding undifferentiated social sea for a multitude of reasons. They grow and last for a certain period, and often die, sometimes before the physical death of their components. They are one of our most pleasurable, satisfying social machines. In the movie *Annie Hall,* Woody Allen says: "A relationship is like a shark. It has to always keep moving forward or else it dies." In other words, the relationship needs to be open to the constant possibilities and opportunities that chance brings.

Take two friends who enjoy movies, conversation, and going to art galleries together. This is a very satisfying structure. But if they are afraid to change their habits, for fear of losing their pleasure, they may end up with a dead shark on their hands. They can be locked into a rut and what was once a pleasure can become an oppressive duty. Eventually one or the other may find a reason to terminate the relationship. The most enduring friendships are those where there is continual growth in the friendship in response to each individual's growth and to accidental external events and opportunities. "Let's invite that new person to dinner! Let's join that club!" They may find that they no longer have as much time as before for movies because they're too busy cooking gourmet dinners with a new group of friends or getting someone deserving elected to Congress, but the friendship will be alive, continuing to enrich their lives. Friends who say "yes" to variety, who take chances, and who welcome new experiences and opportunities rather than acting as a brake on one another will experience a growing, rewarding, fulfilling friendship.

A social machine must be immersed in a rich, random soup of events, opportunities and occasions — the world of chance — in order to feed on them. If we could eliminate chance from its environment, and if we chose to do so, the machine would starve to death. The social machine, in response to the fluidity of its environment, can grow and change by internalizing those random chunks of structure it comes in contact with. Our own growth and development will be encouraged through our roles in these changing, evolving machines.

Try to concretely visualize a social machine of which you are a part.

- Does it have a special language?
- What are its parts?
- Would permanently fixing it exactly the way it is today guarantee your happiness?
- Can you see how its need to grow and change would better contribute to your future satisfaction?

This may seem to be a strange view of reality. When we adjust the level of our vision and look in a certain way, out of the corners of our eyes, we can see these strange lumbering beasts, these social machines. It's humbling. We sometimes think that we are the apex of evolution, but now we find ourselves only part of a richer, more complex system than we had ever imagined. However, our role inside these machines is not insignificant. A social machine is a four-dimensional creature, extending through time. It has a fixed past and a potential future. Think about the friendship just described. Whether this organism (the friendship) grows or dies depends on our free actions in the present moment. Do we let it feed on chance and diversity? Do we take advantage of new opportunities to enlarge the friendship and make it deeper? We are the mouths of these beasts and how well we feed on what Fortuna brings determines whether they will thrive or wither away.

There is another function, associated with mouths, which we perform for these social machines. We pass from machine to machine; we leave our cozy home and go into the marketplace; we ride our bicycles to the polling place. Perhaps we are passed from machine to machine and our will is just a fiction. An interesting speculation is that in the unimaginable meta-levels of the culture of these machines, humanity plays a role which is very much like language. Maybe our daily lives are made out of conversations carried on among these machines. But enough speculation . . .

The world of social machines, reflecting the rapid pace of cultural evolution, is much more fluid and changing than the material world of rocks and water, or even the biological world of animals and plants. Social machines are continually breaking down. This breaking down also contributes to the process of growth. Chunks of structure broken off from one machine are constantly being reabsorbed by others. Even when an empire conquers a piece of foreign territory, that conquered culture does not vanish. It reappears, transformed within the enveloping empire, contributing to the shape of a new, more diverse culture. A broken marriage sometimes contains the seeds of two new families. Large social machines attack and feed off loose pieces of other machines. This picture is like the primitive sea of amino acids described by scientists. Before the accidental creation of the invariance mechanism of self-replicating DNA, amino acids were loosely fitted together, fell apart, and reformed again in constantly new patterns. Who knows what may evolve from this social soup we now inhabit?

Individuals find their pleasures and their purposes in life by being part of these constantly evolving social machines. We enjoy the secure sense of structure we find by performing roles internal to these machines. Because our natural point of view is very small relative to the massive structures of society, we are sometimes led to make mistakes in analyzing and attempting to understand our social space. We describe what a social machine looks like at one point in time and then we begin to believe that this is how it should be, forever. We begin to create myths about the permanence and unchangeability of social machines, attributing static structure to them. (This occurs even though individuals clearly change and grow and in spite of the fact that their roles are never the same from year to year.) Out of these myths of stability, we come to fear change. We decide to try to halt it. But these machines can only be stopped by death. When we shift the level of our perception, we can see these social machines as living, changing entities which take in nourishment from the seas of chance surrounding them. Uncertainty and randomness are foods, necessities of life. The organisms, or social machines, which will be the healthiest and survive the longest and which will provide us with the most happiness will be those whose components (i.e., people) do not react in fear against randomness, but who cooperate to incorporate chance and uncertainty as fuel for growth. Putting it into poetic terms: we, as their mouths, must learn this lesson. To live fully implies that we willingly and joyfully, suckle at the bosom of our mother, Fortuna.

It seems paradoxical that chance is the source of order and structure in the situations described above. We usually think of randomness and uncertainty as destructive forces in the inorganic world, gradually eroding mountains into sand or decaying organic matter into simpler chemicals. But as we have seen, chance and uncertainty, when seen from the proper perspective, can contribute to structure and order. Random errors in shooting an arrow at the bull's-eye yield the smooth regularity of the normal curve. Random interactions of people and objects make up the world of macroscopic social machines.

Imagine the crashing of millions of different waves upon uncountable, different, irregularly shaped rocks, for millenia upon millenia, until there is created a beach covered with nearly uniform, minute grains of sand, stretching for miles and miles. This can either be seen as an increase in chaos and destruction or, by shifting our perspective, we can see it as the creation of a larger, more complex entity, a beautiful beach. Random perturbations can and do build up the order and complexity of nature, eventually contributing to its beauty.

THE MATRIX FOR CHAPTER 13

	A	B	C	D	E	F	G	H	I	J	K	L	M	N	O	P	Q	R	S	T	U	V	W	X	Y	Z
A	18	6	11	17	18	11	6	20	11	20	14	16	14	9	15	19	10	6	15	14	20	5	7	10	3	8
B	9	16	18	11	9	16	11	20	20	19	4	6	18	10	20	6	5	16	3	14	4	16	10	5	5	11
C	18	3	12	14	14	2	3	18	7	10	20	20	12	20	14	18	12	4	3	12	20	5	2	17	16	3
D	7	2	20	7	14	19	17	12	8	20	3	20	6	6	19	19	20	4	15	19	6	9	8	14	12	9
E	19	6	9	12	7	20	2	11	20	9	5	2	17	12	9	11	7	19	16	10	18	18	5	2	12	16
F	11	18	16	2	19	18	17	10	7	12	18	8	15	3	18	10	18	2	15	9	8	14	3	12	12	19
G	9	10	9	19	7	3	15	18	15	8	4	8	8	18	15	2	4	11	12	9	10	14	16	3	5	5
H	2	5	4	5	20	19	18	9	7	12	19	15	19	18	20	3	5	18	15	14	18	5	17	8	19	12
I	7	10	3	16	15	6	17	10	11	2	16	4	15	14	10	10	3	19	8	20	11	17	4	5	15	2
J	6	18	7	15	17	2	14	17	6	16	11	6	19	15	10	8	7	14	15	12	11	2	6	2	12	9
K	14	5	2	5	15	15	20	2	2	11	20	14	5	15	7	11	8	2	11	11	6	14	16	18	8	14
L	14	19	18	12	11	5	17	11	15	20	8	18	14	19	8	2	15	6	2	5	7	5	15	15	6	9
M	18	4	17	5	6	17	19	8	3	11	12	14	4	11	20	12	10	10	19	7	3	9	7	17	19	5
N	7	7	5	11	16	4	17	12	19	10	9	20	16	3	12	3	17	16	10	4	20	18	3	14	14	12
O	14	17	18	15	16	19	2	5	15	2	8	2	2	17	10	19	18	11	2	9	20	4	20	11	20	5
P	17	9	5	20	20	10	19	18	15	10	7	6	11	8	3	16	3	7	20	7	15	17	7	18	4	7
Q	11	16	9	18	4	15	7	20	8	14	8	2	9	9	6	6	20	3	7	20	14	18	8	16	16	12
R	8	8	10	17	15	4	17	11	19	10	12	10	3	18	2	3	4	6	6	20	4	17	2	20	9	17
S	20	18	6	18	6	17	11	20	6	20	14	10	9	10	3	11	11	7	20	16	6	7	6	8	17	19
T	12	8	12	17	10	12	7	3	16	16	5	7	5	4	19	14	2	9	8	18	20	4	4	11	2	19
U	17	9	5	2	9	6	14	17	7	3	2	7	15	9	11	7	16	3	11	8	6	8	12	2	20	4
V	17	15	15	2	17	20	14	5	3	12	8	5	4	2	14	20	9	20	6	11	6	9	14	16	16	10
W	5	2	18	16	6	5	16	2	15	20	15	17	11	10	5	16	11	9	3	20	7	7	6	10	4	16
X	18	11	6	5	16	10	18	12	17	16	16	14	6	14	14	11	7	14	12	18	3	5	6	15	11	3
Y	5	14	2	4	19	8	14	6	9	9	18	11	12	16	9	17	15	8	9	15	20	3	14	19	14	9
Z	2	10	2	8	4	15	18	3	18	16	12	20	2	5	19	9	2	15	2	9	20	16	2	4	7	18

On the chart, find the place where the initials you've chosen intersect. Read the chapter whose number appears at that intersection.

14

ROMANTIC FORTUNA

This chapter describes the world of Fortuna. If an artist were asked to paint a part of such a world, what would he choose to paint? If we wanted to build a Fortuna house, with Fortuna furniture, and with Fortuna landscaping, how would we proceed? If someone wanted to live the Fortuna way of life, and thus become a fortunate individual, what would he or she do to achieve it? We live in a world ruled by chance, so there should be ways to describe what that world looks like. It seems that if we have a clear picture of the world we live in, we will be able to lead happier lives in it.

Our purpose in this book is to try to illustrate the way people can live in the world of Fortuna, a world where chance and uncertainty are positive and beneficial. The fortunate individual makes friends with uncertainty. The Fortuna philosophy helps people deal more effectively with risk. This does not mean that we encourage taking all kinds of risks, but some people cannot live with any risk at all. They are paralyzed in the face of uncertainty. Investment analysts and advisors talk about how investors have different "comfort zones." Some people can't sleep if they own stock which moves up or down with the volatility characteristic of the goddess Fortuna. They prefer to keep their money in a safe-deposit box. However, becoming familiar with the world of Fortuna enables us to take a certain amount of risk with a minimum of anxiety. It contributes significantly to the increase of our "comfort zones."

Talking about "comfort zones" leads us into a playful illustration of a basic aspect of the world of Fortuna. We are going to compare a ball and a box. Suppose that several of us go into the backyard to have a chat about Fortuna. We look around for seats and find several large rubber balls and some wooden crates left there by children. Some of us choose to sit on the crates, others on the balls. Those among us who choose a ball know that such a seat is unstable, unreliable, and unsafe. This sitting position could easily give way. We could tumble to the ground. Note that the words used to describe sitting on the ball belong to the vocabulary associated with Fortuna: unstable, unreliable, unsafe, giving way, tumbling to the ground.

The ball stands for chance and uncertainty. We cannot maintain our balance with certainty while sitting on a ball. This position is lacking in predictability. Furthermore, the ball as a seat involves danger. One could get hurt, for instance, by falling backwards. There are those who claim that it should be possible to predict which people will prefer to sit on a ball and which ones, on the other hand, will remain standing until they find a safe wooden crate to sit on. Analysts will point to certain important factors in the determination of their choices, including general temperament, current disposition, innate or acquired tendencies, physical condition, state of health, and finally age — not age in years — but mental age (the young at heart). Sitting on a ball, we might say, indicates an adventurous spirit.

The rectangular crate, on the other hand, is a more stable and firm seat. Our stability and safety can be entrusted to this rectangular perch with very little effort and attention on our part. Similarly, as we recall, the person who was afraid to take risks left his money in a safe-deposit box. Nothing can happen to the money, but neither does it produce anything. Nothing is likely to happen either when we consistently sit on safe and stable crates. The only major event in such a life (of sitting on stable crates and keeping money in safes) is the absolute certainty of eventually winding up inside the crate and of being placed even more safely six feet under. Life is no fun on or inside crates.

On the ball, however, whether we fall or remain sitting depends on our own participation in the act of sitting. We act more alive on the ball than on the crate. We are, in any case, more active and alert to our state of balance. Sitting on the ball, or actions of a similar nature, place us in the position of exercising our wills and enjoying the pleasures derived from our freedom. It is more fun to do things like sitting on a large, round, rubber ball even though we know that it is probably wiser to sit on square crates. We are playing here with the opposition between a sphere and a cube or, in simpler terms, between a circle and a square. The world of Fortuna is the world of the circle and the sphere. It includes all other objects or actions involving curved lines. There are no straight or angular lines in that world. There is nothing that may cut or prick, but rather there are only shapes that bend around, caress softly, and follow the flow.

This opposition between straight and circular lines has applications in real life. That it has moral implications for the way we should behave in life is explained by French essayist and moralist Michel de Montaigne. In distinguishing between the moral behavior of ambitious, avaricious people, on the one hand, and the behavior of fortunate people, on the other hand, he writes:

"The course of our desires should be directed not in a straight line that ends up elsewhere, but in a circle whose two extremities by a short sweep meet and terminate in ourselves. Actions that are performed without this reflexive movement, I mean a searching and genuine reflexive movement — the actions, for example, of the avaricious, the ambitious, and so many others who run in a straight line, whose course carries them ever forward — are erroneous and diseased actions."

Fortuna and Lady Knowledge

The great Italian poet, Petrarch, wrote an important book on *The Remedies of Fortuna.* In a French translation of this book which appeared in Paris in 1523, there is a beautiful picture (duplicated opposite) showing two ladies sitting face to face. Fortuna on the left is sitting on a ball. Sapientia or Lady Knowledge is on the right, sitting on a cube. Fortuna is blindfolded. In her left hand she is holding a wheel. On the rim of this wheel there are four little people whose significance we now understand. Written on the picture, in Latin, are inscriptions that tell us that "the seat of Fortuna is round, and the seat of Virtue is square." This picture was intended to teach the moral lesson that being adventuresome, taking risks, or experimenting in any way with life is sinful. In other words, you cannot attempt to play an active role in shaping your own life and be considered virtuous at the same time.

Across from Fortuna sits Sapientia or Lady Know-It-All, holding a mirror in her right hand and looking at herself in it. Taking a minute to compare the wheel with the mirror, we see that the wheel stands for what we do; the mirror for what we are. The wheel stands for the experimental sciences and empiricism; the mirror for theoretical science and idealism. In the world of Fortuna, things and people are measured by their actions — symbolized by the wheel in motion — while in the opposite world, things and people are measured by appearance, performance, illusion, and make-believe, the whole syndrome of representation. Fortuna deals with behavior while Sapientia deals with the make-believe world of the theater, as in the ancient plays about Oedipus. Sapientia claims to find universal and eternal truths by looking intensely into her mirror. Her vision of the world is a static one. As she sees only herself in the mirror, she sees no accidents, no happenings, no events, no change, and, in the end, none of the changing nature of life. In her eyes, things are good to the extent that they have no uncertainty. Uncertainty is banished from her world-vision.

Fortuna, on the contrary, does not look into a mirror of wisdom. She holds a rotating wheel with people holding onto the rim to signify that life is made of ups and downs, full of uncertainty. We believe that Fortuna's world-vision is closer to the reality of human existence. Before you choose between the ball and the cube, between uncertainty and certainty, consider the words of Michel de Montaigne, one of the greatest thinkers of western civilization, who wrote this about the idea of certainty: "I know no one but fools who will say that they are certain and resolute about anything."

Even though we usually think of certainty as good (the sun will rise tomorrow) and uncertainty as bad (war, disease, etc.) a little bit of thought will show you that the connection between these ideas is not that simple. Think of

- a surprise birthday party
- the certainty of death

Try to imagine situations where certainty is bad or situations where uncertainty is good. The following may give you some ideas:

- the end of a vacation
- imprisonment
- the thrill of sports and gambling
- the possibility of an afterlife
- the surprise ending of an exciting movie or novel

The world of Fortuna is diametrically opposed to the cold and cruel world of Reason. In art and literature, this opposition stands at the great crux between romanticism and classicism. In attempting to explain these ideas, we will see that Fortuna corresponds to the realm of romanticism while Reason corresponds to the world of classicism. Let us see first what is classicism. The word "classic" comes from the Latin word *"classis,"* which was a call to assemble the people of a town or city in a particular place to get ready to fight an enemy. As the people rushed out of their homes, they gathered in different groups (classes), according to social status: the masters in one group, the servants in another, and each group classified into appropriate sub-groups.

In a world governed by Fortuna, the romantic world, on the other hand, masters and servants would gather all together in the town square and they would elect their leaders on the basis of their ability to defend the town, according to the situation at hand. A strong and smart servant could become the leader in a romantic setting. As can be seen, the word "romantic" does not merely refer to love. It refers to a whole outlook on life. Romanticism translates into a particular way of looking at the world and even a particular way of life. It is the best way to illustrate the world of Fortuna.

THE CLASSICAL AND ROMANTIC THEATRE

Fortuna is a favorite during romantic periods. By comparing two plays, one classical and one romantic, we will illustrate some of the essential nature of Fortuna. Most people already know more about the romantic world than they think they do, so we will let you guess which play is romantic and which is classical.

We are at the theater. The play we are about to see is about love, a subject which we associate, in everyday language, with the word "romantic." But let's watch. A father is telling his son that he, the son, is expected to marry the daughter of an old friend of his, from a family of equal economic and social status. The young man, accompanied by his servant, must travel to the young lady's home and introduce himself to the girl's family. The young man and his man-servant decide to change clothes as a playful deceit and show up in exchanged roles at the house of the bride-to-be.

During the next scene, we see that the same trick has been arranged between the young lady and her maid. They have exchanged clothes and have switched mannerisms and ways of speaking. These artificial switches are comical for the maid fails to accurately mimic the ways of a lady and vice-versa. When the four meet, then, the young lady and gentleman are disguised as servants and the servants have taken the names, the clothes, the speech, and the mannerisms of their respective masters. The young man and his man-servant do not know that the women they are meeting have exchanged roles, nor do the women know that the men are assuming false guises.

What ensues among the couples is a series of very entertaining verbal exchanges and comic situations. The altered situation delights the spectators who, naturally enjoy a feeling of superiority in knowing the truth. After a few scenes, the subterfuge is discovered by the parties involved who have, in the meantime, fallen in love: master with mistress and servant with maid, of course. Everything returns to normal. The parents arrive. Two marriages are decided upon, and the play ends in the traditional manner: with a banquet and music. We have not given you the name of this play because there are really dozens of plays based on this same motif.

Let us go now and watch an entirely different play in another part of town. As the curtain rises, the scene is no longer of a lighted drawing room but depicts a garden at night, with the moon shining through dark clouds in the background. Two characters walk rapidly from both ends of the garden toward the center of the stage. The man wears a cape covering part of his face and a sword at his side. The lady wears a hooded robe. Under her robe, we see that she is dressed like a man. As the couple exchange words, we learn that the lady is none other than the Queen of Spain and that the man is a commoner, a mere servant, who is running for his life from the King's men.

In the midst of a passionate dialogue mixed with tears and embraces, two hooded men appear; a sword fight ensues, and our lover falls to the ground right in front of us, mortally wounded. The queen then stabs herself in the chest with a diamond studded dagger, and falls over her dying lover. The curtain drops.

You have guessed it! The second play was romantic. The first one was not; it was classical. The difference does not lie in the subject matter of love, for both plays deal with love. Nor does it lie in the fact that one play ends happily while the other ends sadly. There are indeed many romantic plays that end on a positive note. Conversely, there are many classical plays that end tragically. Some of the greatest theater in Western literature is romantic, such as the plays of the Spanish Golden Age (the seventeenth century) as well as the plays of Shakespeare. The plays presented by these two great national theaters were permeated with the romantic spirit of Fortuna. But let us not lose ourself in literary criticism. Let us go back rather to the fundamental differences between classicism and romanticism so we can understand better what is meant by the word "romantic," and thus come to understand the world of Fortuna which, in our opinion, is the world we are living in today.

The first play represents the triumph of Reason. Reason was put into question, ever so briefly and playfully, during the course of the play. The rational, orderly, eighteenth-century European social world was turned upside down while the couples were disguised. The authority of the fathers is eventually triumphant as the sons do, in the end, marry the daughters which were chosen for them.

In the play, social "classes" remain separated as is demanded by Reason. The young heir marries the young heiress, and the servant marries the maid. The two marriages form the geometric figure of a square. The classic play is concerned with a square-view of life, a square-view of society, and with a square meal at the end. Comedies such as these, which played in Europe from Madrid to Moscow during the Enlightment (the Age of Reason), always ended with a banquet.

The square meal, the rectangular table inside the rectangular living room, as well as the rectangular check books of the fathers, remind us that the flow of power, of money, and of love are safely boxed in. The play stays within the standard norms of the square and thus speaks for stability.

We need to stress that while stability is usually a good thing, we should not fall into the two most common psychological traps associated with it. First, stability is never permanent; so, we should always keep in mind that instability might be just around the corner. Second, just because stability is desirable does not mean that instability must be bad. Stability and instability can be either good or bad. There are bad instances of stability as well as good ones. One of the obvious beneficial effects of instability is that it brings change, and change is necessary for life. For instance, life in prison is seen as a sort of death because it drastically limits the possibilities for change.

It is sometimes suggested that people return to jail because they seek the stability of prison life; something which they miss in the outside world. The world of Fortuna, although it is risky at times, is full of the richness of life, for as discussed in Chapter 5 of this book, advantageous opportunities can only arise out of instability.

In this connection, it should be emphasized that, while we side with Fortuna in her eternal struggle against Lady Reason, we do not totally reject reason. Reason comes from the Latin *"ratio"* which means cutting things into parts and measuring them, like in the sentence, "he got his ration of water." Rational thinking is one of the important tools necessary for the proper working of our mental processes. We should listen to the voice of reason and we should attempt to be reasonable. However, Lady Reason has her pernicious side too: She invites us to rationalize and to make rationalizations. When we do this, we begin to think that abstract reasoning is all-powerful and we forget to look at nature, to look at reality, to look at experience, and to take into consideration what really happens. While Reason tends to operate in a dream world, Fortuna operates in the real world with all its quirks and imperfections. Fortuna, unlike Reason, does not rationalize; instead, she invites us to look at reality and all its implications. She opens the way to experimental science.

Returning to the theater we see that the second play is romantic because of its essential instability. It is romantic because it depicts the unusual. The romantic artist or writer exploits the mixing, the coming together of extreme differences. Some examples are the queen and the servant, beauty and the beast, a church dignitary and a gypsy girl, the same beautiful gypsy girl and an ugly but good-hearted hunchback, a married woman and a pensive young man who commits suicide in the end, and finally, the model for all of these: a jilted married queen who commits suicide because a young and dashing one-night-stand-lover sails away to start a city which will later be known as Rome.

The romantic couples depicted in these plays break the square mold of Reason. Reality is not square but fluid and full of the curved lines of Fortuna's world. Ironically, the romantic vision of reality is more practical and closer to nature than any possible construct of a rational reality. When describing the romantic world, many authors often use words which seem to have negative connotations. They might perhaps say that a romantic setting is fanciful. The word "fanciful" can be interpreted, however, as highly positive since it belongs to the realm of the imagination which is one of the highest faculties of human beings. What is a person without imagination? The romantic imagination is an organic creative force whose presence is essential in both the arts and the sciences.

It is sometimes also said that the romantic world is fictitious. But what is life without dreams? Fiction might be called the precursor of future reality. Many times it is the poet and the writer of fiction who precede and anticipate the discoveries of the scientists and the concrete realizations of the technicians. Our actual trips to the moon were, at first, pure fiction in the writings of Cyrano de Bergerac, the seventeenth century French author, and in the writings of Jules Verne during the last century. Romantic artists and writers do not limit themselves to describe what they see with their own eyes, but use also their minds' eyes. That second vision is the far-seeing eye of the imagination, an essential component in the creation of anything new.

Other adjectives which are used frequently to describe the romantic world are: marvelous, colorful, extravagant, fabulous, picturesque, and even supernatural. The current popularity of such games as "Dungeons and Dragons" testifies to our fascination with the romantic. Romantic individuals, as well as romantic settings, are, most of all, unique. Never before has there been in the world as much insistence on our desire to be unique individuals, to live our own lives, to do, as we say, our own thing. As the world becomes more and more homogeneous, with fast food chains, gas stations, shopping malls, and office buildings, people, on the other hand, yearn to be different from one another.

One has just to look at an old picture portraying the crowd attending a football or baseball game and compare it with a recent photograph taken at a similar stadium. Instead of the monotonous uniformity of dress and colors in the picture of fifty years ago, the more recent one will show a great diversity of clothing in the stands. Look across the stands and marvel at the fantastic array of colors. There is also an immense diversity of ages, races, ethnic groups, and social classes. Such is the romantic picture of today's world. Such is also the world of Fortuna: colorful, diverse, varied, heterogeneous, pluralistic, full of unique individuals, full of surprises, and essentially, fun.

WAR

Surprise is another delightful asset of Fortuna. It not only has its amusing aspect but surprise is involved in war as well. We saw above that the word "classic" finds its origin in war, that is, in the way people prepared and organized themselves to fight; so it is particularly appropriate to use war as the subject to illustrate another essential aspect of the romantic world. We shall see on which side Fortuna stands.

In classical times, armies used to march onto the battlefield in close formation. This was the "rational" way of doing things. The two opposing armies would face each other in an orderly manner, with the various battalions of infantry, cavalry, and artillery properly and rationally positioned on one side or the other. Then the commanders would have to agree on who would shoot first. It was all very rational, very civilized, very much like organized madness. There is a famous case when the French commander actually invited the English to shoot first: *"Après vous, Messieurs les Anglais."*

The Napoleonic *Grande Armée* was a classical army with a very high level of hierarchical organization. It was a highly rational war machine. All its officers had been raised and educated during the last years of the two-hundred-year-long Age of Reason. That beautiful machine met with its first defeat in Spain. This signaled the end of the classical age and the beginning of the romantic age.

According to many modern philosophers, Michel Foucault among them, this romantic age is with us still today and its way of looking at the world still dominates our own times. Let us go back to the time of Napoleon. In Spain, and later on in Russia, the big classical army, the supreme creation of Reason, was defeated by a new concept of war: the little war — not the normal *"guerra"* (war in Spanish), but the diminutive form of *"guerra,"* the *"guerrilla,"* the "little war."

Thus, Reason and its *Grande Armée* were suitable to fight in the big war *(guerra)*. They were not prepared to fight in the little war *(guer*rilla). This new type of warfare was under the protection of Fortuna. Now, guerrilla warfare was not invented by the Spaniards. The concept is as old as mankind. The practice was revived during the American Revolutionary War and later in Europe, in the wars against Napoleon. The guerrilla fighters had the element of surprise on their side. They made an alliance with an old forgotten goddess: Fortuna. In guerrilla warfare, Fortuna plays the role of Mars, the god of war. (She eventually takes over the roles of all the other gods of the universe.)

The movements of the classical *Grande Armée* were fairly predictable. This made it vulnerable to the uncertainty of the terrain, to the random time of attack, and to the unexpected manner of attack of the guerrilla fighters. Attack could come any time, any place, and in any shape or manner. In the literature of Spanish folklore, we read of the Spanish mayor who invited a group of high ranking French officers to dinner and announced calmly thereafter that they had all been mortally poisoned, including himself. This unexpected type of heroism was unheard of in classical times. It was built on surprise and ruse. It clashed with absolute virtue. It did not make "sense." It was, in one word, irrational.

The Age of Reason died as the *Grande Armée,* a few years later, was struggling through and starving in the snows of Russia where it encountered more "irrational" forms of warfare: guerrilla tactics, retreat, and scorched land. It was not equipped to function in the emerging Age of Fortuna. Later, romantic painters and poets of the nineteenth century began to romanticize the figure of Napoleon. But he was actually a product of the previous age, the Age of Reason.

There is a famous drawing by the nineteenth century Spanish painter Goya showing a man dressed in eighteenth-century garb (the Age of Reason). The man is sitting down on a chair and has apparently fallen asleep at his desk. Above the man's head, Goya has drawn some monsters in a cloud representing the man's dream. At the bottom of the drawing Goya has written: *"El sueño de la razón engendra monstruos,"* which means: "The dream of Reason engenders monsters."

This interesting caption has been translated too simply by many people. The word *"sueño"* in Spanish means both "sleep" and "dream." The caption is usually translated as "when Reason sleeps, monsters are engendered." However, it is equally accurate to translate it as "when Reason dreams, it engenders monsters." In Spanish, both meanings are present simultaneously. The monsters in Goya's painting do not creep in from outside but, rather, they are drawn in the cloud above the man's head suggesting clearly that it is the act of dreaming that engenders the monsters. Furthermore, these monsters are typical of the dream world: owl-like chimeras and nightmarish apparitions. We interpret Goya's drawing as a political cartoon against the rationalistic France of the Enlightenment.

The French Age of Reason produced the French Revolution and, immediately after it, produced Napoleon and his wars of imperialistic expansionism. Goya lived during the Napoleonic Era and captured in a famous painting the shooting of civilians in Madrid by French Napoleonic troops. These atrocities of Napoleon's expansionist wars were the monsters which Reason had engendered. Viewed from Spain, or from Russia, the Age of Reason that the French philosophers had brought about resulted in many good things such as liberty, equality, brotherhood, and human rights; but their Reason had also produced Napoleon and the wars of conquest by the French armies all over Europe. The dreams of the rationalistic philosophers had turned into nightmares.

Reason, throughout the ages, has produced more monsters than is usually realized. Reason rules over communist states. In these cases, Reason leads to many limitations on freedom, to concentration camps, to the Gulags, and to psychiatric prisons for the politically "irrational." In this way, the dreams of Reason, such as the creation of a perfectly egalitarian society, eliminating differences, and trying to eliminate chance and uncertainty, do, in the end, engender the monsters that Goya experienced in his lifetime and which he so skillfully hinted at in drawings and paintings left for posterity. Reason, unchecked by the observation of the facts of nature, leads to the cold and cruel imposition of law and order everywhere: on the stage, on the artist's canvas, in the battle formation, in the dress code ("Sorry, sir, you can't come in without a tie"), in our schools, in the garden, in bed. Fortuna, on the other hand, stands for freedom everywhere.

The romantic view of the world is unfortunately just as simplistic and flawed as the earlier classical view. They have in common the same desperate but vain attempt to deny Fortuna a role in the world. These romantics stripped Nature of her close alliance with Reason but in place of Reason they invented a mysterious force that pushes Nature toward perfection. Many of these romantics believed that the hero — the romantic hero — is protected by a mysterious force. "May the force be with you" is a recent expression of this romantic dream.

Fortuna is romantic but her romanticism differs from that of the traditional romantic. There are no such things as purposes, goals, missions, ends, or destinies towards which living organisms strive. While it is true that a fertilized egg grows into an adult organism, this seemingly purposeful process cannot serve as a model for the evolution of species on earth. Evolution is led by blind chance — blind Fortuna — and no ultimate purpose, no communist man, no superman is in the offing.

A much healthier world-view includes the role of chance. Our romanticism of Fortuna, which we posit as truly scientific romanticism, includes the idea of an organic evolving universe, but the most important facet of our philosophy is that evolution is "without a plan." Men and women are all alone in the universe. As French Nobel prize winner Jacques Monod wrote in the last words of his book *Chance and Necessity*: "Man's destiny is written nowhere. It is up to men and women to choose between heaven or hell on earth."

Our Fortuna philosophy can bring hope to the world by the very fact that it cures us of the teleonomic delusions of traditional romanticism. According to many philosophers, romanticism is still strong among us. The first error we have to correct is that which confuses the development of an individual organism (a single human being or a single fish) with the evolution of a species such as humanity or fish or dinosaurs. The continued growth of mankind is not purposeful and guaranteed. It is, at best, precarious.

So, as we surround ourselves with nuclear weapons, we lie to ourselves by saying that, since the world is not a clock, but an evolving organism with a definite goal, it must continue to evolve in the future. This belief is not only erroneous (as it confuses ontogeny with phylogeny), it is also dangerous. It makes the presence of such things as nuclear weapons and hazardous wastes as somehow "acceptable." The lie that the world as organism will continue evolving is everywhere, and even those who do not believe in God believe that "the force" — that mysterious thing that pushes evolution forward — will somehow continue doing so indefinitely.

While it is true that we are now living in the continuation of the romantic world that began at the end of the eighteenth century, it is also true that the romantic view of the world is only a portion of a more complete description of the world of Fortuna. We could say that the world of Fortuna is a romantic world but without its illusions and myths. Progress is a romantic myth which has worked, so far, in favor of mankind. However, belief in continued and undisturbed progress is a dangerous illusion because it excludes chance as a cosmic force in the universe and it blinds us to the possibility that progress could cease at any time with the annihilation of the human race.

Do you believe that

- science will find the answers to nuclear war and pollution?
- humanity will survive forever?
- progress is inevitable?

IT IS NOT NECESSARILY SO. The future is constantly created out of events, accidents, and the individual's participation, in the present. What are you doing to make that future come out positively?

THE MATRIX FOR CHAPTER 14

	A	B	C	D	E	F	G	H	I	J	K	L	M	N	O	P	Q	R	S	T	U	V	W	X	Y	Z
A	8	8	17	2	5	5	20	11	9	5	16	8	2	18	2	11	17	8	7	4	16	3	8	18	9	3
B	11	4	19	8	3	20	10	4	17	16	11	12	8	19	16	19	2	15	10	19	9	7	9	9	4	5
C	13	18	11	6	15	20	12	11	15	20	10	8	5	3	8	19	3	18	13	18	15	6	4	2	4	19
D	4	6	12	20	20	18	12	4	11	3	5	13	11	5	16	11	6	7	18	3	20	15	5	20	17	2
E	16	17	5	5	20	9	6	4	16	10	15	5	16	8	5	5	5	10	8	12	16	16	13	16	18	10
F	3	20	2	3	3	10	10	19	10	15	20	20	10	5	10	18	6	15	19	10	2	8	16	10	3	17
G	3	8	5	10	15	8	12	16	12	16	8	10	7	9	20	12	5	5	5	5	13	20	11	15	6	15
H	9	4	2	6	3	2	10	8	3	16	16	7	7	5	5	7	15	19	4	19	15	7	15	18	15	8
I	5	13	12	4	16	5	4	8	10	11	2	19	13	19	19	13	18	16	7	7	10	8	2	6	9	13
J	2	8	16	3	13	17	5	7	9	5	13	11	2	10	12	12	18	11	4	4	18	10	13	5	17	19
K	20	9	10	8	5	7	6	10	8	7	19	5	13	2	12	16	6	16	20	20	20	5	19	12	6	18
L	6	6	12	8	2	16	19	3	8	7	6	12	4	11	19	11	3	4	18	20	5	3	20	4	8	7
M	5	7	3	11	18	18	17	17	18	15	18	4	2	20	11	7	20	15	7	6	10	5	11	3	20	6
N	13	2	9	18	19	15	5	6	18	19	6	19	12	13	6	17	4	5	11	5	6	19	17	11	18	2
O	11	3	15	6	11	7	4	20	7	18	15	17	17	5	2	5	6	18	16	4	10	19	17	19	9	12
P	8	8	4	12	16	19	3	6	6	6	20	16	9	2	19	20	16	17	9	16	16	19	12	13	19	17
Q	10	3	20	20	19	11	16	6	15	4	18	4	7	4	4	19	18	16	8	5	9	12	4	15	6	4
R	6	10	16	20	7	8	5	18	5	20	5	6	9	5	9	13	15	10	10	4	15	3	16	15	2	16
S	13	7	5	4	8	6	20	13	20	7	11	20	5	17	4	7	2	4	12	7	13	17	18	15	16	4
T	18	18	2	3	9	8	17	7	20	11	9	18	20	19	12	6	3	5	15	16	11	11	7	6	19	4
U	2	12	2	17	4	13	10	15	10	6	9	4	13	5	7	17	2	4	17	9	12	20	4	16	7	3
V	5	2	10	6	16	12	5	8	20	16	15	4	10	19	2	10	20	2	17	12	18	13	18	20	6	9
W	8	19	9	3	2	9	10	8	19	12	19	20	13	2	15	9	10	16	15	5	13	20	5	15	19	5
X	10	16	3	6	11	8	13	2	10	13	17	7	16	2	19	10	15	17	16	20	11	19	7	4	3	8
Y	20	5	13	3	17	16	4	17	3	11	16	15	20	5	19	18	6	16	8	2	19	18	11	4	5	18
Z	17	16	10	11	9	3	17	6	7	18	10	18	18	12	6	11	11	9	6	3	10	12	8	8	4	12

On the chart, find the place where the initials you've chosen intersect. Read the chapter whose number appears at that intersection.

15

PROBABILITY

For as long as humanity has used language, we have attempted to discover, analyze, and pass on those rules of language which aid us in reasoning correctly. Eventually these rules were encapsulated and summarized in formal logic and then further refined and distilled through mathematics. These linguistic tools have been useful in helping us to understand the world around us. When the philosopher Kant was searching for a means to prove that there were absolute, undeniable, and nontrivial truths about the world, he founded his argument on our intuitive geometric conception of space and on our numerical perception of the passage of time. Science, using rigorous, deductive reasoning based on mathematical truths was able to discover the laws that govern all the important aspects of the physical universe such as motion, electricity, light, gravity, and sound. When we hear words like "thus," "therefore," "consequently," or "hence," we are in the presence of the logical or mathematical type of reasoning.

However, there are many interesting and important questions to which this logical method of reasoning does not apply. Much of our knowledge is not certain. There are many questions which cannot be answered with just a "yes" or a "no." Sometimes, the best answer we can give is, as Sam Goldwyn said, "a definite maybe!" In classical logic, we could only talk about whether a sentence, like "one plus one equals five" was true or false, but there are many statements which fall between true and false, involving unpredictable situations where the outcome is uncertain or where chance plays a large role. In order to reason about these statements, the idea of mathematical truth needs to be stretched; we have to consider the degree of a statement or whether one statement is more or less true than another. This type of probabilistic reasoning is characterized by words like "it is likely that," "it is possible," "perhaps," and "this tends to influence that." It seems a contradiction in terms to say that there could be a mathematical (implying absolute certainty) theory which deals with these probabilistic statements, but there is. As the modern mathematical theory of probability was being developed out of classical mathematics, every step of its evolution was based on purest classical logic. Yet it surprisingly allows us to describe and manipulate ideas from the world of uncertainty.

Since it appeared that the world of Fortuna, filled with possibilities and uncertainties, could not be expressed in terms of absolute, formal logic, mathematicians and scientists were challenged by the puzzle of how the concept of uncertainty could be expressed mathematically. The development of the theory of probability gave a means of describing chance, but this theory turned out to be unlike most other scientific theories. Usually when a situation is analyzed mathematically, it becomes possible to control it. For example, the mathematical analysis of the orbit of a spacecraft provides the means for modifying that orbit in order to make the ship land wherever one wants. But even though the theory of probability describes the outcomes of a random, chance-like experiment, such as flipping a coin, it cannot predict whether it will fall heads or tails and it provides no means for controlling the outcome of the toss. At the heart of the theory of probability is an open space, occupied by chance or, in other words, Fortuna. Her role and power lies in providing events which we can only record and describe. She is the fount of uncertainty. The scientific theory of probability has grown up around her, attempting to understand her, but never controlling her. This theory provides humanity's most precise answer to the question, "What is chance?"

The history of the theory of probability is closely linked with gambling. Thousands of years ago when an important decision had to be made and no one was certain what to do, it was often left up to the gods to decide. An oracle was consulted in the following manner. Various bones (sometimes from a recently sacrificed animal) were marked with signs and scattered on the ground. The pattern of exposed markings would then be interpreted in a standard way, much as a modern-day fortune-teller reads someone's fortune from a deck of cards. Since no one knew beforehand how the bones would be arranged, people were satisfied that the gods were the only influence on the outcome. People, by obeying the bones, could be confident they were being obedient to the gods. Bones of this sort have been found at archeological sites dating from thousands of years ago. Gradually, as the practice evolved, the bones assumed standard shapes and they finally evolved into cubes, each of whose faces was equally likely to end up on the top — our modern dice. The practice of consulting an oracle also evolved into a manner of solving disputes between individuals — by flipping a coin one could see whose side the gods favored — and then finally into modern games of chance using both dice and other randomizing devices, such as wheels or cards.

In the seventeenth century, a gentleman gambler named the Chevalier de Méré was trying to find a system for beating the house in a popular dice game of his day. He consulted a friend, the mathematician and philosopher, Blaise Pascal, concerning certain calculations. Pascal not only answered the gambler's questions but, getting interested, went on to solve the much more complicated question of how to split the prize money if, for some reason, the game had to be halted before it ended. This involved figuring out who would have been more likely to win the game had it been played out. He began a series of exchanges of letters with another French mathematician, Pierre de Fermat, and between them they created all the terminology and notations necessary for a scientific study of chance. It is generally agreed that these men created an entirely new branch of mathematics and, given the natural interest many people have in gambling, the growth of this branch has been vigorous.

This chapter is not intended to be a textbook on probability. We recognize that a large number of our readers are "math-o-phobes," and that too many formulas and numbers obscure rather than illustrate the subject at hand. But there is one simple concept, easily explainable, which can demystify and clarify a lot of the language of probability being used all around us, from scientific announcements to weather forecasting. The key idea behind probability is that when there is a situation whose outcome cannot be exactly predicted, then some fractional or decimal number between zero and one is assigned to each possible outcome of the situation. This number, 1/10 or 1/2 or 3/4 or .95, represents how likely it is that the outcome will occur. It is a way of measuring how certain we are of a particular outcome. It can also be used to compare the likelihood of different outcomes.

Something with a probability of 1/100, a number very close to zero, is extremely unlikely; this outcome occurs on the average only once out of every hundred times the situation occurs. If the probability of a particular couple having a green-eyed, red-headed daughter is 1/100 then, if they were to have one hundred children (not very likely!), probably one would be a red-headed, green-eyed daughter. If they were to have only two or three children, most likely none would fit this description, but it could happen. It would just be a rare, unlikely event. Another way of expressing this is that the odds against this red-haired, green-eyed daughter are 99 to 1 — a long-shot, but a possibility.

Near the other end of the spectrum of probabilities, an event with a probability close to one, like .99 or 99/100, is very likely. If today is Monday, the probability that I will go to work tomorrow is close to .99, which means it is just about certain that I will, but, as in every such case, there is a slim chance (precisely .01 or 1/100 in this case) that for some reason I may not make it to work tomorrow. It is most likely that I will go to work, but it is not absolutely certain.

The number zero is reserved for impossible events, like the probability of a married man also being a bachelor. The number one is used for certainties, like "one plus one equals two." In real life situations, as opposed to mathematical or linguistic tricks, there are no absolute impossibilities or certainties. The probability that the sun will rise tomorrow is .99999 . . . — continuing on for perhaps a thousand nines — but one has to admit that there is always a slim possibility that it might not rise for some unimaginable reason. The fact that we never assign a "0" or "1" to the probability of ordinary events can also be expressed in the language of Fortuna. Her power to cause a virtual certainty to fail to happen or to make happen something which is extremely unlikely cannot be disputed. This fact, that we never assign the probability of one or zero in practice to any event, can be expressed either in the language of mathematics or in the language of Fortuna.

Try tossing a coin ten times. Note how many heads and tails you get. Do it several times. You'll be surprised how rarely you will get exactly five heads and five tails.

When we toss a coin, we say the probability that it will land heads up is 1/2 and the probability that it will land tails up is 1/2. Each outcome is equally likely, so they are assigned the probability halfway between zero and one. This number 1/2 has an exact mathematical significance and definite consequences. It does not mean that exactly half the tosses will be heads. It means that in the long run, if we flipped that coin many times, and divided the number of heads observed (or tails) by the total number of flips, the resulting fractions would get closer and closer to 1/2, or expressed as a decimal, closer and closer to .5000. The table below illustrates the typical outcome of a large number of flips of a coin simulated on a computer using a random number generator. Looking at the numbers in the next to the last column, we see that the more flips there are, the closer the resulting fraction of heads is to 1/2.

However, hidden within this apparent regularity is a wide-open realm of possibilities for the free and capricious actions of Fortuna.

Number of flips	Number of heads	Number of tails	Heads divided by total; fraction	decimal	How far different from ½
10	6	4	6/10	.600000	.100000
100	54	46	54/100	.540000	.040000
1000	495	505	495/1000	.495000	.005000
10,000	5013	4987	5013/10000	.501300	.001300
100,000	50,083	49,917	50083/100000	.500830	.000830

Notice that when we flipped ten times there were only two more heads than tails, but after flipping 100,000 times, even though the decimal was much closer to 1/2, there was a difference of 166 (50,083 -49,917) between the number of heads and tails. That gap will continue to get wider and wider as we continue flipping. It is extremely unlikely to obtain exactly the same number of heads and tails. Because this discrepancy between the number of heads and the number of tails gets larger and larger as more tosses are made, we might expect to occasionally get three heads in a row, or four heads or even ten heads in a row. In fact, it can be shown that if we are willing to keep on tossing coins long enough, a hundred heads or a thousand heads or a million heads in a row will be virtually guaranteed to happen. And the same applies to tails, too. We may have to wait until all the stars in the universe have been reduced to blackened chunks of coal, but it's almost certain to occur sometime.

Gamblers know this — that "you can catch a hot streak of luck" — and by betting on heads when a streak of heads happens to occur, they could win really big money. But gambling is a dangerous business. Psychologically, the most potent reinforcer of behavior has been shown to be random reinforcement. Many beginning gamblers who happen to win early and unexpectedly because of a "hot streak," really get hooked. Sometimes, just to entrap novice gamblers, professionals will even manufacture an early streak of luck for them.

If ten heads in a row have come up, some people think that the streak is likely to continue and will bet on heads. Others, feeling that the coin will remember and try to correct the overabundance of heads, will bet on a tail occurring next. They're both wrong. Mathematicians know that each toss of the coin or roll of the dice is completely independent. The coin has no memory. The next flip of the coin is completely unaffected by the preceding string of heads. One's luck can change at any moment. When we say that "the goddess of luck is fickle," we're expressing exactly the same idea as the idea of mathematical independence. On each flip of the coin, heads and tails are both equally likely to occur, regardless of what has happened previously.

By manipulating probabilities and wagers, some gamblers, both professional and amateur, try to outwit Fortuna and try to find a "system" that will guarantee winning. A simple example of one of these betting systems, sometimes called martingales, is based on the idea of doubling one's wager and is applicable in games like roulette or boule where the payoff is equal to the amount of the wager. You start with a fixed wager, say $1 or $10 or $100, and each time you lose, double your wager. Each time you win, go back to the beginning wager. The success of this method hinges on the fact that if you add up doubled numbers, like 1+2+4+8+16, you get a number, 31, which is always exactly one less than the next double, which is 32. Here's another example:

$$1+2+4+8+16+32+64+128 = 255$$

$$2 \times 128 = 256$$

Suppose you follow this system, and you lose eight times in a row. From the calculation above, you will have lost $255. Following the system, you will wager $256 next time and if you win, you will have a net gain of $1.00 for the sequence of plays. Every time you win, you will be $1.00 ahead (or whatever your original wager was) and every loss will be covered by doubling. Seems like a sure thing, doesn't it?

Well, the pitfall is this, and it's no wonder that this system is called "the gambler's ruin." Those doubled wagers get bigger and bigger at a rapid pace. If you run into a long series of losses, and can't double because you've run out of money, you'll lose it all. For example, if you came into the casino with $10,000 in your pockets and started doubling, you will have to wager $4096 after your twelfth loss in a row. At this point in the game you will have already invested $8191. If you then lose for the unlucky thirteenth time, you won't be able to put up $8192 on the next doubling and you'll be ruined. Just like in the example of flipping coins, sooner or later these long strings of losses will certainly occur. If you play long enough, you'll be ruined, no matter how large your beginning stake. If we want to take advantage of the abundance and richness of Fortuna, gambling is not the recommended way!

Probability also has a more serious aspect than gambling. Probabilistic language has to be used whenever we attempt to speak scientifically about people. In physical science we can say that it is certain that under standard conditions, water will boil at 100 degrees Centigrade (this being part of the definition of the Centigrade scale), but it is impossible to predict with certainty what any one individual person will always do under a given set of circumstances. Science can only deal with general laws concerning repeatable circumstances, whereas the individual is a unique event. We can predict with some accuracy that a particular city will consume a certain number of tons of fish in the course of a weekend; we can say that John Doe will probably eat fish this weekend; but there is no way to predict exactly that John Doe will eat fish at 6 PM this Saturday.

Because of this uncertainty, many scientific conclusions involving individuals can only be expressed in this probabilistic manner: "There is a statistically significant correlation between jogging more than ten miles a week and premature baldness in males." In order to understand what this conclusion means and what it implies for each one of us, we have to understand how it was discovered. First of all, "statistically significant" is a fairly general term. In a scientific publication, this result would have been more specifically reported as "A correlation between these two factors has been proven to exist at the 99% degree of confidence." How is this fact discovered? Suppose we are experimenters who do not know whether or not there is a connection between baldness and jogging. We choose two groups of nonbald men at random, say in their thirties. The men in one group jog more than ten miles a week, the other group consists of nonjoggers. The men are matched so that they have similar jobs, families and other habits, and we try to balance evenly between the two groups any other factors, such as family history, which may contribute to baldness. After a fixed period of time, suppose it is discovered that 5% of the joggers have begun to bald while only 2% of the other group have. By plugging into standard statistical formulas, we figure out that the probability of this difference happening just by accident is one in 100. Unless the rare event has occurred where we accidentally chose groups in which one had more men who were just about to become bald, we can be 99% confident (99 cases out of 100) that there really is a relation between jogging and baldness.

But is there really a relation in this particular case? Does jogging contribute to baldness? Maybe, or maybe not. Even after the scientists report a "statistically significant" result, there is that 1% chance that they are completely wrong. Because one out of every 100 positive scientific results is actually in error, scientists constantly check and recheck their results with new experiments. There are many tragic cases where some drug will seem to be a cure for a dreaded disease like cancer because a positive result has been observed in just one series of experiments. But, when other scientists try to duplicate the result, it turns out to have been only an accident that the people who were treated with the drug improved. Like gamblers, many people get hooked on the belief that some miracle drug will cure them just on the evidence that one or two afflicated individuals recovered after being treated by it. But positive results from a scientific experiment can come about by accident. If the results cannot be duplicated, it's futile to pin one's hopes on a miracle cure, and dangerous too, if conventional treatments are neglected.

We often misunderstand the advice medical science gives us because we misinterpret its probabilistic message. At a party, a pregnant woman was overheard saying, "Well, I smoked all through my last pregnancy and the baby was all right. Why should I quit for this one?" An understanding of probability could help us give this prospective mother some good advice. Medical science tells us that there is a statistically significant correlation between smoking during pregnancy and birth defects. This result has been repeatedly confirmed in many experiments. That means that there is an increased probability of birth defects in the infants born to women who smoke during pregnancy. Suppose that without smoking, the probability of a birth defect is .00100 or 100 in 100,000, while the probability with smoking is higher, say .00175, or 175 in 100,000. This means that if there were 100,000 pregnant women who did not smoke, we could predict 100 babies born with birth defects, whereas if these 100,000 women had smoked during their pregnancies, we would predict 175 birth defects. No one could tell in advance to which women these additional 75 babies with defects would be born. In fact, most smoking mothers (99,825 out of 100,000) have perfectly normal children. That's the crux of the problem because if we're trying to decide whether or not to smoke, and we look around us, we will see hundreds and hundreds of normal babies born to smoking mothers. Not much of an incentive to stop, is it? But, if somehow we could convince 100,000 pregnant women to quit, we could save 75 babies from pain, disfigurement, and possible death. This is what we could have told the woman at the party. "You can be self-indulgent and continue smoking, but there is a risk. Most likely your baby will be okay, but if you love children and are concerned about their possible pain and suffering, then you'll quit, encourage others to do so, and help save those 75 children, one of whom may be your own."

There's another side to this situation. Suppose there is a pregnant woman who isn't aware of the linkage between smoking and birth defects, or perhaps the connection was not yet discovered until after her pregnancy. Suppose she smoked and her child did have some defect and later she learned of the possible connection with smoking. Some people torment themselves endlessly with guilt in situations like this, even to the point of causing emotional damage to themselves and their children. In probabilistic situations like this there is some consolation. We need not continually suffer from guilt. Remember, even without smoking, 100 out of the 175 children would have had defects stemming from other causes. Remember, 999,825 children born to smoking mothers are normal. Smoking may or may not be the trigger for any given birth defect. It's impossible to tell. A child's defect is a possibility that happened, perhaps through the mother's negligence, but perhaps not. It's an event out of the world of chance, largely beyond anyone's control. People feel tormented by it as if it were the moment of descent on Fortuna's wheel.

When something like this happens, there is only one thing for us to do. Accept it. Climb back onto the wheel and look forward to future ascents. We must leave our guilt behind and, starting today, try to make the best of our lives in the future. Parents of handicapped children who have shouldered their extra burdens and gone on living as fully as possible sometimes, paradoxically, report that the birth of that child was the seed for enormous satisfaction in their lives. It becomes an opportunity for discovering the joy of giving and loving, for growing into strength. Rich lives springing out of situations which are initially painful and discouraging illustrate the fact that whether a situation is good or bad depends to a large extent on what we make of it. Accidents in our lives, the gifts of Fortuna, are neutral. It was a medieval distortion of Fortuna that portrayed her face with one fair side and one ugly side — good fortune and bad fortune. The ancients more accurately described her merely as "the one who brings." It's up to us to determine whether the consequences of her gifts will be good or bad in our lives.

Misunderstandings about probability are at the root of the heated controversy today concerning the safety of nuclear power plants. Scientific theories are expressed in absolutely certain terms but, when dealing with variable building materials, possible future human behavior, and occasionally faulty components due to human error, engineers can only speak in probabilistic terms. Citizens' groups complain to the Nuclear Regulatory Commission that the nuclear power plants aren't safe enough, that the one-in-ten-thousand-chance of an accident isn't safe enough. Later, after great expense, the Commission's engineers report that the chance of a nuclear accident has been lowered to one-in-a-million. Of course, to the citizen, that still isn't safe enough!

Citizens are demanding certainty, while the only tool that modern science has to offer is reduction of probability. It's a myth, left over from the days when scientists were guardians and interpreters of the clock-work universe, that science can give certainty. The citizens are wishfully living in the past. However, not to choose sides, the engineers are toying with deception if they try to pretend that they are really meeting the demands of the concerned public for absolutely certain safety.

What can we do? If the anti-nuclear forces are adamant that they will not tolerate the possibility of any nuclear accident at any time, then the only way to satisfy this need is not to have nuclear power plants at all. Because, if there is any possibility of an accident (and dealing with materials and people, there always is) then we can be virtually certain that at some point in the future it WILL happen. If the probability of it happening in any one year is one in a thousand, then there is a fifty-fifty chance of it happening before 500 years are up. The more plants operating, the more likely it is that it will happen even earlier. It could happen this year. Given time, you cannot avoid something that is probable: Fortuna is irresistible. There are only two options available — shut down all nuclear power plants if an accident is unthinkable; or evaluate the costs of an accident and weigh this against the benefits the power generated would bring to society. This is a political choice which voters must make, for it is impossible for the engineers to accommodate wishes for perfect safety. In this futile dialogue, the two sides are speaking different languages.

One of the subtlest roles probability plays is in quantum mechanics. Quantum mechanics is that branch of physics which describes elementary particles like atoms, electrons, and protons, and explains the foundations of matter. In this modern theory, we discover that the elementary particles do not have a material reality in the ordinary sense but are most accurately described as bundles of possibilities. Before we observe an electron, it is no place in particular. It could be in any number of places, some more likely than others. Actually, it is closer to the truth to say that each electron is in every place in the universe simultaneously, smeared thinly and insubstantially over all of physical space. When we observe it, we find it more often in some places than in others. When we make an observation, the electron moves from "everywhere" to "here," and where it will appear can't be predicted, but can only be known with some probability. The electron is a "probability wave" and its motion through space is best described as fluctuations in the probability of its being observed in various places.

This seems like a flimsy foundation on which to build solid tables and chairs, let alone battleships and space shuttles, but perhaps these probability waves can be better understood if we relate them to something on a larger, more familiar and tangible level. In Chapter 13 we speak about all the "social machines" in which an individual has a role — eating dinner with our family, attending church, on the job, at the airport, dancing at a nightclub, lecturing to an assembled group, etc. What is a human personality but the sum of all these roles we do play or could play in all these social machines? In every existing social machine, there are a number of potential roles for each one of us. Even if we never actualize that role, for example, even if I don't sit down with a particular group of people for lunch one day, the role I could have played in that group during that particular lunch hour is an essential part of what I am. Our "personality" is spread thinly and insubstantially over social space, existing sometimes as potential and sometimes realized, just as the electron is spread over physical space.

Life has many rich possibilities. We can dress up or dress casually, take charge or follow, learn or teach, be serious or playful. In different settings our personality presents different aspects of itself. We once spoke with a young woman who was extremely shy at parties while at work, she excelled in organizing people and taking charge. She felt guilty and was lamenting the fact that she hadn't "gotten her act together yet." She thought she was being deceitful and, in one or the other of the situations, presenting a "false face." But, as Emerson said, "A foolish consistency is the hobgoblin of little minds." Great minds, like Montaigne, have acknowledged their own internal contradictions and ambivalence and have welcomed the abundance of this diversity. Looking into his personality and noting its fluctuations, just as the scientist observes the probability wave of the electron, he wrote:

> *I give myself now one face, now another, according to which direction I turn it. If I speak of myself in different ways, that is because I look at myself in different ways. All contradictions may be found in me by some twist and in some fashion. Bashful, insolent; chaste, lascivious; talkative, quiet; tough, delicate; clever, stupid; surly, friendly; lying, truthful; learned, ignorant; generous, miserly . . . whoever studies himself really attentively finds in himself, yes, even in his judgment, this gyration and discord.*

We don't expect a piece of fabric shown under different lights to always appear the same. So with our lives. We have a richer, freer, more varied life to live, showing different faces and being a different kind of person in each setting we find ourselves. The complexity of twentieth-century life draws out of each one of us a complexity of responses. There's no deception here. We are not inconsistent when we express ourselves through different kinds of social activities. Our personality is not one simple thing, but a complex bundle of possibilities seen from many different angles. The more varied aspects we present to the world, the more complex and richer the opportunities which will come to us. The apparently concrete reality of our personality, like that of the electron, is based on the insubstantial foundation of probability.

Probability is not a source of disorder or a cause for anxiety. Instead it contributes to the complexity of the world and to the abundance and variety of our social lives. This complexity, this variety, and this abundance, all issuing from probability, are testimonials to the generosity of Fortuna who is the source of these rich gifts for humanity.

THE MATRIX FOR CHAPTER 15

	A	B	C	D	E	F	G	H	I	J	K	L	M	N	O	P	Q	R	S	T	U	V	W	X	Y	Z
A	9	9	14	8	9	17	14	6	5	18	5	10	6	14	5	3	19	2	16	19	11	17	4	3	5	5
B	2	12	20	7	2	10	20	19	3	9	14	10	20	16	19	4	11	9	9	13	5	6	18	20	8	18
C	14	12	14	12	10	5	8	19	4	4	14	3	6	7	3	12	10	20	16	16	10	16	8	18	6	17
D	3	7	18	6	9	5	3	8	9	7	4	6	8	12	8	13	11	3	14	17	8	19	11	12	16	5
E	3	4	6	20	4	4	4	9	13	3	19	7	8	6	12	12	20	3	17	6	19	17	11	14	20	14
F	14	16	20	18	8	20	20	16	3	19	19	14	8	13	4	19	19	10	8	17	5	10	17	8	16	14
G	8	7	11	6	8	14	2	8	2	6	13	17	10	13	18	5	20	14	7	2	2	6	18	5	9	2
H	12	18	16	19	10	5	8	13	9	18	5	18	10	17	3	12	7	20	19	7	17	4	16	10	5	5
I	9	2	8	6	6	14	10	5	5	4	9	13	17	9	4	2	20	13	20	5	9	7	14	20	6	14
J	17	13	6	14	5	14	12	6	10	11	6	16	13	18	19	4	16	13	20	19	12	4	17	7	9	18
K	16	7	16	6	11	3	16	17	14	17	10	19	8	8	19	3	20	20	19	12	19	8	8	10	17	17
L	16	10	17	9	5	10	7	20	3	17	17	19	2	8	12	4	6	10	11	8	12	14	18	5	14	14
M	7	20	12	6	9	4	8	3	17	5	3	9	10	19	6	20	12	11	8	8	4	3	14	13	2	12
N	3	19	16	2	2	20	20	9	8	17	13	18	6	19	5	8	3	9	14	3	16	6	18	9	11	20
O	7	8	8	3	19	8	17	6	5	17	11	4	7	16	18	18	8	19	19	19	13	14	6	14	19	13
P	2	7	11	13	4	8	17	17	2	7	12	8	3	20	2	19	9	9	18	3	12	3	19	10	9	11
Q	2	19	7	16	9	5	8	10	13	16	14	6	12	11	14	3	11	13	13	17	8	13	20	4	12	10
R	5	4	2	2	18	10	16	20	17	8	11	18	19	19	20	4	11	14	9	18	8	16	14	18	11	20
S	4	12	14	17	17	10	7	10	11	19	8	17	14	18	7	13	8	13	5	2	11	18	9	13	6	3
T	16	10	17	13	6	7	4	19	8	2	11	13	11	8	6	19	14	20	19	19	6	17	2	5	5	16
U	3	14	18	18	14	8	11	3	14	19	7	20	5	11	13	8	19	10	12	4	14	14	11	13	2	13
V	12	12	20	18	11	7	20	2	19	18	7	3	17	16	10	18	17	17	5	16	3	8	5	10	10	7
W	14	18	5	17	17	3	4	14	10	5	8	18	17	16	10	4	7	11	11	14	11	16	12	2	10	2
X	5	4	18	9	2	2	6	4	7	7	2	6	8	10	17	19	4	5	14	13	5	4	18	18	12	2
Y	13	4	10	13	4	13	13	13	16	20	20	16	16	20	12	10	18	14	19	9	10	16	7	3	10	19
Z	11	20	7	16	7	5	4	5	2	12	6	16	12	3	7	4	16	7	13	11	11	10	11	13	3	5

On the chart, find the place where the initials you've chosen intersect. Read the chapter whose number appears at that intersection.

16

ACCIDENT

It's fascinating to watch small children playing a board game as they get ready to roll dice when the resulting throw will determine which square they will move next. On one occasion there was a six-year-old boy whispering "Give me an eleven" to the dice and shaking them for a very long time with a serious expression on his face before he carefully threw them. How he makes the throw, he believes, determines what number will turn up. If he can only do it just right, and wish hard enough, maybe he can make the dice give him what he wants! The boy probably had a lot of experience learning how to control things by mastering very subtle cause-and-effect linkages — if you push the pedals, the bicycle moves forward; if you turn a knob, the television starts; if you flip the switch, the light goes on. The scientific viewpoint which he is intuitively using is a natural way of looking at the world, trying to find the key, the cause, that will bring about a desired effect. The child assumes that the shaking of the dice and the number that comes up must be linked somehow and he acts accordingly, in a naive, scientific manner, searching for the key, the perfect toss. Quite a few adult gamblers share his belief!

Our technologically advanced civilization is founded on a belief that nature is regular and dependable. Every effect has a cause. Steam, for example, is caused by the application of heat to water and thus can be dependably harnessed, brought into existence at will, and manipulated to create and control machines powered by steam engines. Our control over nature is based in our belief in the close and necessary relationship between cause and effect. Looked at from a global point of view, our present scientific era, which began in the Renaissance, is characterized by a particular world-view called scientific determinism which envisions the physical universe operating like a giant clock, ticking from moment to moment with each effect preceded by its cause.

I have described this earth, and the whole visible world in general, as if it were a machine in the shape and movements of its parts . . . for example, when a clock marks the hours by means of the wheels of which it is made, it is no less natural for it to do so than it is for a tree to produce its fruits.

DESCARTES

In theory, if one knew exactly the position and state of any complex material entity, one could predict exactly what would happen to it in the future. All the laws concerning cause and effect and the motion of physical particles which are needed for that prediction were discovered by Newton in the eighteenth century. According to this scientific determinism, even our thoughts, which correspond to movements of particles in the physical brain, could be predicted. There was no role for the immaterial in the day-by-day workings of the universe. God was conceived only as a First Cause who had wound up the clock of the universe and left it running. Moment by moment, the clock-work ticks forward, working out the inevitable predetermined consequences of the original God-given state.

This scientific viewpoint was so incredibly fruitful — fueling progress, leading to discoveries which enabled humanity to vastly increase its control over nature, culminating in air-conditioned houses with running hot water, television, telephones, computers, airplanes, and moon landings — that it came to be the undisputed, most natural, intuitive way of looking at things. If we were to ask a man on the street, "Does every effect have a cause?", he would say, "Sure," and look at us as if we were crazy!

Taken out of the world of physical science and applied to ordinary events, however, this world-view leads to some absurdities. There are gamblers who, thinking like that little boy, believe that they can force the outcome of the dice. In the extreme, this belief can lead to superstition or paranoia. For an example of how erroneous this way of thinking is in ordinary situations, consider a young man who spills catsup on a suit he needs for the next day, and has to spend Saturday evening at a laundromat. There he meets a young woman who also just happened to be there. Later they marry. He finds it hard to believe that he came so close to having missed someone who has since become the most important person in his life. He tries to imagine a cause for this event, so he says, "I think we were fated to meet. It was written in the stars. My horoscope said that I would meet someone very important that week and it came true!" On a similar but sadder note, a young mother whose child died of a rare blood disease becomes convinced that she is being punished for having had an abortion several years earlier. We all imagine connections and suspect hidden causes. We see Fortuna in the role of Nemesis. This is where the paranoia begins to come in. When bread prices go up or stocks go down, we're quick to blame the monopolistic oil companies, or the bureaucrats in Washington, or the Trilateral Commission, or the

"Gnomes of Zurich," or the Communists. We know that major events must have a cause and we search endlessly to try to locate these causes so that we can possibly control them and moderate their painful impact on our lives. This is the scientific method, a method of proven past successes.

But searching for the causes to events, and finding answers in something like "the stars" or "vengeful fate" doesn't always seem to help our understanding of a situation at all:

For want of a nail, the shoe was lost;
For want of the shoe, the horse was lost;
For want of the horse, the rider was lost;
For want of the rider, the battle was lost;
For want of the battle, the kingdom was lost;
And all for the want of a horseshoe nail.

TRADITIONAL
based on Benjamin Franklin

In the chain of events from the loss of the nail to the loss of the kingdom, one event logically follows the other, one event is the immediate precursor of the next, but we balk at saying that the loss of the nail "caused" the loss of the kingdom. If we knew, as a scientific fact, that loose nails imperiled the kingdom, then public safety could be significantly improved by a decree imposing a regular program of blacksmith checkups. How absurd! Before this chain of events had occurred, no one could have foreseen the consequences of the loss of a nail. Even if the nail hadn't been lost, other chains of events, just as unlikely, may have led to the loss of the kingdom.

There are connections between the series of events in the above rhyme but these linkages are not cause-and-effect relationships. They are temporal and accidental. The consequences at each step are not necessary, but contingent; it could have been otherwise. We can only figure out the sequence of events in retrospect; it could not have been predicted in advance.

Chains of events may be linked either causally or accidentally and it is important to distinguish between the two types of linkages. In order to picture a purely accidental event, imagine a doctor taking a stroll in a small village and passing below a sloping roof where a workman had earlier left a hammer. The hammer slips off the roof, falls on the doctor's head, and kills him. His death is declared accidental. One of the characteristics which help us identify accidental events is the disproportion in importance between the earlier and the later linked event, i.e., when a very small thing is followed by and linked to a very large result. This is what is so beautifully illustrated in the above nursery rhyme and keeps it an enduring part of the cultural heritage of

English-speaking peoples. In the anecdote about the doctor, it was probably a tiny wisp of a breeze which sent the hammer tumbling down, but its consequences, if perhaps he had been the only doctor in that region of the country, may mean death and suffering beyond his own. Accidental chains of events move from the smaller to the larger, as from the loss of the nail to the loss of the kingdom. On the other hand, necessary or causal chains of events generally move from the large to the small, like a giant hydroelectric generator costing millions of dollars, grinding endlessly, so that I can heat enough water for a cup of tea.

To say that something is caused by accident is, however, psychologically unsatisfactory. We don't like to accept this because it means we cannot have control over some event. Given our scientific world-view, we are not content with small causes engendering large effects. We search for something that seems to be lacking, some cause that is sufficiently large. Just as we derive from ancient morality the principle that the punishment must fit the crime (an eye for an eye), we want the cause to fit the resulting event. In order to find a satisfactory explanation for such a serious event as the doctor's death, we create abstractions like "the workman's negligence," or we say that with close enough scientific investigation covering the weight of the hammer, the texture of the roof, the weather, the doctor's pattern of behavior, etc., we could have predicted the moment of his death (and hence prevented it).

But accidental cause is indeed a full explanation of what happened here. To say that an event occurred "by accident" is a rich explanatory device, not just a way of avoiding the question. Accepting this type of explanation can help clear up a lot of puzzling aspects of modern life. Many things really do happen just by accident — like meeting your future wife in a laundromat. Once we begin to see the role of the accidental in everyday life, many myths can be debunked, shadows lifted, and we are better able to cope with all the events in our lives. For example, some things can be controlled, some cannot. It is not within our power to manipulate those events that occur purely by accident. Science cannot be helpful in these areas. A large part of wisdom consists in trying to find out what is and what is not within our control, what is causal and what is accidental, and concentrating our efforts towards modifying the future in those areas where we do have some chance of being effective. We will be happier and more contented by acknowledging the domain of Fortuna and not attempting to contest her power there. There are ways by which we can have some influence in the world of Fortuna (which are more fully discussed in other chapters), but in that world we can never have complete control.

Before we can fully comprehend the notion of accidental cause, we need to stretch our language. We need to extend the domain of the word "cause." When Aristotle was analyzing the physical world and laying down those dichotomies which have shaped Western thought for generations, he gave accident a major role in determining the shape of reality. His third major category of causation consisted of those things which occur "by accident." At the present time, if we say that something is caused "by accident," most people understand that statement to mean that the event didn't have a cause, or that we don't yet know its cause. This is a consequence of the pervasive world-view of scientific determinism. But when Aristotle used the words "by accident" he meant a concrete type of causation. We need to become comfortable with statements like "accident caused the doctor's death" as a full and complete explanation of the circumstances surrounding his death. We can also say: "Accident caused the loss of the kingdom; it was a concatenation of accidental events that no one could have predicted." It is precisely because it is difficult to comprehend how an abstraction, like accident or chance, could "cause" something material to happen that personifications of abstract forces were created by the Ancients. "Fortuna caused the doctor's death" fits our idea about how a sentence concerning causation should be structured. The cause is the same size as the effect. (Why did she do it? No particular reason. It's just her nature to be capricious.) Using language like this, Fortuna (or Accident) encompasses a complete description of the cause of the event and gives us a convenient shorthand for talking about this complex set of circumstances. We don't have to believe in the concrete existence of a pagan goddess tooling around naked on a round ball in order to use this language. One cannot deny that there are events that are caused by accident. Rehabilitation of the "language of Fortuna" will give us a vocabulary to express these events. Language shapes how we see reality and therefore, using this language will provide us with a fresh outlook on the world around us, one that was lost when the scientific viewpoint of cause and effect became all-pervasive.

Let's try to look at the world around us through eyes newly opened by the use of this language, distinguishing between accidental and causal linkages. Imagine a typical morning: The clock-radio goes off at a determined moment, part of a causal chain of events that we put into effect by setting the alarm the previous night. The fact that one particular tune awakes us rather than another is an accident. Our mood, which may be gloomy or happy, depending on a causal chain that has to do with our state of health, our dreams, and how well we slept, clashes in an accidental manner with music and world news, another causal chain that originated all around the world, and this accidental event changes us, making us become happier or sadder, in a completely unpredictable manner. That we have a bowl of corn flakes is a determined part of our regular schedule, but it too is the end product of the combination of several causal chains, including insects, the sun, the generation of seeds, distribution of food, stocking patterns in our local grocery store, and many others, leading to the accident of this particular bowl of cereal consisting of these particular flakes of rolled corn. That we are swallowing this cornflake is a major coincidence, requiring the coordination of thousands of independent causal chains, a wildly improbable and unpredictable event, but one that is actually taking place.

Almost all the details of an ordinary life, where we go, the people we meet, what we see, what we do, what happens to us, etc., are rarely predictable results of conscious planning and control, but are extremely improbable accidental events. It's sobering to reflect on the fact that many Americans fear — and it is possible — that World War III, a nuclear holocaust, will commence with some accidental error in our high technology defense systems. Ordinary life is made up of chance events which are created by the unexpected crossings and recrossings of myriad causal chains weaving the essentially accidental nature of the world as we experience it. Lifting the blinders of scientific determinism allows us to see that Fortuna has a major role in shaping the reality of our daily lives.

Look around you. Look at the details of your physical surroundings. How did this book come to be in your hands? Your furniture, your personal mementos — most of these came into your life by accident. If you can't attribute at least 50% of your surroundings to accidental causes, then look around again. Determinism is blinding you!

How we perceive accident, or whether we see it at all, is a critical factor in the debate between communism and capitalism. Communism is a scientific system, treating economic and social systems as giant causal mechanisms. Its followers believe that by far-reaching and careful planning, every tiny detail of the economic process can be controlled and directed. Their five-year plans include everything, from number of tons of steel to be produced to size and quality of the standard toothpick, each home to be provided with thirty-seven toothpicks per family member per year. This results in some families of heavy toothpick users always running short while others accumulate unused rations which go to waste or get sold on the black market. In some years, perhaps when the proper forms are lost or a new clerk is in charge, maybe no one will remember to remind the lumber industry to produce toothpicks, and no one will have any that year!

Trying to scientifically manage a large, complex organic entity such as an economic system is like an individual telling his heart "Beat now, stop, beat now, stop . . ." Some things are better left to happen by themselves! And things that happen by themselves are the domain of Fortuna. Renaissance humanists equated the word "Fortuna" with the word "automatic," meaning that which happens automatically or, as we say, by itself. Except for God, Fortuna is the only force in the universe which can be its own cause.

The theory behind the capitalistic free market is quite different. Capitalism recognizes the key role of accidents in ordinary life. With profit as a motive, the system works by itself without much direction. Instead of attempting to control events, accidents are encouraged to happen. Each time the retailer stocks his shelves with a wide variety of goods originating from many different places and each time the consumer makes a choice from the various products on the shelf, an accidental event occurs. When a stereo aficionado buys a Sony (Japanese) receiver and a Tandberg (Swedish) tape deck and takes them home to listen to a prerecorded Capitol (American) tape of Bizet's (French) opera Carmen (Spanish), a beautifully rich and individual event has been created out of the accidental intersections of a world-wide network of causal chains. It could not have been planned for or entirely predicted. A planned economy cannot make events of this type happen. The free enterprise system, with its myriad accidents, touches our lives yielding variety, abundance, and freedom.

Compare these two scenes: Two hundred years ago, small villages would have to depend on touring shows and musicals for their entertainment. Everyone in the village would attend these infrequent occasions. They would all hear the same music at the same time and each individual's stock of musical experiences would be virtually identical. But today, nearly every home has a record collection, sometimes consisting of hundreds of disks. It's very unlikely that any two collections are the same. In addition we have AM and FM radio, tapes, TV, and movies. One person can be a country-western fan, while her next door neighbor, or even her husband or son, may listen to classical music or attend operas. By letting the system work by itself, responding to consumer demands and to the profit motive, the free market has created a remarkably diverse world of possibilities. It recognizes the essential role of accident. We're free to find individual means of expression, and our lives are full of variety and opportunity in the realm of consumer goods.

Especially in the United States today, we live in a world of opportunities. Because of the variety and diversity inherent in our economic and political systems, we are truly free. Most things that happen here are accidental, touched by Fortuna. With the coming together of these multitudinous possibilities and opportunities, it seems that just about anything can happen, and does. Even the former astronaut, John Glenn, can become a U.S. Senator, and the former actor, Ronald Reagan, can become president!

When we take off the blinders of scientific determinism, we see that in a profound sense the essential nature of the world around us is accidental; Fortuna is a powerful goddess. Each individual is created out of an immensely improbable coming together of parental germ cells. Each moment brings us fresh, new, unexpected encounters which shape our lives. Death, birth, health, wealth, where we go, what we become — these vital but unpredictable elements are all in the realm of accident. And we're lucky that it is this way. Accident brings variety, abundance, and riches. The cornucopia which is always in evidence in ancient statues of Fortuna illustrates this fact. But even more importantly, recognizing the role of accident can free us from paralyzing regret and futile planning. Things generally happen by themselves. Our impact on many events is often limited to that of reaction and self-control. There is no inevitable destiny, but instead we are free to create our individual futures in cooperation with Fortuna.

And not only are we, as individuals, not able to control everything that happens; apparently, no one is. What happens in the world is too big and complex to be controlled; the communists tried with their economic system. People do influence events, but neither OPEC nor the Trilateral Commission nor the World Bank is running the show. Things happen mostly by themselves. The destiny of the human race is being worked out through the individual choices and interactions of ordinary men and women, each reacting as well as they can to the events which come their way. It's frightening to know that no one is in charge; no one can save us from the consequences of our foolish actions. Frightening, but it's perhaps the most essential component of our freedom.

THE MATRIX FOR CHAPTER 16

	A	B	C	D	E	F	G	H	I	J	K	L	M	N	O	P	Q	R	S	T	U	V	W	X	Y	Z
A	7	4	7	10	19	9	3	13	3	12	19	14	8	12	7	10	2	10	12	2	3	7	3	6	19	19
B	13	5	12	15	4	12	2	15	12	4	13	20	14	8	13	13	7	17	6	18	12	20	6	11	19	6
C	6	10	13	19	20	19	15	5	10	11	15	14	2	4	10	3	7	5	2	3	14	14	6	6	17	15
D	6	5	8	9	17	13	14	13	20	8	2	8	4	7	7	14	19	2	4	9	5	20	20	11	19	7
E	18	12	11	10	10	18	11	15	3	20	8	17	20	10	20	4	3	13	18	20	9	11	8	19	6	9
F	6	5	19	20	12	15	3	7	11	6	4	5	17	17	7	5	2	3	9	18	7	19	6	5	19	3
G	12	17	10	11	6	10	5	20	13	10	11	12	5	11	2	19	6	3	14	4	12	3	2	4	14	19
H	3	11	18	11	5	11	6	17	10	2	17	9	13	10	13	20	13	8	7	18	4	20	4	19	2	19
I	15	3	20	17	3	17	12	7	3	14	19	5	7	4	11	7	19	6	14	13	2	14	7	3	10	8
J	4	10	12	9	11	12	7	14	20	2	8	9	14	11	15	5	4	4	5	8	15	7	18	15	20	13
K	11	19	17	9	2	19	14	18	5	10	3	20	19	5	4	7	11	5	15	6	14	6	20	7	11	7
L	17	2	20	2	14	11	14	10	5	9	20	7	5	6	2	3	18	2	4	7	14	11	8	7	20	8
M	15	18	11	13	13	12	14	9	12	14	9	2	9	12	10	15	8	20	9	11	5	7	20	10	14	9
N	17	5	14	8	11	9	8	17	12	5	18	12	11	17	20	12	9	20	20	10	9	9	4	17	5	19
O	15	9	14	5	4	5	9	8	11	15	20	11	15	7	7	4	10	17	18	3	18	12	14	15	18	3
P	4	3	8	11	7	13	18	8	17	8	10	10	19	9	6	3	2	15	10	17	13	4	15	20	17	20
Q	8	12	12	19	15	7	13	3	18	13	13	10	13	5	11	10	5	6	2	2	4	17	17	20	20	8
R	9	6	20	4	12	11	20	7	3	18	20	19	2	6	6	14	12	9	4	19	12	20	20	14	4	19
S	14	14	19	10	11	12	2	5	14	14	17	15	20	5	15	3	4	18	18	11	2	13	20	7	13	8
T	4	20	8	4	2	19	2	20	10	9	10	4	17	5	7	2	5	7	7	20	9	18	15	8	9	13
U	5	8	6	14	17	7	13	11	20	17	6	19	6	10	3	5	4	18	9	10	10	10	6	4	9	12
V	9	8	11	19	19	2	19	3	9	17	18	8	12	7	20	11	14	18	18	7	17	5	20	17	19	20
W	10	17	20	4	13	17	8	3	11	13	3	12	15	18	9	14	18	7	4	17	15	3	11	19	12	12
X	9	13	10	3	3	3	5	3	4	6	11	11	7	5	6	7	12	19	3	4	2	17	17	8	7	14
Y	9	3	19	7	15	15	5	5	17	10	10	20	13	11	6	15	11	11	14	20	18	5	10	11	9	12
Z	18	17	8	10	3	14	13	10	17	15	13	13	15	6	20	15	19	20	4	13	8	7	5	5	2	7

On the chart, find the place where the initials you've chosen intersect. Read the chapter whose number appears at that intersection.

17

THE POLITICS OF FORTUNA

Beginning at random on this complex topic, it is not far fetched to say that Fortuna protects the United States from dictatorships, whether they be dictatorships of the proletariat (communism) or dictatorships of the elite (fascism). In true democracies the last word in decision-making must always be left up to Fortuna. Accepting the results of an election based on majority rule is a lot like accepting the result of a tossed coin when a decision has to be made. Elections must contain an element of chance for people to respect their outcome. It is as though some mysterious or divine or cosmic entity, in this case Fortuna, has to play a part in the process before this same process is considered valid.

In the United States, Fortuna plays a role even in the Supreme Court, which gives this country the religious characteristics of a democratic papacy. There, Fortuna and her numbers, the tool of majority rule, rule supreme. After the justices have exhausted the resources of human reason, they resort to Fortuna by a simple vote for or against a decision. There, as always, a majority vote of the justices marks the fate of a judicial decision, and gives it its legal, and, in a deeper sense, its religious validity under Fortuna.

Chance is a subject which has been greatly neglected in the vast body of writings about politics. From Plato's *Republic* to Santiago Carrillo's more recent *Eurocommunism,* with such diverse theoreticians as Montesquieu, Rousseau, Marx, and John Stuart Mill in between, the role of chance in political processes has been largely ignored. One reason for this may be the very newness of their science. Unlike physics, mathematics, and biology, which are generally accepted as "established" sciences with cummulative bodies of knowledge, new areas of inquiry like psychology, social science, economics, and political science are still trying to gain respectability. While mathematicians, physicists, and biologists publish books and articles on chance, there is scarcely anything being said about chance in newer disciplines, especially in the social sciences. Political science is no exception to this rule. If a professor of history or political science were to come into the classroom and say that this or that event happened by chance, the students would not see any point in taking notes and the lecture would be over in five minutes. Instead, a network of causes, forces, counterforces, systems, and effects has to be developed and sustained in order to give the appearance of a science. Only in the most advanced sciences is the theoretical structure strong enough to allow for chance.

The time will come, however, when social scientists, psychologists, anthropologists, economists, and political scientists will feel safe in dealing seriously with events, accidents, and chance. It is not our intention to detail theories explaining exactly how the element of chance can be injected into political theories. We shall leave this to the specialists. We shall adopt the point of view of the amateur, the essayist, the speculator, and shall deal with politics in a poetic and playful manner. We would like to remove our language as far as possible from that of such monuments of reason as Kant and Hegel for whom everything comes structured in groups of threes. The roundness and fluidity of chance suggest that we avoid all triangular or square types of theorizing which exist in rationalistic language.

Chance is not something irrational and unscientific. Chance is an essential part of a scientific description of the universe. In this book chance is called Fortuna. Fortuna is often contrasted with another allegorical entity, Ratio (reason); hence, many people feel that Fortuna does not have any place in scientific discourses. This book attempts to bring Fortuna and Ratio back together. We are in favor of the peaceful scientific coexistence of chance and reason just as we are in favor of the peaceful political coexistence of the United States and the Soviet Union. These two oppositions are not unrelated as we shall see in this chapter.

WATERGATE

Many explanations of the American political tragedy known as Watergate have already been attempted. Ours, we hope, differs from the others in examining it from the point of view of chance. The success of American democracy may be attributed in simplified terms to a combination of preparedness, or Ratio, and tolerance of the inherent disorder of things, Fortuna. A balance between these two entities is difficult to achieve. Yet it has been achieved in American society, is ingrained in the minds of the American people, and forms the basis of the political freedom enjoyed by Americans. The laissez-faire principle applied here is derived from the philosophy of Fortuna, while planning belongs to the rationalistic world often represented by Hermes. An easy way to understand Watergate is by comparing and contrasting these two mythological figures, Fortuna and Hermes.

In our elections, each party or person who is running has a chance to win by getting the most votes. These uncertain processes where the outcome is not known in advance are protected by Fortuna. Fortuna presides over the sanctity of the ballot box. She punishes any tampering with those systems which should be left to fall as they may, such as roulette, dice, tallies, surveys, polls, vote counts, etc. Fortuna is the mysterious — almost religious force — that lies behind the electoral process. Of course, she is banished from the ballot boxes in communist or fascist regimes where only a single slate of "approved" candidates is presented to the voter.

In the United States, the democratic electoral process is at the basis of our freedoms. American elections can be seen as a sort of religious ritual. To get a glimpse of what we mean, one would have to imagine a Martian walking into the hall of the Democratic or Republican National Convention at one of those dramatic moments when the band is playing, banners are being hoisted, and people are shouting at the top of their lungs, wearing strange looking hats with animals on them.

Our Martian would not immediately understand the fine line between what is permissible and what is not in the apparent confusion. In order to understand what is not permissible in the democratic world we have to examine Hermes who is the opposite of Fortuna. Hermes is the god of artifacts, of things like electronic gadgets, listening devices, tape recorders, and other tools which were used by the political burglars caught on the premises of the Watergate Building. For the electoral process to remain within the realm of Fortuna it must follow certain rules. The first rule is that Hermes must not be allowed to interfere. Any tampering with the electoral process or any violation of the ballot box can be viewed as a violation of the rights of Fortuna, the right of things to be left to chance.

It is Fortuna who chooses the leaders in the free world. The offices of the election committee of a party fall under the protection of Fortuna and a break-in there is akin to a sacrilegious act. The Watergate incident can be interpreted as a violation, an attempted rape by Hermes of the goddess Fortuna. The national uproar was enormous and the punishments given to the accomplices of Hermes, who included the President of the United States, were unprecedented.

At times when punishments follow hidden wrongdoings, as in this case, people are led to believe in the existence of a cosmic force called Nemesis who sees all, remembers, judges, and punishes. Nemesis, the goddess of retribution, is then confused with Fortuna, the one "who brings." But the nature of Fortuna is accidental. She does not remember and she does not judge. Sometimes wrongdoings are followed by punishments, as in the case of Nixon, but just as often crimes are unreported and unpunished. In this case, the wrath of the American people, following upon the accidental discovery of the Watergate burglary, was the force that led to the downfall of Nixon and his cronies.

It became clear to the American people when the existence of the secret tapes was revealed that Nixon and his men had made too close a pact with Hermes. It is in the nature of Hermes to work in secret or, as we say, in "hermetic ways." With the electoral process, just as with playing cards, people must have their hands above the table and the deck should not be stacked. In sportsmanlike endeavors there is an implicit understanding that an element of chance must be left in the game.

People must be assured that Fortuna is still in control and that she has not been kidnaped and tied up in some basement. As W. C. Fields sat down to play cards, another character once asked him "Is this a game of chance?" to which the famous comedian quipped: "Not the way I play it." The Watergate burglars attempted to play democracy like W. C. Fields played poker. The underlying evil behind cheating is that it does away with chance. When we know in advance what the outcome will be, the fundamental uncertainty is lost.

In order to show the role of Fortuna in democracy and particularly in the electoral process we have relied on a simple opposition between Fortuna and Hermes. The opposition need not lead to a narrow interpretation of the roles of Fortuna and of Hermes in the world. Hermes has been narrowly, and perhaps even unfairly, depicted in our illustration as the maker of gadgets used in a third rate burglary. But he is more than that. He presides over a great and advantageous technology which can unfortunately be put to bad use. Because we put Fortuna and Hermes in opposition we need not conclude that Fortuna stands opposed to science and technology. She is not against the gadgets themselves; she only objects to their misuse. In the Watergate incident, they were used in secret, at night, and in ways that were an attempt to eliminate the element of chance.

DEMOCRACY AND COMMUNISM

A vital and underlying reason why people believe in the electoral process is precisely because it does encompass a definite element of chance. The importance of the Watergate incident is that it was somehow sensed by the public as an attempt to remove Fortuna from the elections. Western democratic societies, and in particular the United States, are founded on chance and opportunities. The totalitarian regimes of the Eastern bloc stand opposed to Fortuna, who, whether as an abstraction or as a personified goddess, is essentially anti-communist.

Communist systems, ranging from Plato's *Republic* to Thomas More's *Utopia* to Marx's *Das Kapital,* are engineered to minimize the influence of Fortuna on the affairs of men and women. These systems leave as little to chance as possible. They are the exclusive products of Lady Reason and they ignore completely the role of the other woman, Fortuna. Our philosophy shows that it is possible to bring them together and that this is in fact the strength of democratic systems.

The role of chance can be incorporated within rational discourse without fear of falling into irrationality. Political theorists, not recognizing this, have built neat and tidy systems that do not conform to the chance-like nature of life. For political rationalists, and for Marxists in particular, everything is regulated, regimented, divided, analyzed, shared equally, properly measured, and eventually "rationed." Communist systems are nightmares of Lady Reason gone mad. In practice, the theories of these rationalists rarely work smoothly or successfully, and end in limiting the role of individuals, curtailing their actions, and eventually robbing them of freedom.

In the free world, chance and individual incentive play significant roles. It is the world of Fortuna. The greatest good in a free state is not unity but its opposite, variety. The strength of the United States is, to a significant extent, the wide variety of its institutions and the diversity of opinions expressed freely by its citizens. Variety and diversity are some of the most outstanding features of Fortuna.

The principle that every citizen has the right to be as different from her fellow citizens as she pleases, and that a wide variability is possible, is protected by the Bill of Rights. If people were to look for a divinity to oversee these fundamental guarantees, they would find Fortuna. That we have reintroduced ideas related to Fortuna in political discourse does not mean that we should chase out Reason. Many have thought that the two principles are incompatible. For instance, in the sixth century, Boethius writes of calling in Reason and chasing out Fortuna. There are two opposite dangers posed by excluding either Fortuna or Reason. On the one hand, the anarchists chase out Reason while rationalists and their disciples, the communists, chase out Fortuna. The anarchists want no police, no army, and no governmental structure. Communists believe, on the other extreme, that all facets of society can be governed rationally. Both extremes are ridiculous; we should attempt to accommodate both Fortuna and Reason.

While the Bill of Rights encourages people to be as different and diverse as possible and to do as they please, it is not an anarchistic document. The exercise of the freedoms it guarantees is only feasible within the limits set by law. This is an outstanding illustration of the fruitful cooperation of Fortuna and Reason. The French philosopher Montesquieu defined liberty not as the right to do whatever one wishes but as the right to do whatever the laws permit. When people break the law they make other people less free. Laws are thus mechanisms through which the largest possible number of citizens can live in liberty and receive the fruits of bountiful Fortuna.

One might expect that laws which place limits on the freedom of individuals are the product of Reason only. Indeed, those are precisely the bad laws. The good laws are written jointly by Reason and Fortuna — by counting votes. A law has to pass a test under the watchful eye of Fortuna. It has to come before an assembly and be put to the test of a majority vote. In the face of uncertainty as to whether a proposed law will be put into effect or not, thus in the presence of Fortuna, the voters agree in advance to abide by the results of the tabulation. This process was explained by Jean-Jacques Rousseau in his book *The Social Contract.*

Rousseau, one of the first romantics to bring back Fortuna after she had been cast out by the classicists, and one of the initiators of our modern age of Fortuna, wrote, in an often misunderstood passage, about this quasi-religious consent that a citizen gives to laws passed by the majority:

> *The citizen gives his consent to all the laws, including those which are passed in spite of his opposition, and even those which punish him when he dares to break any of them. The constant will of all the members of the State is the general will; by virtue of it they are citizens and free. When in the popular assembly a law is proposed, what the people are asked is not exactly whether they approve or reject the proposal, but whether it is in conformity with the general will, which is their will. Each man in giving his vote, states his opinion on that point; and the general will is found by counting votes.*

Rousseau must not be made into a forerunner of communism, as some believe, for he wrote that "it is against the natural order for the many to govern." He was aware that such things as "the dictatorship of the proletariat" are dreams of Reason gone mad. He saw clearly that "it is unimaginable that the people should remain continually assembled to devote their time to public affairs," he warned that "so perfect a government is not for men." Instead, his theories support the democracy of Fortuna, the democracy as practiced in the United States, which technically is a republican form of representative government. It is a delusion to think that Reason alone can suffice to run things. Instead, Reason and Fortuna must work together.

Rousseau writes: "When therefore the opinion that is contrary to my own prevails, this proves neither more nor less than that I was mistaken, and that what I thought to be the general will was not so." In this passage, he explains that we must yield to a higher authority outside of ourselves. No matter how powerful our own Reason might be, we must yield, in this instance, to the decision arrived at by counting votes. This decision is unknown before counting the votes. It could have gone either way. It is chance-like and mysterious. Reason in this case must yield to Fortuna. Democracy thrives under the peaceful coexistence of these two great forces, structures, personified ideas, or divinities: Fortuna and Reason. All else leads either to anarchy or to tyranny.

Belief in majority rule has an almost religious tenor. This faith, as we have seen in our discussion of Watergate, seems to emanate from a fundamental trust and acquiescence in whatever the outcome might be of an uncertain situation, an election. An apparently logical explanation of this trust is that whatever is believed by a lot of people must be better or truer than whatever is believed by only a few. But this is neither logical nor completely satisfactory; it is merely a convention issuing from a simple rationalization process which is based on the unproven hypothesis that more equals right and less equals wrong. Everyone knows that it is possible for a lot of people to be wrong about something and for perhaps only a few to know the truth. The simple rationalization behind majority rule is that a certain thing is right since so many people desire it. But, if this was all there is to majority rule, there would be no reason for people to obey it. There must be something besides mere counting that explains why people tacitly accept the decisions of a majority vote.

Why do people respect majority votes? We will explain this by examining at what stage in the electoral process the belief in majority vote arises. This critical building up of belief occurs before the vote takes place. Before people gather in an assembly hall or go into the voting booth, they make a pledge to obey whatever comes out of this mysterious process. This build up of trust in the process occurs long before the actual voting begins. The vote could go either way. It is almost like flipping a coin. Chance is present in the process. Fortuna gives us her verdict which we can read by counting the votes or by looking at which side the coin fell on. The vote of confidence in this process takes place before, not after, the result is known. This helps explain the current controversy concerning exit polling and the rush by the networks to be the first to announce the winners of an election, sometimes even before the polls close. These premature announcements conflict with that pseudo-religious moment when voters cast their votes and thereby place their faith in an unknown outcome.

We dare say, putting it into poetic terms, that voting is an act of faith performed in the temple of Fortuna. This act of faith (the pledge to abide by whatever comes out of the ballot box) occurs before the results are known. If a citizenry cannot make this pledge, it means that it is not yet ready for democracy.

THE THIRD WORLD

The foreign policy of the United States has failed in the past, and will continue to fail in the future, in these instances when it insists that democracy can be achieved by simply bringing in ballot boxes and organizing elections in countries where the citizenry is not yet ready to pledge faith in the mysterious forces underlying the electoral process. When the ballot boxes then fail, as when elections are ineffectual, a further mistake is often made by sending in, first, military advisors, and then combat troops. The original mistake is thus compounded, leading to situations like the Vietnam War. Instead of soldiers we should be sending political missionaries or, at least, believers in the democratic process to these countries which we fear are about to fall under communism. The Peace Corps is an idea very much along these lines. Money for the Peace Corps and for cultural exchanges is a better investment in democracy than guns and bombs.

Many countries are still under the firm grip of the despotic father image. They have not yet reached the level of a democratic understanding of Fortuna which requires an act of faith to tolerate the uncertainties of electoral processes. A common statement heard from the best believers of this democratic ritual is the promise to work together with the winning candidate and to heal wounds. These and other conciliatory feelings are expressed in rhetorical stock phrases which true democratic politicians commonly use right after elections.

In order for Fortuna to make her entrance, a certain social, economic, and political mood must be in place. Such favorable conditions do not exist in countries where people must limit their freedoms and regiment themselves in order to keep from starvation. Our American foreign policy should recognize that socialism — something which we ourselves made use of in order to help take us out of the Depression — may be a viable temporary solution in many underdeveloped countries.

Countries may have to achieve a certain plateau of social progress through socialism before they can aspire to enter the Age of Fortuna where individuals may be given wider and wider ranges of freedom.

Diversity and democracy first require a certain level of abundance and an educated citizenry. It seems to us, from this point of view, that the United States may be making too much fuss about the spread of socialism in the third world, and wasting too much energy on trying to prevent that process. The United States does not have the winning hand in countries like Vietnam or Nicaragua, but can be most influential in Poland or East Germany where centralization of power, rationing of resources, and restrictions on entrepreneurial ventures by individuals is no longer necessary. These industrialized countries are ready to step into the World of Opportunity, the Land of Fortuna. Other countries, like Cuba, will have to wait a while under socialism until they reach a higher level of affluence.

Already, Fortuna is penetrating deeper and deeper into the political fabric of the more developed nations of the Soviet Bloc. One of the most interesting aspects of the diffusion of Fortuna is the huge increase in international commerce and finance by the communist countries of Europe which now invest directly in the Western economy. Any essential differences between an American and a Soviet representative meeting in the board room of a London bank to discuss oil imports are rapidly disappearing. However, the differences between these two negotiators and a peasant from Nicaragua are enormous. Taking this peasant by the hand to a voting booth does not solve the problem. That peasant cannot yet pay allegiance to abstract political processes like elections or democratic laws. Instead, he bows to people, to bosses, whom he believes are different from him and have a divine right to rule over his destiny.

Perhaps we should separate the issue of national security from that of the spread of socialism. It's right to insist that no Russian missiles be placed in places like Nicaragua. We did this with Cuba and everybody supported us. But we should let these countries choose their own form of government, even if it be socialist, and still continue trading with them, just like we trade with China and Yugoslavia. Eventually they will be ready for democracy and simultaneously, they will have become familiar with the American culture and will have been exposed to the influences of Fortuna.

Communist countries do not form a single bloc of stone. Again, rationalization deceives us here because Reason, when used by itself, makes us think in terms of unifying wholes, transforming everything into "one" as in the term "Communist Bloc." On the other hand, fortunate individuals are encouraged to think in terms of multiplicities, varieties, nuances, differences. There are indeed many shades of communism. By increasing our contacts with these societies through cultural and commercial exchange we will introduce them to the abundance and opportunities of democracy and pave the way for bringing them into the present Age of Fortuna. In this way we will avoid enormous military expenditures, and also the dangers of confrontational politics. We should take advantage of divisions which do exist among communist countries, but instead, we seem to be the ones who contribute most to their consolidation by our own monolithic opposition.

Instead of throwing bombs, as we did in Vietnam, we should bomb underdeveloped countries, which are presently socialistic, with books, magazines, color televisions, refrigerators, blue jeans, cassette players, and current films. We should place them directly into the flows of consumerism and production, paralleling their own desires. Economic assistance goes a long way towards bringing people into the Age of Fortuna. The threat of bombs makes them withdraw into regimentation, fierce nationalism, and paranoid anti-Americanism. The United States can win the ideological war against totalitarian regimes without firing a single shot. We seem to forget that it was the communists who built the Berlin Wall. The West has all to gain by increasing international contacts and exchanges. The tides of Fortuna will make their rational sand castles crumble.

From this perspective, it is quite possible that the Russians are pleased by the fact that we have imposed an embargo on travel and trade with Cuba. China has been de-communizing its society, deemphasizing communal life, and widening the private sector, partially encouraged to do so by the opening up of trade with the West. Our foreign policy protects Cuba from these corroding effects which Fortuna could have on its totalitarian regime. The abundance, the freedom, and the democracy of America, the Land of Fortuna, have a powerful captivating effect on the minds of visitors from other lands. The Soviet bloc does not have this captivating appeal. Quite the contrary is true as people in this decaying Byzantium must be kept from fleeing it.

INDIVIDUALISM

How do fortunate individuals manage to escape being dragged into a totalitarian herd? They achieve this through their strong sense of individuality. No one explained this relationship between individuality and freedom better than the great English philosopher John Stuart Mill. In order to fight tyranny, he asserted, people should push their individuality all the way to eccentricity. Eccentricity is the ability to escape these forces which push us toward the center, the center of a political tornado-like fascism, nazism, communism, fundamentalism, or any other magnet-like "isms." In *On Liberty,* Mill wrote:

Precisely because the tyranny of opinion is such as to make eccentricity a reproach, it is desirable, in order to break through that

> *tyranny, that people should be eccentric. Eccentricity has always abounded when and where strength of character has abounded; and the amount of eccentricity in a society has generally been proportional to the amount of genius, mental vigor, and moral courage it contained. That so few now dare to be eccentric marks the chief danger of the time.*

Suppose we are in a crowded stadium where a politician delivers a speech full of inflamatory rhetoric. It may happen, as it did in Hitler's Germany, that a lot of people become hysterical and stand up giving the Nazi salute. On such occasions, the people whom we call "fortunate individuals" are most likely to stand back and become independent observers of what is happening around them. Whenever too many people start doing exactly the same thing, wearing the same clothes, speaking the same words, watching the same things, going to the same places, then people who enjoy the diversity of Fortuna begin to separate themselves from the herd and take refuge in their own individuality. Fortunate individuals are inoculated against the Orwellian virus of submission to tyranny. They sense that standardization and homogeneity are the opposite of diversity, heterogeneity, and plurality, all of which are essential components of the freedom which Fortuna brings.

Montaigne, our epitome of the fortunate individual, often advises "going with the flow." "Thus," he writes, "I am fit only to follow, and I let myself be carried away easily by the crowd." Like many positions stemming from a belief in Fortuna, this one has to be moderated. Fortunate individuals do not let themselves be carried to extreme behavior by crowds. Specifically, during the holocaust, they would not have become passive accomplices of mass murder. Accordingly, in the next sentence Montaigne, after having said that "he lets himself be carried away by the crowd," makes the appropriate adjustment when he states: "And yet I am not too easy to change, since I perceive a like weakness in the contrary opinions." The fortunate individual keeps a healthy distance from extremism in political opinions. People who understand the role that Fortuna plays in human affairs are the opposite of zealots.

We have shown (in Chapter 14) that the world of Fortuna is romantic as opposed to classical, and it is a well-established notion that a primary distinguishing feature of romanticism is individualism. The romantic hero is first and foremost an individual. Examples of this include not only Ulysses, Alexander the Great, and Napoleon, but also the Lone Ranger, Rocky, E.T., and all modern rock stars who strive, with more or less success, to capture the imagination of the modern romantic public through their eccentricities. The romantic hero or heroine is, by definition, different from the rest of us. On the other hand, the classical hero or heroine is reduced to standardized and uniform patterns.

Some people have great admiration for the classical. They may view our defense of the world of Fortuna, of chance and uncertainty, as a glorification of chaos and irrationality and a denigration of classical accomplishments. But this is not so. The classicists, particularly the ancient Greeks and the French of the seventeenth century accomplished great things including great artistic and literary works. Our preference for the romantic world of Fortuna has little to do with the beauty of the Parthenon.

Classical art in Greece was a reaction to a turbulent historical past. People had suffered greatly because of constant political and social upheavals. They had lived in a state of constant anxiety for too long and they desperately wanted order, stability, and certainty. Solon of Athens, a writer of the time, wrote:

> *In every activity there is danger, nor does anyone know, when he undertakes to do something, how he will end up. One man, striving to do what is right, falls headlong into great hardship, while to another who acts wrongly, the divinity gives good luck, rewarding him for his own thoughtlessness.*

We do not need to take refuge in the safety of a geometrical world of reason to escape the dangers of living in the real world which, by nature, is full of uncertainty. Instead, we can combine both approaches. We can use the achievements and the learnings of the classicists and also venture into the apparently chaotic domain of the romantics. The classicists, while they gave us objects and systems of great beauty, made very little progress in dealing with the real world. Similarly, our modern rationalists, the Marxists, have great difficulty adjusting to the chance-like nature of human beings with their desires for individuality and self-improvement.

Fortuna is beginning to enter the monolithic soviet bloc through its iron curtain. Into these planned and centralized economies she brings the profit motive, new fashions from the West (emphasizing eccentricity), and modern music, especially rock music, which is characterized by diversity. The wide diversity of tastes and the volatility of new musical trends disrupts the feeling of order, uniformity, and continuity which centralized, planned, rationalized, and totalitarian regimes attempt to foster. The Fortuna philosophy is the political solvent of tyranny in all its shapes and forms.

FREEDOM

Fortuna is the protectress of the individual. She is as diverse and powerful as a huge computer that can perform billions of operations per second and can thus deal with the random wills and desires of every individual on earth. Until recently, people did not know that this was possible. In order to simplify the task of dealing with millions of different individuals all wanting different things, the state was invented and became the centralized unit of desire, the only free entity. Instead of having to deal with millions of individual wills, it was considered much simpler to deal with only one will, the will of the state. Under state-centered regimes, individuals don't count, not because of any evil plot to deprive them of their individual freedoms, but simply because the individual is too complicated and too unpredictable. It is possible to predict with a great degree of accuracy how many people will go to the beach on a hot summer day, but one cannot predict that Jane Doe will be at the beach on that day. Rationalistic political systems do away not only with the individual but also with individual events. The modern computer provides us, on the other hand, with a model of a state which can deal with billions of different wills at the same time. The existence of differences is a distinct possibility.

Just as the individual is erased and the multiplicity of individuals is ironed out in a rational system that can be logically represented as a unity, in a similar fashion, events are denied their own existence. Rationalistic regimes deny that events happen by chance. Instead they give events "rational" explanations for their existence. Events are denied their legitimate filiation to Fortuna: "Things don't just happen," they say. It would be too destructive to their rational worldview to admit that events can happen just by chance, and so they sew the events neatly into the rational fabric of history where everything has a cause, a reason, a purpose, and an end.

These rationalistic regimes and philosophical systems must eventually topple because they are built upon a fundamental error: the error of excluding the role of chance in their programs. We are not the first writers to have decried the vanity of human rationality. All political systems based exclusively on rationality will sooner or later crumble. However, our aim is not to do away completely with rationality in political science but to marry it to chance. We are not falling into the trap of irrationality. Instead, we want to humanize and naturalize Reason by inviting her to live in harmony with Fortuna.

The ideology of the free world allows for a maximum of subjective freedom while at the same time preserving some measure of objective freedom. Communist ideology facilitates a considerable amount of objective freedom with a minimum of subjective freedom. Subjective freedom is individual freedom with some limitation set by laws.

Within these limits the individual finds a great deal of room to move and exercise his or her will. He can become a millionaire; she can become President of the United States. Objective freedom, on the other hand is the "freedom" to do what the state tells you to want to do. For Hegel and for Marx, freedom, rationality, and the state are one and the same thing. For instance, in Poland, you are supposed to want to join a union which is approved and planned by the state, not a union like Solidarity which sprouted by itself, without plan, with unknown leaders, out of nowhere as though it had been created by chance. A union like Solidarity which comes into being spontaneously and haphazardly, breaks the mold of a totalitarian state and threatens its existence. Such a union threatens the stability of the planned state by the very fact that it was created from the will of the people, by chance, at random — by Fortuna. It is also because of the very uncertainty of its future course of development that such a union is threatening to the stability and existence of the totalitarian state. This social movement is not in the works, not on the mapped-out charts that lead inexorably toward the advent of a mythical being: Communist Man.

The free world is the world where chance and individual incentive play significant roles. The free world is the world of Fortuna. Among the many countries which make up the free world, the United States is distinguished by its special and privileged relationship with Fortuna. This is not only because it happens to be the most powerful nation in the West, but also because of the specific nature of the American democracy. No other country in the world today is as politically advanced as the U.S., especially in its increasing ability to function as a grass-roots democracy. Here, power ascends from below, in unexpected, unpredictable, and chance-like ways, adjusting to circumstances rather than following a plan. This is the way of Fortuna. Under other systems, power descends from above, from the committee or from the Party. These systems are under the realm of human reason behind which, unfortunately, lies human folly.

In America, we often fail to realize how "fortunate" we are. It may take an outside point of view to remind us of the uniqueness of this true land of the free, this land of opportunity where people still have a chance to do and to become almost anything they want. The Spanish editorialist and political commentator Manuel Blanco Tobio wrote the following lines for Madrid's *ABC* on the occasion of the American Bicentennial: "Providence (Fortuna) has saved the American democracy from the infection of dialectics (rationalism) and hence its simplicity; which does not exclude, in any case, fervors and devotions. Americans would even prefer disorder if order had to be achieved at the expense of freedom." And he added: "We, Europeans, on the other hand, have always been ready to sacrifice freedom for the benefit of an utopia. This is why America has had two hundred years of democracy and Europe does not know whether it will be able to hold on to it after the coming elections."

Written in 1976, these lines seem prophetic when we reflect that five years later France elected a socialist president, François Mitterrand, and, more recently, Spain also went socialist with the election of Felipe González. It would seem that Fortuna and her sister Liberty are still having difficulty establishing a firm foothold in Europe.

CHANGE

This is not completely so, however, since European people have essentially been voting in favor of Fortuna by voting for change. They will probably continue to vote for change (a chance at something new) at an ever increasing rate. Commenting on the election of Mitterrand, the following view was expressed by a director of the London School of Economics in a 1981 issue of *Time* magazine: "It's not a question of conservatism or socialism being ascendant. It's that people have been voting for change. The French electors might have preferred a different sort of change, but the one they got was the only one available." Similarly, in the United States, many commentators observed that Jimmy Carter was elected president because he offered an opportunity for change. By campaigning as an honest person, as someone who, as he promised, would never lie to the people, he presented the electors with essential "change." The question of substance was not at issue. What the people wanted was an indication of change in the system.

Change is an integral part of the politics of Fortuna. And yet this political ideology does not advocate change merely for the sake of change. The fortunate individual is not a rabid revolutionary who seeks constant change. While being open to the possibility of change, the fortunate individual is still at heart a political conservative. His guarded attitude toward change was expressed by Montaigne with the following words: "To my mind, in public affairs there is no course so bad, provided it is old and stable, that is not better than change and commotion." As a devoted disciple of Fortuna, as someone who often said that he surrendered himself into the good arms of the goddess, Montaigne was far from taking any philosophical or political issue too seriously. He espoused a healthy level of skepticism in these matters. He often repeated the old piece of popular wisdom that he was ready to follow a position all the way to the fire, but not into it.

A healthy skepticism is what is needed to become a fortunate individual and to live a successful life in the present age of Fortuna. We can be happy and successful in such a world if we are able to make uncertainty and change our friends. Montaigne said that he thought about politics much like he thought about the weather. It is a business upon which one should not place too much faith: "I have the same opinion about these political arguments (as with the weather) provided you do not bump up against principles that are too plain and obvious, like predicting extreme heat on Christmas or snow in August."

There are other specific ways in which Fortuna is related to the American political process. The American presidency is an office which is closely, historically related to Fortuna. As we have seen, President Nixon was punished by Fortuna-Nemesis, and President Carter was brought in through a desire for change under the aegis of Fortuna, but it is really the life and then the tragic death of that romantic hero John F. Kennedy which suggests most strongly the role of Fortuna in the political process.

Since President Kennedy's administration, American voters have been voting for more and more frequent and rapid change. Change has been constantly on political, social, and economic agendas. It may even be ingrained by now in the American psyche. In the September 1981 issue of *Psychology Today,* William Watts stated that, "Change is now taken for granted. It may be the only permanent feature of life in America today." His article was based on a survey which found that, "in 1964, 12 percent of the respondents said 'maintaining the status quo' was one of their hopes. Two decades later, only 2 percent said so. Change has become acceptable to most Americans."

Is this good or bad? We believe that it is good. We are entering into the age of Fortuna and we should become comfortable with change. We should view change as beneficial; we should accept uncertainty as a natural fact of life and not be obsessed with worries because of it. In the same article, Watts sounds alarmed when he writes that, "The pervasive concern with economic issues, overshadowing all else, must be counted as worrisome. It is, in fact, a kind of national obsession." We would not go so far as to be alarmed about this concern. It is true that economics is quite often on the front page these days. But behind all this talk about money, what people are really discussing is the nature of uncertainty. They are getting a basic education in the Fortuna philosophy. As a result of this education, people are beginning to acquire a healthy skeptical attitude about planning for the future. Without saying so specifically (perhaps because they do not yet know how to verbalize it), they sense that the future is under the domain of a mysterious and sometimes capricious force. This is the force which we call Fortuna. The ancient Chinese ideogram for "crisis" is a combination of the ideograms for "danger" and "opportunity." In the present crisis over the Federal deficit, Americans sense both the danger of the situation and the opportunities for changing and restructuring past economic practices.

VENTURE CAPITAL

To symbolize the idea that the politics of Fortuna are more likely than any other to bring about prosperity, the ancients used to depict the goddess carrying a cornucopia, a horn of plenty. She stands ready to dispense its abundance to all those who place their trust in her. This trust cannot be expressed by a mere silent and passive prayer. The trust must be demonstrated by actions which are in line with the philosophy and the politics of Fortuna. One of the best examples of actions which illustrate this kind of trust is what is known in the United States as venture capital. The word "venture" itself is related to chance and is an important element in the language of Fortuna. Venture, adventure, and even Bonaventure are words meaning luck or good luck. *The Christian Science Monitor* carried an article on page one about venture capital in its issue of January 13, 1983. Among the most interesting points made about venture capital is that, "venture capital funds are an almost uniquely American phenomenon."

In this article venture capital was defined as seed money. A San Francisco financier calls it, "the pilot light of American industry." Another financier is quoted as saying that, "there is no remotely comparable venture capital activity anywhere in the world." Why is this? "Why such rapid growth in venture capital investments over the last five years?", asks the article. All sorts of economic reasons are given but we might answer simply that we are witnessing an activity which flourishes under the reign of Fortuna. The article hints in that direction when it compares the attitude of American businessmen with that of Japanese and German businessmen. It indicates that, "many point to the American willingness to risk failure." Mr. Stanley E. Pratt, president of the Venture Economics Division of the Capital Publishing Corporation of Boston is quoted as saying that, "In Japan and Germany, failure is an absolute no-no. Americans, (he notes), are more willing to view failure as a 'learning experience'."

An indication of the return of Fortuna may be that venture capital is rising rapidly; the existence of this activity out of the world of Fortuna underlines the vigor, the strength, the promise, the potential of the United States in the present Age of Fortuna. The article continues: "Sometimes the ideas fail, taking 100 percent of the investor's money with them. Sometimes they splutter along for years and just break even. But when they succeed, they can provide healthy returns on the initial investment. Winners include Wang Laboratories, Federal Express, Apple Computers, and hundreds more — all started by individual entrepreneurs with little money but plenty of imagination." The key words in this passage, which come from the language of Fortuna, are "individual entrepreneur," and "imagination."

EQUALITY

A healthy society should make it possible for its citizens to seek power, fame, or wealth within the limits set by laws which guarantee that others are not injured. The Land of Opportunity is the land of Fortuna. Here, achieving these individual goals becomes a possibility for each and every citizen. Michael Walzer has just published a book called *Spheres of Justice: A Defense of Pluralism and Equality.* His solution to the problems posed by equality, what he calls a "complex equality," seems to be in line with our philosophy of Fortuna.

Walzer states that "no citizen's standing in one sphere or with regard to one social good can be undercut by his standing in some other sphere, with regard to some other good. Thus Citizen X may be chosen over Citizen Y for political office, and then the two of them will be unequal in the sphere of politics. But they will not be unequal generally so long as X's office gives him no advantages over Y in any other sphere — superior medical care, access to better schools for his children, entrepreneurial opportunities, and so on."

This idea of spheres is very similar to the one we present in other chapters, primarily Chapters 5 and 7. As we explain there, life is divided into bubbles (spheres) which we called "kairoses" or "occasions" which are portions of time during which things happen. We recommend there that it is wise to keep our "kairoses" (our life experiences) separate from one another. In other words, one should not attempt to mix together the distinct experiences of being a lover and an office manager, or a good father and a successful politician. A powerful political leader, who may inspire fear in his opponents, should be able to play horsey on all fours with his young child in the privacy of his own home. On a different level, Walzer recommends practically the same thing: keeping the flow within separate individual spheres. This separation between kairoses or spheres is necessary for life. It may be based on the model of life itself. In healthy body tissue, the cells are separated by their cell membranes. When the cell walls break down and the cellular fluids mix together into a big, undifferentiated mess, death occurs.

Similarly, sanity may also consist of keeping our mental processes apart instead of what is often attempted, with little success, of keeping it all together. Multiplicity and diversity of opinions is more healthy than constrained thinking. This point is most significant when we apply it to politics: a society, like a living tissue, is more or less healthy to the extent that it is pluralistic, when its citizens (its cells) are able to affirm their own individuality and their own differences.

Under Fortuna, experimentation is maximized. Her motto is "Why not?" Ronald Reagan himself is a politician of fortune, in the same sense that we say a "soldier of fortune." It is out of the ordinary, an unlikely occurrence, for an actor to become President of the United States. To this, Fortuna answers "Why not?" President Reagan is thus a fitting president for this current age, the age of Fortuna.

If the pilot at the controls of the airliner is a woman, "Why not?" If the Chairman of the Board is a kid in his twenties, "Why not?" If he should come into the board room in blue jeans and sneakers, "Why not?" None of these things are understood yet by Europeans, for they have some catching up to do before they enter the dawning of the age of Fortuna.

The French, for instance, cannot take advantage of the fruits of Fortuna in the realm of politics: almost all their leaders come out of one school, the *École Nationale d'Administration.* These leaders, known as "Enarcs," are trained, and perhaps even born, to lead. The French government consists almost entirely of people who have known one another since school-days. It does not matter whether they are from the left or the right because their intellectual background makes them socially equal. They are all out of the same mold and there are no "individuals" among them. Their state is still under the reign of Ratio. The reign of Fortuna may eventually come to France but, in order to free themselves from the clutches of rationalism, they would have to start by figuratively killing Descartes, the father of rationalism, their intellectual father.

PARALLELS WITH THE PAST

How do we sense that we in the United States are entering the age of Fortuna? What are the signs? Are there any historical parallels? Does our present world resemble the past? Language is the key to this investigation. The language of Fortuna contains the words: uncertainty, instability, but also: discovery, adventure, conquest, experimentation, dabbling, and skepticism. All things that do not have a firm footing belong to the world of Fortuna. (Let us not forget that a "firm footing" is not something to be automatically desired, as it may come from wearing a ball and chain around the ankles.) When these words are current and common, the era can be recognized as one in which Fortuna is active.

The election of President John F. Kennedy signalled the dawning of the Age of Fortuna in the United States. Kennedy possessed many traits that broke the standard presidential mold: his youth, his religion (first Catholic president), a glamorous family, and, most of all, an individual style. His initiation of the Space Age in America, with his promise to have man walk on the moon within ten years, was perhaps the event that best heralds the advent of the age of Fortuna.

The assassination of President Kennedy brought us face to face, in a most violent manner, with the instability, the uncertainty, and the precarious nature of human affairs, society, and politics. Similarly, after the death of Alexander 2300 years ago, and after the assassination of Caesar 2000 years ago, uncertainty was rampant and Fortuna made a vigorous comeback. The war in Vietnam further emphasized the uncertain nature of the present age. The history of the United States is beginning to resemble, in an eerie way, those periods in the historical past of Greece and Rome when Fortuna made a vigorous return into the world. We do not believe that history repeats itself. However, the past has lessons and parallels from which we can learn.

The parallels that we will suggest between Ancient Rome and the present-day United States are not exact. In different ages, Fortuna returns always under different sets of circumstances. She would not be Fortuna if she repeated herself exactly. She may produce different results, combining different elements into a new political reality yet unheard of. However the environment which characterizes her return is always the same: instability, uncertainty, movement, flexibility, novelty, and, most essentially, freedom in all its aspects.

In Ancient Rome, during those years when uncertainty was at its height, Fortuna became so prominent that people actually began believing in her as a powerful divinity. The educated classes had almost entirely lost their faith in the ancient pagan gods and goddesses. Fortuna came into the void created between these departing deities and the coming God of the Christians. She flourished in the crack between two religious systems. W. Wade Fowler, a scholar who has studied Fortuna wrote: ". . . a belief in blind chance, whether conceived as a deity or not, gained ground steadily in the century after Caesar's death." When we consider the present political conditions in the United States, then the position of Fortuna during the period of the Roman Revolution and the early Empire becomes an extremely interesting one.

According to another scholar, Howard Patch: "The Empire was an essentially romantic period, when Rome, with a limitless ambition for worldly conquest, ventured forth into the unknown, and in nearly every turn of human life felt the risks which imply chance. It was, moreover, a time of religious skepticism, with a general dabbling in foreign creeds, and without much spiritual depth. At such a time Fortuna came into her own." To make the analogy to today we must translate the word "conquest" in terms other than territorial ones. There are new frontiers and new fields of conquest. Venturing into the unknown today has a wider meaning than it did in Roman days. It includes ventures into space, computers, and genetic engineering. A sense of excitement is also generated by current ventures in experimental artistic and literary endeavors.

The religious skepticism of Ancient Rome is alo widespread today, together with a revival of religious interest which we could qualify as wide, scattered, although sometimes only skin deep. John Naisbitt, author of bestseller *Megatrends* (1983) extrapolates this trend into the future: "And there will be a continuation of the current religious revival, although not necessarily abetting established traditional churches."

There were two other periods, besides the period of the Roman Empire, when Fortuna returned in full force. Centuries before the Romans, the Greeks experienced a powerful and lasting return of Fortuna. In the Alexandrian Age, Tyche (Fortuna), the capricious goddess of chance, was reborn of skepticism and the difficulties of reconciling experience with belief.

She returned many centuries later, during the Renaissance, some 500 years ago. Again, the social and political conditions resembled our own. Wrote Montaigne: "In an ordinary, tranquil time a man prepares for moderate and common accidents, but, in this confusion that we have been in for thirty years, every Frenchman, whether as an individual or as a member of the community, sees himself at every moment on the verge of the total overthrow of his fortune."

During the Renaissance, the words, chance, fortune, luck, destiny and others were in common daily usage. The plays and sonnets of Shakespeare are filled with references to fortune. Well-known passages abound and are familiar to all students of The Bard. References there to chance and Fortuna are not just outdated habits of language but carry significant meaning. There were also long periods in history when Fortuna went underground. These are the various periods when Classicism, not Romanticism, was the prevailing philosophical spirit.

FORTUNA REDUX

When we say that Fortuna returns today, we are not alluding to the return of an old creed like an old style of clothing that happens to be once more in fashion. We are talking instead about a recurring phenomenon which emerges regularly in historical periods with certain characteristics. The present social and political circumstances indicate that we are in one of those periods which is ripe for the return of Fortuna either as a scientific abstraction or as a divinity. Whichever people adopt (abstraction or deity) depends upon their own individual temperamental, emotional, or intellectual predisposition.

The fortunate individual, the person of the future, is a cosmopolite, no more French or Spanish than Arab or Jew. This vision of the future, fully-achieved World of Fortuna is still far off but we seem to be heading in that direction. The current period may be more precisely called one of transition. Fortuna thrives in periods of transition. Professor Howard Patch studied the transition period between Republic and Empire in Ancient Rome: "Civilization was necessarily in a state of skepticism and transition. It had too much of the youth's universal wonder to be held by any well-knit, dogmatic belief. It was the time of the beginning of the Empire; and in this period Fortuna, born long before, really came into her own."

America is still young. It contains within it borders of the widest diversity that mankind has ever known. You can travel from the pre-World War II Jewish quarter in Warsaw to a sidewalk in Naples by just walking a few blocks in Brooklyn. Our contacts with the Orient have been extensive and our experiences with Japan, Korea, and Vietnam have marked whole generations of Americans.

Fortuna thrives in today's cultural and religious diversity just as she did in Ancient Rome. Writes Patch: "With the riches of all countries in the cargo of Italian ships, came new religions by the score. The element of chance would naturally be felt to play a large part in life; and Rome was most susceptible to foreign suggestion, dabbling in new faiths and creeds, and reviving the old for hardly more than idle pleasure."

Fortuna may be our first modern goddess. Without actually naming her, perhaps because mankind has forgotten her name after centuries of attempting to deny the existence of chance in the world, people are constantly making indirect references to her. The themes of chance, of variety, diversity, change, and uncertainty are becoming more and more prevalent in American life. The personification of Fortuna, as we see it in this book, provides an umbrella for all these concerns which we now see as essentially interrelated. She may be the only deity acceptable to modern man. Again, the comparison with Ancient Rome is worth noting: "Fortuna flourished on the skepticism which might corrode any well organized religion." In one word, she is paradoxically the goddess of people who no longer go to church. Furthermore, as Patch observed, "She appealed to man in moments of his greatest weakness and greatest strength. Her variety appealed to poetic fancy. The tenacity of her hold on the popular mind worried the philosophers. Such are her charms in Rome; and with such brilliance the long pageant of her career begins."

Today, there is no reason to worry as did the philosophers of old; no reason, unless some leaders wish, in abhorrent paternalistic fashion, to keep the people away from the "perils" of chance and inside the fences of their dogmatic and rationalistic corral. Fortuna has returned and is commencing a beautiful career.

THE PRESIDENT AND LADY LUCK

There are a few interesting coincidences between the United States and Ancient Rome which we would like to mention in conclusion. These should be read with a good dose of healthy skepticism and with an awareness of the playfulness which is characteristic of the way Fortuna often touches our lives.

Fortuna became the goddess of the Roman people but she also became the tutelary, guardian, goddess of the emperors. Among the many emperors of Rome some were religious, others were unbelievers, and others still were more notably superstitious in public, in private or in both arenas. Some Roman emperors carried a golden statue of Fortuna wherever they went. It may be that they, while believing in chance, were not overly superstitious but carried the statue of Fortuna just like modern leaders carry flags, presidential seals, Lenin hero-medals, or copies of the Bible or of the Koran. Many citizens came to believe that their leader was under the special protection of Fortuna. In the year 19 A.D., a new temple of Fortuna was dedicated to the emperor Augustus. This was on the occasion of the Emperor's return from a long voyage to the Middle East. Because the trip had been a success and the Emperor had returned safely (would we dare to send Ronald Reagan to Beirut nowadays?), the temple that was erected to celebrate his return was dedicated to the Fortuna of the Return. In Latin this Fortuna is named *Fortuna Redux*. She is, in a sense, the Fortuna of all returns, including her own in our modern world.

Fortuna was always closely associated with the national leader who, in Rome, happened to be the Emperor. And in our time she has certainly has been associated with Ronald Reagan. The reports of the May, 1981 attempt on Reagan's life make interesting reading for anyone even vaguely aware of the history of Fortuna. The reporters, essayists, commentators, and journalists who informed the world about this event used an abundance of words dealing with chance like "luck," "lucky," and "fortunate." Says Jeff Greenfield, "It staggers the imagination, and it proves beyond doubt, that the 40th President of the United States has been blessed by Providence, or the Good Witch of the North. (The Sprinngfield Massachusetts Morning Union, 11-27-85).

We read in the May 31, 1981 issue of *Parade* magazine (seen by millions of readers as it is an insert in most Sunday papers): "It is interesting to note that each of the five attending physicians described Reagan as 'lucky' in that he was shot near a hospital where an experienced trauma team could promptly provide him with care of the highest standard."

The reporter does not actually "explain" why "it is interesting" even though he repeats the phrase several times. It is as though he felt, and the readers as well, that the "luck" of a President was a subject of interest even though the reasons, which have to do with the ancient belief in a special relationship between a leader and Fortuna, had long ago been forgotten. The bullet "was lodged," according to medical reports, "about an inch from both the President's heart and aorta." The attending physicians were reported to have said: "The President's a lucky guy."; "God sure smiled on him."; "What we had for us was luck, time, experience and preparation."; and, "We were all lucky."

In the United States — the Land of Opportunity — the Office of the President, and Ronald Reagan in particular, with his fortunate rise to power and his fortunate escape from assassination, we see a profound and close relationship to Fortuna. The President of the United States, the most powerful nation in the world, is the fortunate world leader par excellence. So, when President Reagan is said to have been helped by Lady Luck it is just as thought-provoking, curious, and even as puzzling a coincidence as if Reggie Jackson had an automobile accident with a truck loaded with baseballs, or if a famous pianist were killed by a falling piano as he walked down the street.

This coincidence — for those of us who know that Fortuna is the natural protectress of the leader of the free world — had a startling impact, sending shivers down our spines as if we sensed the presence of a ghost. We felt as though an abstraction, the idea of chance, had actually become personified and had tried to communicate with us. We were left with the eerie sensation of seeing the most powerful man in the modern world, the equivalent of Augustus of Ancient Rome, walking once again on this earth hand in hand with the goddess Fortuna, his own Fortuna Redux.

THE MATRIX FOR CHAPTER 17

	A	B	C	D	E	F	G	H	I	J	K	L	M	N	O	P	Q	R	S	T	U	V	W	X	Y	Z
A	11	18	2	4	4	20	7	18	20	4	12	9	3	11	10	15	11	18	20	20	9	19	13	7	16	9
B	4	8	16	12	12	18	4	8	9	14	5	11	16	5	2	8	4	7	5	10	16	14	14	12	10	13
C	5	5	18	16	4	8	7	7	6	8	6	11	16	16	5	5	18	15	10	11	4	3	15	10	3	14
D	13	20	15	15	7	12	11	5	12	12	12	4	15	2	9	12	7	18	12	6	11	12	18	7	15	14
E	13	16	18	14	3	16	15	2	2	19	12	6	7	13	6	15	12	11	9	3	2	13	18	4	7	15
F	2	12	8	5	13	11	6	18	13	9	12	9	6	7	2	13	9	6	6	5	15	4	10	16	7	5
G	10	3	4	4	13	18	7	4	14	7	3	5	4	20	13	8	16	6	15	20	11	12	13	20	12	10
H	4	2	13	14	12	15	4	12	14	9	7	12	12	20	6	5	14	10	2	5	2	13	20	5	9	13
I	12	12	14	11	14	8	5	11	7	15	12	16	4	2	16	6	15	7	18	9	15	15	19	14	19	16
J	5	15	20	13	3	16	18	3	11	18	20	14	3	7	7	10	12	20	19	15	2	5	9	6	5	11
K	9	15	20	16	6	2	12	6	20	6	4	11	18	4	10	9	7	11	8	3	15	11	9	3	20	3
L	11	7	4	18	8	2	9	16	12	16	2	3	12	12	6	13	16	8	14	2	20	2	2	14	13	13
M	3	14	10	2	12	10	11	12	8	20	5	12	13	13	3	13	13	18	12	16	20	19	9	18	13	19
N	15	4	3	19	20	14	2	2	13	16	4	9	19	5	2	11	15	13	19	12	10	3	12	12	6	16
O	13	20	12	20	13	3	11	10	16	14	5	20	10	14	15	15	9	20	14	14	16	20	18	6	8	15
P	3	19	15	15	6	15	9	11	10	12	4	20	2	15	16	11	11	18	7	4	18	14	3	11	14	12
Q	20	11	15	15	14	19	2	19	3	15	9	7	11	12	19	2	13	18	5	19	7	20	9	10	4	16
R	4	14	11	16	20	6	12	14	6	3	16	13	4	12	14	11	6	7	15	13	6	18	9	16	7	10
S	19	15	13	5	9	15	13	3	13	16	12	4	11	9	20	14	7	11	7	14	16	8	11	19	3	5
T	6	7	7	9	19	2	5	14	11	14	8	16	2	18	10	18	11	6	14	4	13	20	13	9	8	20
U	12	18	3	19	11	14	9	8	12	5	10	6	16	13	12	16	8	14	18	20	2	3	15	18	10	8
V	7	6	18	12	10	5	10	14	5	15	11	15	5	9	7	9	12	9	20	20	4	11	12	15	7	12
W	16	15	2	12	10	2	9	11	12	2	5	3	12	13	8	3	19	15	19	9	12	2	9	13	11	9
X	2	10	20	13	4	20	9	7	20	10	8	19	11	13	20	14	10	10	20	15	16	6	5	7	2	12
Y	10	13	18	10	12	11	8	3	2	6	6	2	11	19	10	8	3	20	16	13	11	10	15	15	13	16
Z	10	13	16	2	8	9	8	7	11	11	8	6	13	4	10	6	13	6	10	12	7	13	4	20	9	15

On the chart, find the place where the initials you've chosen intersect. Read the chapter whose number appears at that intersection.

18

THE GOOD LIFE

These are troubled times. The world is changing at a dizzying pace. We are uncertain of the future: nuclear war, inflation, energy crises. Will we be forced to change our way of life? Divorce, the breakdown of the family, new lifestyles, television — will any of the ideas we live by still make sense fifteen years from now? How can we plan? How can we live? Are there guarantees any more? Where is there a safe and secure harbor for our lives? How can we find it?

Self-help books sell by the thousands, each one with a different answer, all trying to help us find this haven. Traditional answers aren't even tried any more. Lottery madness sweeps those states where they have been legalized and people dream of instant wealth and gratification while personal savings drop and consumer debt rises. The religious solutions of faith and inner peace when practiced today either seem old-fashioned and out of touch, or wild-eyed and cultish. New solutions are proposed and discarded at a rapid rate: EST, TM, Zen, back to the land. For a while they seem to offer a solid foundation for the direction of our lives. But individuals continually move from one new idea to another which seems to indicate that the peace these solutions bring is fleeting.

Perhaps there isn't a haven where we can cease struggling and find peace. We have to give up that hope. But there is a way of life which can bring happiness. It is not an easy solution, because these are not easy times. It's a real challenge to live in a sea of continual change. Living this good life will not transport us into a perpetual state of bliss but, through a process of continual change, growth, fluidity, and movement, we can find satisfaction. We must cherish freedom, have courage, and most of all, come to terms with the powerful, yet paradoxically, almost invisible forces of uncertainty which surround us and buffet us. This way of living which leads to the good life is referred to throughout this book as the Fortuna philosophy. Because the times today are so tumultuous we must begin to recognize the powerful forces of uncertainty surrounding us so that we can perhaps learn better how to live with them.

FREEDOM

Freedom is an essential component of the good life. But our attitude towards freedom reflects a fundamental ambivalence. On the one hand, we aim for personal independence and autonomy, striving to make our own place in the world. On the other hand, for safety or companionship, we often willingly submerge ourselves in groups, giving up some of this precious self-determination.

A rat in a maze has less freedom of action than a rat in a meadow. Loss of freedom of action means a constriction of the number of possible choices available to a person. When the possibilities for action narrow, and we're required to follow one path, whether physically or mentally, we have lost our freedom of action.

Some people are uncomfortable with too much freedom of action, because when there is an abundance of opportunities, one has to make choices. When there are so many possibilities, it seems impossible to be confident of choosing the best one. Such a situation provokes much anxiety.

There are several ways to avoid this anxiety. If we live in a highly structured society that relieves us of many choices, there is no problem. If not, we can convince ourselves that the social structure in which we are embedded is more rigid than it actually is by making definite plans for our lives which cannot be changed, or by having fixed opinions and attitudes. In this way we limit the multiplicity of options which need to be considered in situations wherein too much freedom leads to anxiety. We'll see as we go on that avoiding uncertainty in this way has clearly undesirable consequences. It is the fear of making mistakes in the face of so many possible choices that leads us to consider so limiting our freedom. That imprisonment is universally considered a punishment indicates that if there were any other way to alleviate this anxiety, we should find it.

A ship in harbor is safe, but that is not what ships are built for.

Our language tricks us into this dead-end path by giving us words to formulate the concept "the best choice." To say that one choice is best implies that in some way all the other choices are mistakes. It is precisely the fear of making mistakes, the desire to be safe and secure, that leads us to pay the price of giving up freedom. But, to say that there is "one best choice" implies that somehow, theoretically, someone could see forward into the future and determine the consequences of all our potential actions, and choose the one that is best. There are two reasons why this idea doesn't make any sense. First, how can one determine what is best? Suppose we're talking about a young married woman trying to decide whether or not to have children. Suppose that through some miracle of technology, she can look forward in time and examine her possible futures. Let's take two simple possibilities: she can see herself either as a mother or as a career woman. Which one would be better for her? Even if she could see them clearly, it's impossible to say which is better. Her happiness, which is the goal of these deliberations, depends more on her reactions to her circumstances at the time than on the details of those circumstances themselves. Montaigne said, "Every person makes his own happiness, and no one suffers long except by his own fault." We have control over our reactions to events in our lives. The future happiness of this woman does not depend on the choice she makes today, so much as on her future attitude toward her life circumstances, whatever they may turn out to be. This future life might even turn out to be a creative combination of these two scenarios, perhaps as a mother and career woman, juggling jobs and finding great satisfaction in both.

The second objection to the idea of "one best choice" is even more fundamental and realistic. We cannot see the future clearly. Indeed, it is usually impossible to see the future even murkily. As individuals, a society, and a culture, we are in a period of immense change and variability. Sometimes it seems like anything could happen. We've seen too many life histories that are filled with change, that progress from college student to soldier to hippie to drop-out and, eventually, to happily married insurance salesman with two kids and a house in the country, to be surprised at anything. Rarely were any of these changes anticipated. In one generation, America has gone from a young, powerful force united for good, ready to sacrifice everything in order to rescue the world from fascism, to a soft, uncertain, selfish nation, full of narcissistic people, barely and grudgingly willing to rescue people left homeless by the war it was responsible for. Planning requires stability, and if we hold fast to the hope of stability in a world of shifting forces, we will be like a sail, which when tied in a fixed position will be tattered into shreds by the tempest. The world of Fortuna is the world of the ever possible tempest. (In fact, the words tempest and fortune were interchangeable in the Renaissance. It is to Fortuna that Shakespeare refers in his play *The Tempest.*) There are too many uncertainties surrounding every possible choice to try to predict what the many possible futures will be like and choose from among them the "best possible" one.

If events in the world were predictable, if one could make the "best choice," one would be justified in trading one's freedom for safety and security. Many people yearn for this solution: "We need a leader." "Why don't the scientists get us out of this mess?" To get off this mad rollercoaster, to have someone say, "This is the future, here is what we must do to get there," these anxious, tired people would be willing to surrender not only their freedom of action, but all the traditional American freedoms as well. But it doesn't work. For a while, faith in the leader alleviates collective anxiety but, as the German people found under Hitler, the step beyond faith into self-deception can be far too subtle to detect and fatal to follow.

No politician can lead us into a secure future. The scientists do not know what effects their discoveries will have on the basic structure of our society. No eighteen-year-old has the foggiest idea of what the world will be like when he's forty, or even if it will be here. The times are too variable, and will continue to be so.

All of this is incredibly anxiety-producing. The traditional solutions, planning for the future, or giving up one's freedom to have someone else — dictator, scientist, father, or husband — plan for you won't work. What is needed is a new philosophy, a new attitude to face this variability in which we find ourselves immersed. What we need is another way of looking at uncertainty.

MAKING FRIENDS WITH UNCERTAINTY

Uncertainty is a potent force. Let's be realistic. We can deny its existence and hide from it, or we can accept it, adjust to it, look on the bright side of it, and learn to know it. Every person is only as well or as badly off as he thinks he is. Uncertainty need not be thought of as a blight that mars an otherwise perfect existence; instead, the existence of uncertainty implies the possibility of obtaining freedom's profound and satisfying rewards. A mature attitude towards uncertainty can lead to an appreciation of freedom which cannot even be conceived of by those who are anxious to abandon theirs. Even if the world were certain, and the future predictable, no amount of preparation could take into account all the contingencies, so we suffer the anxiety of ever striving for knowledge and knowing we will never know enough. Granted, this drive for knowledge has fueled modern science, yielding unimagined wealth and mastery over the physical world. Because it has been so successful for so long, it is difficult to abandon. But some phenomena cannot be mastered by this tool. The intricacies of individual actions in a social web are too complex to be predicted deterministically; the inescapable elements of randomness in complex systems cannot be neglected. We must acknowledge this and abandon planning in those areas where our anxiety gives us warning.

No amount of maneuvering can guarantee happiness, companionship, material comfort, or even life twenty years from today. If we'd studied harder or planned more carefully, we still couldn't guarantee these. Let's give up the inappropriate planning. Let's give up the anxiety. We need to accept uncertainty, exploit its positive aspects, and cease denying it.

The fruitless search for certainty in an uncertain world can easily lead to rigid planning which only denies the variability of the world and unnecessarily limits our future options. Trying to guarantee today that our spouse will continue to love and care for us ten years from now can lead to decisions about making friends of the opposite sex, or not changing jobs that could destroy the very future happiness we seek to preserve by clinging to our spouse. Instead one should say, "It's impossible to know now, at this moment, what I should do in a future situation. It depends on how I'll want to act then, which is dependent on what will then be my past; but that is unknown to me now because it is my future." To bind our actions because of an anticipated future limits freedom with no certainty of a desirable outcome. And we should not abandon freedom for an empty promise.

Since indeterminacy is inescapable, variability should be relished as one of the positive aspects of life. We don't plan for a happy situation in life but, instead, keeping our eyes open, we wait for an opportunity to pass by, and if it looks good, we grab it. The more varied the situations we find ourselves in, the more opportunities we will have, in the present, to make our future lives more pleasant. For example, instead of planning for a specific career where jobs look plentiful (as many did in the sixties with teaching, and in the seventies with law, and in the eighties with computer programming), many successful, happy people kept their eyes open, jumped at a chance in business or some exotic field they could not even have imagined themselves involved in, and by creative career changes have made themselves quite comfortable. Let us relish variety, because the more varied our lives, the more chances for happiness will come our way.

DEAD-ENDS

In order to feel safe and secure, some people

- avoid change
- give up freedom
- have rigid and fixed attitudes
- avoid choices for fear of making mistakes
- look to others to lead them
- plan rigidly for the future
- become fatalistic and passive

But none of these will guarantee security and happiness!

We should approach with zest, not fear, a point in our lives where the future is unknowable, a place where there is a branch in the road and we have to choose. At no other time are we more alive; at no other time are we expressing more what is the fundamental human activity — to experience the present in freedom and to choose the future. Let's relish uncertainty, because in a deterministic world, we would not be free.

We don't need a long-term plan for our lives in order to find happiness but, moment by moment, we need to act in a way that maximizes variety and uncertainty. This will provide opportunities for choices and changes. For example, in the face of a disintegrating marriage, where unhappiness and bickering obscures all the previous happiness, it is futile to sit at home together, to continue old patterns, and to hope that even though the people are changing, old structures will rescue the marriage. Instead, cultivate new friendships, take a vacation (together or separate), go to a marriage counselor, change your job, anything! One can be confident that the old patterns will continue to lead nowhere but downwards. Maybe one of the new circumstances will bring happiness. Take a chance and try something. Take a leap of faith into the future, trusting that with enough variability, something will come along that can contribute to happiness. Let us act, and we will be in harmony with the changing world around us.

It takes courage to act in the face of uncertainty. Courage is an old-fashioned virtue which is much in need of revival today. But courage is fostered by necessity, so it should come easily to most of us as we have no choice but to live with uncertainty today. It is only one more step in learning to become the friend of uncertainty.

COURAGE

It is not easy to find the courage to act. Fear tends to make us passive and quiet. Some people make a virtue out of inaction, fatalistically accepting whatever comes their way. Some might be sufficiently lucky, and have low enough expectations in life, that whatever comes their way will suffice for their happiness. But, to experience life to its fullest, to experience growth, to learn, and to reach our full human potential, it is necessary to act. By our acts we increase the variability of our environment and hence increase our freedom. But how does one break away from the passivity of fear and begin to act? The answer is not difficult. The fear we feel is the fear of the unknown, of uncertainty. We are paralyzed and unable to act because we cannot confront uncertainty. However, acting in the face of uncertainty builds our confidence and makes it seem less fearful, while if we passively avoid a confrontation with uncertainty, it will loom even larger in our nightmares. Only action itself will free us from the fear of acting. Once we realize this, there is no choice left but to act. Again, courage arises from necessity.

To make some of these ideas more concrete, and to learn more about courage, consider the process of taking an extended trip to some place we have never been before. This is very much like life itself. Our goal is enjoyment; the path ahead is known to us only through the uncertain reports of others who have been that way before us. We must act in order to make the trip, and it requires courage. Because of our fear of uncertainty, millions of Americans who have the means for wide-ranging travel stay at home, or only visit places well-known to them. Many, though, harbor in their hearts a wistful wish to visit exotic places like Paris, London, Dublin, Madrid, Israel, Mexico, or Africa. One alternative which some elect, the package tour, promises to take us through all the places of our dreams, while insulating us from the uncertainties of language, lodging, unfamiliar food, and differing customs. They offer American-style hotels, air-conditioned busses, and the companionship of people exactly like ourselves. They may even insulate us from the thrill of adventure we are seeking in visiting that far-off land, while also exhausting both our pocket-books and our bodies. The package tour exploits our fear of the unknown. It guarantees to protect us from uncertainty but, in the process, it dulls the experience. Many tourists wish they could find the courage to travel independently; they wish they could discover how it is possible to live with and relish the delightful uncertainties and unexpected encounters offered by exotic people and places.

The goal of most travelers is to visit interesting places, have unusual experiences, see up-close a kind of life and culture different from their own, thereby returning with a deeper understanding of their own culture. The fears that keep most people at home, or travelling in groups, usually revolve around uncertainties: "I know Rome is an interesting place but, when I get there, where should I go and what should I do? I don't want to miss anything interesting. What if I can't find a hotel?" But these fears are ridiculous grounds for avoiding going to Rome or for surrendering freedom to a group tour. Suppose we do arrive in Rome on our own, not knowing any Italian. Immediately we are immersed in another culture and ripe for adventure. With the help of a phrasebook, our first experience can be finding a hotel, which usually involves making contact with a native, practicing our arm-waving, letting him or her practice their English, and becoming personally involved with someone from another culture. The taxi driver, the proprietor of a small hotel, dinner at the small restaurant around the corner — all of these will be experiences we can bring home with us.

Some people might complain that to make one's own arrangements is time-consuming and wastes the time that could otherwise be spent on touring. These are often people who have a narrow, rigid conception of what constitutes pleasure and whose acceptance of life is limited. They have blinders on during the time spent on the airplane, the bus to the hotel, checking in, unpacking. This is not unreasonable: their accommodations are just like those at home so there is little reason to pay much attention to what is happening. When they enter the tour bus and travel around Rome, their blinders lift, and they begin to allow themselves to enjoy their trip. But the view from the tour bus windows is no different from that of picture postcards or their home TV screen, and they never really touch these new surroundings. No wonder they find little pleasure in it.

If we can be courageous, and act, and accept with pleasure whatever comes to us in our travelling, we will find the adventures we all hope for. It is impossible to plan ahead of time, because the experiences we seek can only be brought to us by chance. The train that is delayed, making us arrive in a strange city late at night, or the couple whom we'll never forget, who invite us to share their lunch because we didn't know we had to bring one, are memories to cherish. Having preconceived notions of what our trip must be like leads to regrets. If perhaps we miss seeing the Parthenon because we are sitting at a sidewalk cafe listening to strolling singers, we can't say that we haven't fulfilled the purpose of the trip which was to enjoy ourselves. And if it's really important to see the Parthenon, we'll find a way to do so. At worst, the price paid for these adventures in travelling is sometimes a slight physical inconvenience, a seedy hotel, or a slow train. But that's only because we're living life rather than remaining in the womb at home or on a guided tour. The rewards belong to the courageous.

Still more lessons in courage are to be had from studying the creative process. The successful poet or painter is not troubled by uncertainty. Quite the contrary, she cherishes it as an essential component of creativity. The poet has no preset idea of the poem before she sits in front of a blank piece of paper to write it. Instead she is guided by an idea that has touched her and by the structure she has chosen. As she acts, the poem is born out of the unpredictable interactions between that poetic idea and the images and words which spring forth from her mind. Without uncertainty there would be no creative process. The writer witnesses chance creating novelty and sees beauty emerge from under her pen. Bravely, she must venture into uncharted regions, filled with uncertainty, to bring back the prize. Without her action, there would be no poem. Hers is a joint authorship with chance. To let fear of uncertainty inhibit one from writing would be like letting hunger keep one from eating. Since we can only discover this truth through action, we must be courageous.

Life is like a poem or a journey. The richness, beauty, and texture of a full, satisfying life is only possible if one is active. Uncertainty, or fear of uncertainty, is not a reason for inaction but, instead, it is a partner with us in creating that fullness of life. To try to live a life where everything is known and planned and where we are protected from uncertainty is like forever travelling in air-conditioned busses or copying other people's poems out of books. We must embrace randomness and accept the role of chance as an enhancer of life. Once the veil is lifted from the face of uncertainty and we see her as a friend and helpmate, rather than as a fearful force intent on destroying our plans, then it's easy to act. It's not necessary to generate courage out of thin air in order to act. On the contrary, with Fortuna as our friend, we find it easy to act, and therefore we become courageous.

HAPPINESS

Some people appear to be luckier than others. Speaking to them, we hear about interesting friends, harmonious family life, challenging work situations, all related in an optimistic manner. Sometimes it doesn't seem fair for one person to have so much. Later, however, we might discover that much of this happiness arises out of situations which were initially painful and discouraging. The successful businesswoman might have been a young widow who raised a family alone and simultaneously retrained herself. The athletic star might have struggled with a debilitating handicap as a child. Not all success stories are founded on tragedy, but enough of them are to teach us the lesson that present happiness is not based solely on lucky circumstances. It depends just as much on an acceptant attitude toward life. In order to move beyond their pain, these people have made the inward decision to come to terms with whatever was brought into their lives by uncertainty. Through that decision they have gained peace of mind and happiness.

One has to be careful in making acceptance into an unqualified virtue, however. To passively accept your life circumstances without attempting to move beyond them is a fatalistic, self-defeating attitude. Unless acceptance is closely coupled with action, one can create a mental state wherein one is dominated and oppressed, and yet meekly submissive. Change and growth are necessary. Positive acceptance of a situation means that we must free ourselves from the prison of self-deception. If the situation is painful, acceptance will often entail action to change that situation. Many women who have had the courage to honestly examine their marriages have also found the courage to change them, and hence, have been led to happiness through independence. On the other hand, men and women who have discovered the shallowness of the "sexual revolution" have had the courage to face the emptiness of promiscuity and to choose monogamy and commitment. Acceptance means learning to love ourselves. If we cannot learn to love being Irish, Jewish, American, old or young, black or white, male or female, it will be difficult — at at times impossible — to structure a life of happiness upon these unchangeable foundations.

We make our own happiness by accepting whatever and wherever the uncertainties of life have brought us. But happiness is quite different from passive acceptance. Some of the happiest people are profoundly dissatisfied in various ways: a scientist wanting a better answer, a poet seeking a better metaphor, an introspective youth trying to understand himself. Dissatisfaction, coupled with action to relieve that dissatisfaction, can sometimes, paradoxically, make for a rich and happy life. Happiness comes from accepting the fact that one has embarked on a search which, even though it may have no clearcut end, is, in and of itself, a joyful process.

PAIN

The picture painted so far is perhaps a bit too rosy: sailing into the future with a bright smile on our faces, content, experimenting, accepting whatever Fortuna sends our way, brave, happy. Let's not kid ourselves. As we take action, as we open and become receptive to our experiences, and as we grow and change, some of the events we encounter will be just as painful as others are pleasurable. Bad events will probably come our way just as often as good events do. The essence of the good life is not in avoiding pain — there's no reason at all to think that's even possible — but derives in large part from how we deal with all the accidents out of which our life story is woven, be they happy or sad.

Following the death of her mother, Judy experienced a painful period of adjustment. Because she was an only child, she had quit school when her mother became seriously ill and had come home to give her the round-the-clock nursing which was needed. Her parents had been divorced for a long time and her mother's relatives were scattered. She gave her mother the best possible care and did not regret at all abandoning her personal plans for a while. Especially since she had been uncertain about what to do next in her life, she welcomed a period for reflection and growing intimacy with her mother. When the last moments came, they welcomed together the relief from pain that it brought. But afterwards, when she discovered that because of her mother's substantial insurance provisions she would have enough money to realize a cherished goal she had long ago set aside — finishing her undergraduate education at a top-notch Ivy League college, followed by medical school — she became profoundly depressed. Somehow, it did not seem right that such happiness should arise out of such pain. She found it hard to profit from her mother's death, and was almost convinced by guilt not to use the money for her education, but to give it instead to some charity.

Eventually common sense won out and she did use the money for her education. But for many years, memories of her mother were painfully tainted with guilt. Later she came to understand why this was so, and she explains herself this way: "I knew I would eventually have to come to terms with my guilt over using the money from my mother's death for my pleasure. The old saying 'Every cloud has a silver lining' sums it up for me. Life offers us a banquet of possibilities, some good, some painful, all inextricably linked. We have to reach into the web and pull out the good, that which pleases us. I didn't wish for that money. I didn't even know about the money. I never wished my mother dead so I could have the money. After she died and I had a chance to get the education I had always wanted, I had to pass beyond the pain of her death to choose the pleasurable opportunity presented to me. I had to turn the black cloud of grief around to see its silver lining. That the money and her death were linked had to be accepted. I could not linger at the pain, but had to continue to live my own life by moving on to the pleasurable."

Science teaches us to look for relations between events. "What causes what?" And, indeed, few would question the assertion that wisdom resides in understanding the causal linkages between events. But, especially in areas of life where strong emotions are involved, the faculty for finding regularities sometimes works overtime. Because her mother's death and her acquisition of a cherished goal were so closely linked together, she expected and feared that there was a causal linkage in the other direction, that her pleasure at acquiring the money in some way contributed to her mother's death. The searching mind, examining the world around it, constantly projects and tests cause-and-effect relations on adjacent events. In Judy's case, just the consideration of that possibility was extremely painful. When she came to terms with her unnecessary guilt she intuited a fundamental truth: Life is an accidental mixture of good and bad, and events of both kinds come tumbling into view in a random mix.

There are more things not related by cause and effect than so related. Relationships are often thrown together by chance; they are married by Fortuna. When faced with a painful situation, it's not very productive to use the energy generated by tension to speculate on how this bad event might have been caused by other events. Often we will be deluded by the strong emotions involved and end up spreading the poison of pain unnecessarily. Instead, recognizing that most of the events surrounding us are accidental and independent of one another, we can use our energies to encapsulate the pain, confine it, and not allow it to contaminate surrounding pleasures. A human being who is healthy in body and mind seeks positive experiences; the wearing of a hair-shirt and unnecessary denials of the positive aspects of life benefit no one. Darkness and silver linings are just accidental consequences of the play of sunlight on a cloud. We can choose to linger on either aspect.

As a thought experiment, remember some bad event that happened to you. Obviously it had bad consequences. Now, to practice the Fortuna philosophy, take a pencil and paper and try to list at least three consequences of the event which were positive. We guarantee that they will be possible to find if you keep trying! This exercise will help you recognize that every event is mixed, both bad and good, and we err when we call the event just bad or just good. Practicing this outlook will make you a happier, more optimistic person.

People who believe in astrology carry to great extremes the belief that all events are causally linked. Most of us would be willing to admit that perhaps it would have been possible for scientists, using fantastically sensitive instruments, to have measured the gravitational influence of the planet Jupiter on the surface of the earth at the moment of our births. But to imagine that this physical influence plays a role in determining whether or not we will be successful in business is inconceivable.

Yet it is interesting to ponder on the fact that without the ancient belief in the influence of the stars on earthly events, it is unlikely that Newton would have developed his theories of gravitation, which were the genesis of modern science. Science seeks to find the cause of all events, and does so by first trying to discover all the possible influences on an event and then by trying to weed out the essential from the inessential. But in terms of the ordinary events of personal life, there are influences much stronger than the stars which account for what happens in our daily lives. A careful study of the world around us will show that many of the events that surround us are caused by chance. In other words, they are purely accidental, especially when they touch on the lives of people, their interactions, love, family, health, and success or failure in the material world. It is a desperate mind, seeking a possible cause for these important events, that hits upon the influence of the stars when every other possible cause has been ruled out.

We don't have to look to the stars to account for the causes of so many puzzling aspects of life if we can recognize the essentially accidental nature of daily life. For example, suppose we stay home from work one day because of a minor illness and a radio talk show calls up with a trivial question. We answer and win $500! The cause of our staying home was the illness. The cause of our being called was determined somehow by the radio show host choosing our number to call. But there is no cause for our winning the $500. It is not because our horoscope said we would be lucky today, nor is it because we were kind to our elderly neighbor. The winning of $500 is an accidental event — it was just an accident that the two causal chains, our being at home and the phone call, happened to intersect at that moment of time.

We have to stop thinking of the absence of a direct cause as a lack or a void. Not every event necessarily has a cause. Instead, we can conceive of the existence of accidents as evidence of the positive presence of an active, natural force, personified as Fortuna. Once we clearly visualize this force, and understand how it works in the world, we can realistically comprehend the lives we have been dealt, in which accident and chance play a much more significant role than most people realize.

Life is a series of events. We find ourselves in a situation, whether good or bad, and the question is, "What should I do now?" Recognizing which events we can influence and have some control over, as distinguished from those situations which come our way purely by accident, can help us maintain our stability and avoid unnecessary anxiety. There is our domain, where we can exercise some influence, and there is the domain of Fortuna. We often err in over-estimating the extent of our domain and minimizing hers. This caution is echoed in a familiar prayer:

> *God grant me the serenity to accept the things I cannot change, the courage to change the things I can, and the widsom to know the difference.*

When twelve-year-old Sally broke her hip at camp and had to spend painful months in physical therapy learning how to walk again, her parents continually blamed themselves. "If only we hadn't allowed her to go to camp last summer, she would be laughing and dancing with her girl-friends, instead of this." It's clear in this case that the parents are accepting responsibility for something entirely out of their domain, something which is purely accidental. Yet this attitude is not uncommon, and those parents who feel that they bear responsibility for preventing pain in their children's lives can expect a painful time of parenting. A careful distinction needs to be drawn between "pure accident," as in this case, and a linguistically similar term, "careless accident," implying an event which could have been prevented by the application of foresight. Illness is one of the events that often comes to us entirely from the world of chance. People are very uncomfortable about the fact that a disease like cancer can strike anyone, anytime, without any prior warning. Which one of us will get cancer is probably 95% accidental, influenced moderately by personal health habits (like smoking), family history, and environment. But there are no clear-cut causal patterns. Without smoking, we still might get lung cancer. On the other hand, we may work in an asbestos factory all our life and live to be 99 years old. This uncertainty is so painful — it's as if our nose is being rubbed in the fact that we cannot control the onset of this dreaded disease, and we can't stand it! So we grasp at anything that claims to put this back into our domain: preventive megavitamins, stringent controls on environmental pollution, a massive research effort to conquer cancer the way we did the moon. But when Adele Davis, one of the most influential advocates of a balanced healthful diet for the prevention of disease, died of cancer, and when James Fixx, author of *The Complete Book of Running* which spread the idea that active people live longer, died of a heart attack while jogging, everyone had to realize that death still is and may always be a lottery, and we can only influence the odds.

A certain amount of pain in life is inevitable. No one can avoid it entirely. First of all, even the most content person in the world has to deal with the anxiety of knowing that whatever it is that makes him so happy — his money, his health, his loved ones, — could be taken away from him at any moment. Secondly, we appear to be headed for hard times — inflation, recession, energy shortages, a paralyzed government, the possibility of nuclear war. We are entering a period of uncertainty out of which no one can be confident of escaping unscathed. Lastly, every one of us must face the supreme event, our own death. Only rarely is death caused by some clearly responsible agent, such as in war or in an automobile accident caused by carelessness. Usually it just happens. It is an accidental concatenation of the fragility of our physical body and some harsh aspect of reality. Our attitude towards death is typical of our attitude towards all those unavoidable, undesirable events which chance sends our way. It's useless to fear this pain. Some people are so paralyzed by the thought of death that they're afraid to live. What's the use of that? There is very little we can do to avert what bad luck may be coming our way, so it seems the only reasonable thing to do is to be cheerful and enjoy the good and pleasurable things of life while we have them. Don't poison the beauty of these moments by anxiously worrying about that which is clearly seen to be out of our control. Pleasure is sometimes dropped into our laps, and sometimes it is taken away; we should enjoy it while it is here. Montaigne, in the following words, puts forth a beautiful thought borrowed from Seneca.

> *Fortune does us neither good nor harm; she only offers us the material and seed of them, which our soul, more powerful than she, turns and applies as it pleases, sole cause and mistress of its happy or unhappy condition.*

In these increasingly uncertain times, we cannot expect to have the same ideas about what constitutes the good life as our grandparents did. Kay, a young mother in her thirties, who recently entered college after ten years as a homemaker and part-time bookkeeper, has had experiences which are not unusual: "I used to think that everyone grew up, got married, settled down and had a family and a job. After a while nothing really happened to them and they just grew older and grayer. Maybe it used to really be that way but, as I grew older, I realized that I kept changing. When I started working after my divorce, I met a lot of people, and no one seemed to be settling down anymore. And if they did, it didn't last for long and it didn't make them happy. I decided I wanted to keep changing. I don't know what will happen tomorrow but I want to be ready for it. It used to bother me that I didn't know what I'd be doing ten years from now, but now I find this way of life exciting. That's why I'm going to college now. I don't know specifically what I'll do with my education but, after I've learned a lot more than I know today, maybe I'll get some idea of how to get the most out of life."

To practice the good life:

- Relish variety
- Make friends with uncertainty
- Practice courage
- Be flexible and accept change
- Accept who and where you are in your life; move forward
- Accept contradictions
- Look for the "silver lining" in every event
- Recognize the role of chance in the outcome of events; mistakes are not fully your responsibility
- Be ready for opportunities
- Prepare flexibly instead of rigidly planning
- Cling to freedom

The good life is not a static state that can be achieved and maintained, but is a process, a type of movement, that implies growth and fluidity. Instead of trying to force one's life to fit a preconceived pattern, at every moment the structure of our lives is newly created and emerges out of our interactions with experience. What or who we are in the next moment grows out of the accidents of that moment in a way that cannot be predicted in advance by anyone. Students of evolution will appreciate the fact that in fluctuating environmental circumstances, adaptability requires this type of constant responsive variation.

If we dare open ourselves up to the world of uncertainty, we will be involved in the frequently frightening and frequently satisfying experience of living with greater range, greater variety, and greater richness. We will live intimately with feelings of pain — for growth and change are never easy — but also more vividly, with ecstasy. Events, both good and bad, will impinge on our lives and our organisms will respond. We must be always attuned and expectant, ready to receive the favors of Fortuna, ready to savor them fully when they come our way, ready to manage ourselves and "look on the bright side."

The pursuit of happiness is not easy for the faint-hearted. It requires courage. We must accept that we will change, moment by moment, in response to the events Fortuna brings into our lives. We must acknowledge that we do not control our changing but only experience it. Our future is not written in the stars; we are, instead, involved in its creation. No other way of living makes any sense in this uncertain world we live in today. We can find the courage to live this way. The Fortuna philosophy advocates that we do live this way. And when we do, we will enter into the hopes, joys, freedoms, pains, and pleasures of the good life.

THE MATRIX FOR CHAPTER 18

	A	B	C	D	E	F	G	H	I	J	K	L	M	N	O	P	Q	R	S	T	U	V	W	X	Y	Z
A	5	12	3	19	20	15	11	10	19	3	11	11	10	16	9	12	12	11	4	9	17	12	20	15	20	6
B	17	11	15	4	19	19	19	10	16	7	19	7	7	7	9	15	17	3	4	3	10	4	12	8	17	17
C	2	11	19	4	2	4	2	16	2	14	12	2	14	12	7	7	5	9	5	17	5	15	17	19	15	4
D	8	13	14	17	15	4	16	16	14	9	14	16	20	9	20	3	2	19	3	20	14	16	13	19	4	15
E	4	10	3	8	9	2	8	5	12	5	3	20	14	5	3	7	8	20	10	11	15	3	4	17	15	7
F	12	17	12	16	16	5	13	4	5	20	7	12	4	4	16	3	14	14	14	11	6	17	5	20	5	4
G	19	11	13	17	3	2	10	10	5	12	14	11	13	8	11	3	15	20	11	16	19	17	12	14	19	14
H	10	10	7	20	7	16	14	3	16	17	9	14	4	2	16	13	11	3	8	4	20	11	5	15	11	4
I	3	14	17	3	12	9	16	16	12	3	20	11	10	5	7	14	8	15	9	6	7	16	8	7	8	5
J	16	20	19	19	10	11	13	11	14	7	3	12	15	4	16	16	8	15	14	7	17	9	15	13	2	17
K	17	20	9	17	3	16	10	3	16	13	6	2	9	17	5	2	4	14	7	17	9	7	15	16	3	19
L	5	14	16	20	9	12	13	6	11	14	5	4	8	10	10	20	5	20	9	17	4	8	9	16	16	5
M	2	5	6	20	7	2	4	19	16	4	6	10	16	10	19	6	7	12	11	9	11	6	5	7	5	16
N	9	13	7	9	14	11	3	7	7	12	10	11	2	14	11	10	19	8	17	16	12	14	11	2	20	3
O	19	2	20	17	10	6	12	16	4	13	3	13	11	3	3	10	16	9	13	2	8	11	7	20	15	14
P	20	6	13	9	5	9	14	3	7	20	3	4	14	11	17	13	6	10	6	12	8	13	10	12	12	14
Q	5	17	13	9	17	2	12	7	9	10	20	8	2	13	20	16	4	12	16	6	11	3	19	7	7	19
R	20	16	15	10	6	19	14	9	9	17	7	3	15	20	12	7	5	17	12	8	7	4	17	8	12	12
S	17	6	7	14	14	19	15	16	17	15	9	12	13	6	10	19	16	8	15	10	8	14	10	2	19	11
T	13	4	16	20	17	20	19	15	3	5	14	15	19	2	4	20	4	15	5	6	10	19	16	17	11	2
U	10	11	9	13	12	5	5	16	17	15	3	2	2	19	16	12	17	7	5	11	3	6	17	3	6	2
V	6	13	8	11	6	16	17	20	14	5	10	9	13	13	12	3	10	7	2	8	12	17	3	5	3	4
W	2	14	10	2	12	13	19	9	13	15	4	14	4	19	6	17	9	3	8	13	5	6	17	7	17	6
X	4	6	17	19	19	11	20	11	8	2	15	12	3	3	11	15	2	3	10	19	17	13	3	16	10	15
Y	2	17	9	11	16	7	10	12	7	3	11	6	14	9	7	6	16	17	10	7	12	17	16	7	6	11
Z	6	15	11	3	16	2	10	13	16	6	4	12	3	19	17	3	3	2	11	19	19	9	10	14	14	10

On the chart, find the place where the initials you've chosen intersect. Read the chapter whose number appears at that intersection.

19

THE FORTUNATE INDIVIDUAL

While the abstract idea of Fortuna is sometimes difficult to grasp, each individual must somehow come to terms with uncertainty and change in his or her life. Personifying the idea of Fortuna allows us to talk more easily about how each individual can deal with these forces. Someone who is sensitive to the presence of Fortuna and who has successfully adapted to it will henceforth be called a fortunate individual. Four hundred years ago, Michel de Montaigne described this type of person in interesting detail. Talking about himself, he wrote: "I am the sort of man who readily commits himself to Fortuna and abandons himself bodily into her arms." Montaigne is our prototype of the fortunate individual and examples from his life and writings will be used to illustrate how one can successfully adapt to the presence of uncertainty and change.

Fortunate persons do not necessarily possess fortunes, although many fortunate individuals are indeed wealthy. Rather, they are people who have a very special and close relationship with Fortuna, so close that they throw themselves into the arms of the goddess. Without any intention of being sacrilegious, let's use the famous statue of *The Pietà* by Michelangelo to preserve this idea in our minds, the idea of letting ourselves be held in the arms of a maternal figure. *The Pietà* shows Jesus, after being lowered from the cross, lying in the arms of His mother, Mary.

You need not be a Catholic to use the Pietà as a memory device — not even a Christian for that matter — for true art possesses a universal message applicable to all persons. Some may hastily object that Christ is dead in the scene depicted, and thus that the idea expressed by the statue is not relevant to our lives. However, He is dead only to the things of this world and only for a brief period of time. In a similar fashion, although not in such a divine and grandiose way, we humans may wish to detach ourselves temporarily, in a sort of brief death, from the things that worry or torment us and may wish to abandon ourselves into the arms of Fortuna, for a moment, leaving the outcome of things entirely to chance. Montaigne says: "I foster as best I can this idea: to abondon myself completely to Fortuna." This does not mean that we do not care about the outcome of events. On the contrary, we should console ourselves in the fact that Fortuna is a benevolent and charitable mother from whom nothing but good can come. The crux of the matter lies in the trust that we place in Fortuna.

ONE FORTUNA OR MANY?

In relating to the personified Fortuna, the problem arises of deciding whether we should view Fortuna as one and the same goddess for everyone or as a different goddess for each individual. Is there one Fortuna or many? Both ideas have a basis in history.

The notion of a private goddess of chance who takes particular interest in one, and who dispenses her gifts to an individual has always been very popular, appearing in many periods of history, from antiquity to modern times. The ancients used to say that as soon as we are born, we are put under the guard and trusteeship of a *genius,* a sort of guardian angel. This idea is still alive today in Catholic countries where people celebrate their namesake's day, a day of the year for each saint. Many people think it more important to celebrate their saint's day, for instance St. Joseph which falls on the 24th of June, and they do so with more pomp and ceremony than on their birthday. (Incidentally, the 24th of June is Fortuna's Day in the Roman calendar.) However, for most Christians today, birthdays have replaced Saints' days in the same manner that Santa Claus and the Christmas tree have replaced the Nativity scene.

The idea of having the persona of a powerful guardian associated with the moment of one's birth is infinitely more powerful than our connection with a date in the calendar. The date of our birth is an abstract numerical construct which can be manipulated using the tools of astrology. But with its attempted personifications via the signs of the Zodiac, its scorpios, rams, and scales, astrology provides us with a pale substitute for the powerful idea of the guardian.

In Ancient Rome, the idea of a personal Fortuna enjoyed great popularity. We read of the personal Fortuna of powerful individuals, such as the Fortuna of Augustus or the Fortuna of Pompey. Various families of the upper class also had their individual Fortuna, such as *Fortuna Juvenia, Fortuna Flavia,* and *Fortuna Torquatiana.* Roman Emperors were known to have an individual Fortuna which they carried with them on their travels in the form of small statues made of gold. The modern good-luck charm is reminiscent of that practice.

Whether we think of Fortuna as a personal friend or as a universal force, or even in both these ways alternately, one of the most beneficial gifts we can receive from her is freedom from fear. Fortuna acts as our guide in many ways, guiding us across new and dangerous grounds or leading us through the completion of a particular task. Indeed, she allows us to be ourselves, to act naturally, and to open our hearts to others about our deepest feelings. Montaigne expressed this very idea when he wrote: "Therefore I give myself to being candid and always saying what I think, by inclination and by reason, leaving it to Fortuna to guide the outcome."

SHARING RESPONSIBILITY WITH FORTUNA

The question might be asked: How much of what we achieve do we owe to ourselves and how much to Fortuna? Only fools think that they owe nothing to circumstances. It would likewise be foolish to think that we owe everything to Fortuna and nothing to ourselves. Again, Montaigne suggests an answer: "There have been some actions in my life the conduct of which might justly be called difficult, or, if you wish, prudent. Even of those, put it that one-third was my doing, truly two-thirds were richly her (Fortuna's) doing." We could modernize Montaigne's statement and say that responsibility and merit should be shifted in part from the individual autonomous man to the environment. What happens to us, what we do, and all our actions are consequences, to a great extent, of circumstances — and when we say circumstances we immediately think of Fortuna. A fortunate individual sees the problem of the sharing of responsibility in terms of proportions and not in terms of black or white, right or wrong. The self, or rather, the many social, psychological, or linguistic selves that we are comprised of have partial responsibility for their actions. This responsibility is limited to a certain percentage, leaving the rest to chance-like environmental circumstances, in other words, to Fortuna. Montaigne, our model for the fortunate individual, claims with humility and, of course, with great wisdom, that he owes two-thirds of his accomplishments to the goddess.

Whenever Montaigne has to make difficult decisions, he shows us how the fortunate individual can involve Fortuna in his or her actions. This individual waits until the very last possible moment to see if the matter will be decided by the contingency of events (again, by Fortuna). This is not to be taken as an excuse to procrastinate but is recommended only as a delaying tactic when facing very difficult decisions. Many of us can remember occasions when we felt sorry for not having waited a little longer before coming to a decision. Popular wisdom also reaffirms the caution against making hasty decisions. Many times, something happens unexpectedly which solves the problem at hand.

At other times, again, making no decision at all may turn out to be the best solution. The fortunate individual is not fazed by such entreaties or criticisms as, "What are you waiting for?", or "Can't you make up your own mind?", or even by such things as, "Are you afraid?" In poetic terms, the fortunate individual is essentially a courteous person who lets Fortuna lead, not because she is a lady, but simply because she is more powerful. She is wiser and completely in tune with all the other forces in the universe. Montaigne stated this point: "So I keep within me doubt and freedom of choice until the occasion is urgent. And then, to confess the truth, I most often toss the feather to the wind, as they say, and abandon myself to the mercy of Fortuna; a very slight inclination or circumstance carries me away."

THE NEUTRALITY OF FORTUNA

One of the most important points to remember is that Fortuna is neutral. Fortunate people do not believe that there are two Fortunas, one good and one bad. Our modern Fortuna is the one the ancients described, the one who brought things and events to human lives. The notion of a double Fortuna is a perversion which was made popular by the sixth-century writer Boethius. He believed that humanity was made up of some people who were fundamentally good and others who, from birth, were irremediably bad. He knew nothing of democracy and lived in a world where there were wide gaps between classes, from the privileged ones all the way down to the wretched and destitute. All good people, said he, had a good Fortuna; all bad people had a bad Fortuna. Some were rewarded with a good Fortuna and others were punished with a bad one.

Boethius had put the cart before the horse. One is not a fortunate individual because one is born good. On the contrary, one becomes a fortunate individual by learning how to live like one. This takes practice; it takes education; it takes courage and effort. People are not born good or bad. Instead all babies, at birth, are fundamentally neutral but with the necessary instincts for good or evil, for cruelty or compassion. How these instincts develop depends on what they learn later in life and how they are raised. It is circumstances, or Fortuna, that may turn one child into a criminal and another into a saint.

From a purely scientific point of view, Boethius' position that there is a good Fortuna and a bad Fortuna is untenable today since we know that an abstract force like chance cannot possess anthropomorphic values of good or bad. Furthermore even the terms "good" and "bad" are misleading because the good and the bad arise at the surface of contact between Fortuna and ourselves. We are the ones who affix the labels of "good" or "bad" to the things that Fortuna brings into our lives. Hence it is up to us to turn all her gifts into good ones

— or at least into bearable ones. What we must avoid is despair.

The first step in this direction is to realize that while Fortuna is indeed neutral, we have the power to control the labeling of that surface of contact between Fortuna and ourselves. We should convince ourselves that the contact is a good one. In other words, we can convince ourselves that Fortuna is generous, benevolent, and kind because we have the ability to manage our own reactions to events. Every event that occurs can be seen as a happy opportunity, an occasion for something good to happen. Those who think that way are called fortunate people. During the Hitler era, for instance, the priest who took the place of another man condemned to the gas chamber seized on the opportunity to gain eternal happiness, called beatitude, through his own sacrifice. His action showed him not only to be a fortunate individual but also made him into a recently canonized saint of the church.

THE APPEARANCE OF FORTUNATE INDIVIDUALS

Is there a way, we may ask, to tell which people are fortunate and which are not? Are there some external features by which others may be able to tell whether you are fortunate or not? To say that fortunate individuals trust Fortuna means that they trust events, circumstances, other people, and the outside world. It appears that such an attitude may be discernable from the outside. People should be able to tell whether you are a trusting person or a distrusting one. This distinction of face, general bearing, and an attitude of trust is acquired through education and by imitating role models of fortunate individuals. Montaigne says: "It seems as if some faces are lucky, others unlucky." This is not a scientific statement, of course. It is impossible to predict the degree of success which will come to an individual who exhibits a confident attitude and a trusting disposition. "As for prognosticating future events from them (from external appearances such as a lucky face)," said Montaigne, "those are matters that I leave undecided." Nevertheless, a trusting face, a confident attitude, an optimistic outlook on life, a penchant for thinking positively, all of these can contribute significantly to success and happiness in life.

Women who have learned karate have said that they are confident enough to walk at night on streets where they did not dare venture before. Some of them believe that they are almost never attacked because of the way they walk, with a confident and steady pace, exuding an aura of assurance. Essentially, they show no fear and their subsequent "lucky" appearance may discourage attack by possible muggers who prefer to pounce on an easy victim. Every mailman knows that if he runs away, even the most timid pooch may chase him.

What do fortunate individuals look and act like?

They have
- a trusting face
- an optimistic outlook
- a confident attitude

They
- do not automatically react defensively
- think positively
- act with assurance

Fortunate people learn early in life that a show of trust and of self-confidence exerts great influence on others. Their confident attitude issues from their conviction that Fortuna loves them and that everything will come out all right in the end. Acting this way can make a real difference at critical moments. "It has often happened," said Montaigne, "that on the mere credit of my physical appearance and manner, persons who had no knowledge of me have placed great trust in me, both for their own affairs and for mine. But the following two experiences are perhaps worth my telling in detail." Montaigne goes on to tell us two fascinating and dramatic episodes of his life. We will paraphrase his beautiful but somewhat archaic style into simpler and more modern language, adding a few necessary historical and geographical details in order to place these two episodes in their proper perspective.

MONTAIGNE AND ADVERSITY: TWO STORIES

The events about which Montaigne writes occurred during one of the darkest periods in the history of France; the time, some four hundred years ago, when lengthy religious wars between the many sects of Catholicism and Protestantism tore the country apart. Montaigne lived in a château in the south of France, near Bordeaux, in an isolated region away from cities. Bands of brigands, with the excuse of religious or political motives, would roam the countryside attacking isolated châteaux and pillaging them whenever they could enter by force or surprise.

Montaigne was quite influenced by his readings of classical writers such as Seneca who wrote that, "locked places invite the thief. The burglar passes by what is open." Reflecting on this wise observation by the Roman philosopher, Montaigne noted that "perhaps facility of access seems, among other means, to protect my château from the violence of our civil and religious wars. Defense attracts enterprise; and mistrust, offense. The fact that so many guarded country châteaux have been lost, whereas my own château endures, makes me suspect that they were lost because they were guarded. That gives the assailant both the desire and the reason. Any defense bears the aspect of war."

Of course the point made here is not that we ought to be careless and leave our doors wide open or go out and expose ourselves to danger. Fortuna has no sympathy for fools or daredevils. The point is rather that, given difficult circumstances such as violent arguments, family fights, and national wars, it is most often wiser not to let oneself be caught by the apparently automatic escalation of violence. Garry Wills, in reviewing Carl von Clausewitz's *On War* (1832), writes that, "where a state of hostility exists, 'deterrence' becomes provocation. Each side's defensive measures become offensive to the other side. Any move taken to keep ourselves invulnerable is perceived by the foe as removing power from him, an act that must be redressed. Perfect security for one side makes the other feel insecure. To place myself outside your power is to rob you of power, until I am placed back within your power." Wrote Clausewitz: "So long as I have not overthrown my opponent I am bound to fear he may overthrow me."

These lines remind us of the current nuclear arms race between the United States and the Soviet Union, and that the possibility of a nuclear war with its subsequent world annihilation is one of the major causes of the uncertainty that plagues mankind today. Other causes of today's uncertainty are the threat of economic collapse and the more devious and disquieting threat caused by the long-term effects of environmental pollution from industrial dumps or the spread of such diseases as AIDS. In the face of such awesome potential catastrophes, faith in Fortuna is both a powerful antidote against despair and a rich source of strength.

Let us go back to the two episodes when Fortuna protected Montaigne from harm. This was during the religious wars, a civil war where everyone in France was in daily danger of losing property and life. Quoting from the great English translation by Professor Donald Frame, we will let Montaigne tell of his first episode.

A certain person made a plan to take my house and myself by surprise. His scheme was to arrive alone at my door and press rather insistently for entry. I knew him by name and had reason to trust him as a neighbor, and to some extent a relative of mine. I opened to him as I do to everyone. Here he was completely terrified, his horse out of breath and all worn out. He entertained me with this bit of fiction: that he had just been set upon a half a league away by an enemy of his, whom I also knew, and I had heard of their feud; that his enemy had been wonderfully hot on his heels, and that, having been surprised in disarray and weaker in number, he had sought safety at my door; that he was greatly troubled about his men, whom he said he supposed to be dead or captured.

I tried quite naively to comfort, reassure, and refresh him. Soon after, up came four or five of his soldiers, with the same bearing and the same fright, wanting to come in; and then others and still others after them, well equipped and well armed, until there were twenty-five or thirty, pretending to have the enemy at their heels. This mystery was beginning to arouse my suspicion. I was not unaware in what sort of an age I was living, how much my house might be envied; and I had several examples of others of my acquaintance to whom similar misadventures had happened. However, feeling that there was nothing to be gained by having begun to be pleasant if I did not go through with it, and being unable to get rid of them without ruining everything, I abandoned myself to the most natural and simple course, as I always do, and gave orders for them to come in.

Besides, the truth is that I am by nature little given to distrust and suspicion. . . . And besides, I am the sort of man who readily commits himself to Fortuna and abandons himself bodily into her arms. For which I have up to now had more occasion to applaud myself than to complain; and I have found her both wiser and more friendly to my affairs than I am.

These men remained on horseback in my courtyard, the leader with me in my main room; he had not wanted to have his horse stabled, saying that he had to withdraw as soon as he had news of his men. He saw himself master of his undertaking, and nothing now remained but its execution. He has often said since, for he was not afraid to tell this story, that my face and my frankness had disarmed him of his treachery. He remounted his horse, his men constantly keeping their eyes on him to see what signal he would give them, very astonished to see him go away and abandon his advantage.

Why didn't the intruder attack? Behind the reasons that Montaigne gives us, and which we understand quite well, for most of us have had similar experiences in life, or, at least, have witnessed similar things happen to others; behind those reasons of cool assurance, of courageous confidence, there seems to appear the vision of Fortuna watching over her protégé, the fortunate individual, in this case, Montaigne. The ancient writers used to say that fortunate persons wear on their faces the sign of the protection of the goddess Fortuna. Perhaps the intruder could somehow read that sign on Montaigne's face. Perhaps, the intruder imagined that he too might come under the protection of the goddess at some time in his life, that he too could hope to become a fortunate person. He sensed that Montaigne, at that particular moment, had placed all his trust in his own good Fortuna. Attacking Montaigne would therefore destroy the intruder's own possibility of ever being able to depend on the protection of the goddess.

Montaigne had treated the intruder as an honest man, like a person worthy of the attention of Fortuna. The intruder was, of course, master of the situation and had but to give the order to have his men ransack the place. Montaigne showed so much trust in him, however, and was so frank and open that the intruder was unable to lose face and harm someone who was now his host. He may have followed the popular conception of good and bad Fortuna, and feared that were he not to behave like Montaigne — that most fortunate individual — the goddess would turn her bad side to him and he would become unlucky. The intruder was afraid of losing face not only in front of Montaigne but also in front of Fortuna. Montaigne knew that he was enticing the intruder into believing that he, the intruder, looked like an honest person and could pass for one. This so pleased the intruder that he preferred this pleasure to the gain he could have derived from ransacking the place and looking like a villain in front of his host, the world, Fortuna, and, in the end, himself. Be it as it may, Montaigne's fortunate composure saved his life.

Another time, during the same civil war, Montaigne had to travel through a dangerous part of the country. A truce had just been declared between Catholics and Protestants in that region, so Montaigne decided it would be safe to travel there. He was accompanied by a group of his personal servants and soldiers, all on horseback. Being a rich and somewhat important person — he was in his lifetime twice mayor of Bordeaux — three or four bands of brigands started from different places in order to capture him.

On the third day of his journey, a band of about twenty masked horsemen accompanied by a small army of mounted archers attacked him and made him prisoner. He was taken into the thickest part of a forest and the bandits divided among themselves all his possessions: his coffers, his money, his horses, and equipment. The bandits talked for a long time, fighting over the matter of his ransom. They also had a big argument among themselves over whether or not they should kill him. In short, the circumstances were dangerous in the extreme and Montaigne found himself quoting from Vergil:

Now you need all your courage, now a steadfast heart.
AENEAS

"After a few hours had passed," Montaigne notes, "behold, a sudden and unexpected change came over them. I saw the leader return to me with gentler words, taking pains to search for my belongings scattered among the troops, and having them returned to me as far as they could be recovered, even including my money box. The best present they made me was finally my freedom; the rest did not concern me much at that time."

Montaigne thought for a long time about this happy and sudden turn of events. The world is ruled both by Reason (Ratio) and Fortuna. So, being a rational as well as a fortunate man, he attempted to find a rational cause for his having been freed. He tried to imagine the possible motives that might have influenced his captors. He was, however, unable to find any logical, rational, political, economic, or social cause. What he found — and he gives us the oral testimony of his captor — was that it seemed to have been, again, the air of assurance, of trust in his own Fortuna, this ambiance of optimistic outlook on life, that made him "undeserving of misfortune." Wrote Montaigne: "The true cause of so unusual an about face and change of mind, without any apparent motivation, and of such a miraculous repentance . . ., I truly do not even now know. The most conspicuous among them, who took off his mask and let me know his name, repeated to me then several times that I owed my deliverance to my face and the freedom and firmness of my speech, which made me undeserving of such a misadventure; and he asked me to assure him of similar treatment should the occasion arise." The leader, with these words, reveals his deep-seated hope that when Fortuna comes to him (should the occasion arise), he will not have to suffer her wrath.

The confident person, like Montaigne in this episode, believing in the protection of Fortuna, creates a powerful impression on the people with whom he or she deals. Fortunate people are admired, respected, and emulated. The leader of the brigands wanted to be like Montaigne and, in fact, even fancied himself in a similar situation being treated in a similar manner. Since the word "occasion" means chance or Fortuna, the expression "should the occasion arise" used by the leader is another way of saying "if Fortuna decides that such a thing should happen to me." So the brigand is trying to protect himself by entering the society of the fortunate. The desire to be a fortunate individual is deep-seated in all people, even brigands. In order to succeed, people should behave as the goddess would wish them to behave, that is, honorably, generously, and humanely.

When trapped in a difficult and dangerous situation, fortunate people do not just worry about how they will get out of it, they also think about whether it really matters to them at all if they get out of it or not. They build themselves a fall-back position in case they do not succeed in escaping, while, at the same time, they wait for the proper occasion, chance, or opportunity to remedy the difficult situation. Therefore, when things outside of our purview cannot be changed, we can at least attempt to change ourselves in order to adapt to these external circumstances, be they conditions, events or people. "Not being able to rule events," wrote Montaigne, "I rule myself, and adapt myself to them if they do not adapt themselves to me. I have hardly the skill to dodge Fortuna and escape her or force her." Fighting against Fortuna, or, worse yet, forcing her, is the last thing a fortunate individual wants to be caught doing. To rule or manage oneself and to adapt are two standard behavioral patterns which are common to the fortunate individual.

THE FORTUNATE INDIVIDUAL TODAY

Let's see how these principles can be applied to life in present day America. John Naisbitt, author of *Megatrends* and publisher of *The Trend Report* gives the following example: "Here you have one unemployed worker. He's the victim type. He believes that some day the automobile industry will come back." So this worker stays in Detroit collecting his unemployment check week after week, getting poorer, more anxious, and more depressed about the future. "Then you have another unemployed auto worker who says, 'Well, I'm not sure this is ever going to happen. Doesn't look too good to me. Let's go where the jobs are.' The jobs are in the Southwest and Florida. So that person moves there, gets into another line of work, and is gainfully employed again." The second unemployed worker is a fortunate individual. We can recognize him by the fact that he is flexible and adaptable to new circumstances.

Are you a fortunate individual? Do you have these traits?

- Do you act with confidence and trust?
- Do you think positively?
- Do you share responsibility in decision-making with Fortuna?
- Are you generous?
- Are you flexible and adaptable?

It is not easy to suddenly acquire the traits of variability, flexibility, and adaptability. It is not easy to accept circumstances as they are, to sell our house, move to another part of the country, and learn another trade. In order to be comfortable with physical changes such as moving, going back to school, and getting another job, one must have practiced being mentally flexible and adaptable to new ideas and new trends in life. Montaigne describes this other type of flexibility — psychological flexibility — which is at the root of practical flexibility with these words: "We must not nail ourselves down so firmly to our character traits and dispositions." Montaigne means here that if we are known to be hardworking, economical, brave, and sober, or if, on the contrary, we are known to be lazy, a spendthrift, a coward, a drunkard, or a womanizer, we should not remain nailed to these "humors." If we do remain so fixed, we get what's coming to us when we are depicted on the comic stage as fools such as the miser, the jealous husband, the workaholic, the Don Juan, the prude, or the misanthrope. The list of inflexible fools is endless. "Our principal talent," wrote Montaigne, "is the ability to apply ourselves to various practices. It is existing but not living, to keep ourselves bound and obliged by necessity to a single course. The fairest souls are those that have the most variety and adaptability."

Four hundred years ago people might have aspired to be a "fair soul," a gentleman, or a lady, but today it is important to understand that we no longer should aspire merely to "be somebody." We should recognize instead that in addition to acquiring the traits of the fortunate individual we must also practice behaving in a fortunate way. This is a question of survival. Says Naisbitt: "The advice I have for young people is learn how to learn, because you are going to be involved in a lifelong learning process, adapting and changing. Maybe changing careers, etc." The advice is commendable and we hear it more and more often today. But how do we learn how to learn and, more importantly, how do we learn how to adapt?

THE SELF AND THE ENVIRONMENT

In order to become an adaptable, fortunate individual we have to be sensitive to the nature of the relationship between ourselves and Fortuna, between ourselves and the contingent world that surrounds us. Perhaps even more difficult than understanding the idea that events in the world are largely determined by chance is accepting another disquieting idea, stated by B. F. Skinner, in his book *Beyond Freedom and Dignity,* that "a person does not act upon the world, the world acts upon him." Since we can interpret "the world" to mean

"Fortuna," what this means is that we do not act upon Fortuna, Fortuna acts upon us. This does not mean that we are powerless victims for, as is explained scientifically by Skinner and poetically by Montaigne, there are roundabout ways of influencing Fortuna. We do this when we take preventive measures and try to modify the conditions under which we live or when we master our responses to events. Until we understand this basic principle and until we stop believing that we can act directly and change Fortuna (the environment), we will not have become fortunate individuals. On this important point, Skinner is emphatic: "Science has probably never demanded a more sweeping change in a traditional way of thinking about a subject, nor has there ever been a more important subject." Essentially, individuals do not act unilaterally; they only respond to stimuli coming from the contingent world around them. The responses of the individual are shaped by the environment. This environment may consist of things outside of us or may be right under our own skin like a headache or a silent soliloquy. We put on seat belts as a response to the probability of an accident. We use a rubber mat in the bathtub, just in case we should slip and fall, as a response to the slippery nature of the bathtub floor. Those who do not buckle-up in cars respond to other sets of circumstances such as the habit of not ever having worn seat belts before in their lives. When the cold wind blows, we button up our coats, and when the sun gets warmer we remove our coats. We do not act; we respond!

Philosophical underpinnings of the Fortuna philosophy:

- Chance exists. It is an abstract, cosmic force in the universe which is equally as real as space, time, gravity, or light.
- Outcomes of events in the world are to a great extent decided by chance.
- We do not act unilaterally; we respond to circumstances.
- The self is multiple, not unitary.

There is a very old fable about the wind and the sun: There was once a traveler walking down a lonely road in the country and wearing a coat. The wind and the sun made a bet on which one would be able to remove the coat from the man's shoulders. The wind started blowing hard and could not succeed for the more the wind blew, the more the traveler would hold tight to his coat. The sun then tried. It started to warm the traveler with its hot rays and eventually caused the traveler to remove his coat. The moral of this fable, that gentle ways are more effective than violent ones, is obvious. However that is merely the surface meaning of the fable. A more important lesson to be drawn is that the traveler is the toy of external forces, the wind and the sun. The traveler responds to things that happen around and to him. In this fable, he responds in a fairly predictable manner. In real life, however, the variety of possible responses is increased by the complexity of the environment; for instance, the traveler could also have taken refuge under a tree or even inside an air-conditioned limousine. Under well defined sets of circumstances, however, we could repeat the experiment with other travelers who would behave more or less in the same manner. Writes Skinner: "Folk wisdom and the insights of essayists like Montaigne and Bacon imply some kind of predictability in human conduct, and the statistical and actuarial evidences of the social sciences point in the same direction."

Fortuna is our code word to replace the element of chance existing in the wind, the sun, and all the other external forces present in the environment. Fortuna could be said to represent an important aspect of all the forces in the universe. Sometimes, these external forces, which the ancients personified as Venus for love, Mars for war, Neptune for the seas, Minerva for learning, Mercury for commerce, Apollo for the sun, and so on, became so unpredictable that they were identified with Fortuna. As a matter of fact, it is interesting to note, in this connection, that historians say that Fortuna is the last goddess to have survived the fall of the Greek and Roman mythological systems because she took over the roles of all the other gods. She is a survivor who stands for an all-pervasive cosmic force in the universe: chance.

THE MULTIPLE SELF

Earlier we said that a standard behavioral pattern of fortunate individuals is that they control themselves in the sense that they master their responses to events. But we have to specify what we mean by "self" before we can learn how to manage it. The Renaissance separated the idea of man out of the world of God and made the self an independent entity. Man was thus conceived as a new entity which was neither an angel nor a horse, as Montaigne used to say. According to this novel Renaissance way of seeing the relationship between man and God, every person was made into the center of their own solar system. Before the Renaissance, people had looked above them, in front of them, in any case, outside of themselves, in seeking for the center of truth, peace, and happiness. They were essentially looking for God by any means. During the Renaissance, the discoveries (or rediscoveries) of other worlds, other astronomical systems, other literatures, other cultures, and other religions destroyed the notion that there was only one center for everything. In its place was created the idea that there were not one but many systems, each with its own individual center. Montaigne was naturally drawn to look for his own center existing within himself: "Everyone looks in front of him; as for me, I look inside of me; I have no business but with myself; I continually observe myself, I take stock of myself, I taste myself. Others always go elsewhere, if they stop to think about it; they always go forward; as for me, I roll about in myself."

In the Renaissance, there was something like an explosion which created the independent self. Within the last fifty years, a new explosion, this time within the self, has created the notion of a multiplicity of selves within each individual. While the idea of the individual was born in the Renaissance, scientific explanations of the self are of very recent origin. The most fruitful insight into the nature of the self comes from modern behaviorism which is the primary scientific approach in psychology. Freudian psychoanalysis is still more literature than science. While Freud may still be read for the pleasure of his clear insights into specific case histories, he is far from being a scientist of the personality. It is presently felt, by psychoanalysts themselves, that Freudian psychology does more harm than good when applied, for example, in the courtroom.

The ideas of Skinner, a scientific psychologist, have not been well received by humanists, many of whom believe that his style of experimentation in behavioral psychology denies the obvious existence of the individual self. Mentalists, Freudians, Marxists, Fundamentalists, Kabbalists, monks of all hues, and peddlers of quintessence deplore the demise of "man as a person," of "man qua man," of "man in his humanity," of the man of Hamlet "How like a god!" all at the hands of Skinner! To limit the human role merely to that of response to one's environment is anathema to those who believe in the ultimate dignity and freedom of man.

The reader may think that we have strayed away from the fortunate individual in engaging in a digression about behaviorism. We are, however, still focussing on our main concern, articulated by Montaigne, which is to see how fortunate individuals may manage themselves when they realize that they cannot control Fortuna. We must come to grips with the questions: "Is there a self to manage?" and, "Who manages that self?" Skinner supports the idea that the self is not unitary but multiple. He writes that a person "plays two roles: one as a controller, as the designer of a controlling culture, and another as a controlled, as the product of a culture." He goes on to define these two selves (using the terminology of Freud in parentheses): "The controlling self (the conscience or superego) is of social origin, but the controlled self is more likely to be the product of the genetic susceptibilities to reinforcement (the id, or the Old Adam). The controlling self generally represents the interests of others, the controlled self the interests of the individual."

To clarify these ideas, consider this example. Most of us prefer to be slim rather than fat because of the pressures of the internalized others. The self that pressures us to diet is called the controlling self. It comes from the others, from outside influences which we have internalized. Note, by the way, that "the others" whose influences you have internalized may also include you. So the controlling self pushes you to watch what you eat and how much you eat because you want to please that controlling self (the others, yourself included). Now, on the other hand, the controlled self (the Old Adam) may love apple pie which happens to be very fattening. Our body may have what Skinner calls "genetic susceptibilities to reinforcement," in other words, our body may naturally crave for the rewards of sweet, juicy apple pie and thus we have an internal war going on between two sets of selves.

There is hope, however, because we ourselves are one of those who constitute "the others" so that we are part of the controlling self. It is most important to note that we are only one part of the controlling self. The controlling self is a social self. It is like an assembly hall where decisions are being made and where we are only one of the many people who sit in that hall. By being able to rule themselves, by managing their reactions and emotions, fortunate individuals are often most successful at having their motions passed in these settings (the place in the brain where the selves meet to reach decisions involving actions). Going back to our apple pie example, we can exert some control over our situation by not buying any pie so that it won't be available in the house, or we could control our behavior by learning more about how we eat.

The crucial point here is to realize that the controlling self is multiple, made up of many interdependent selves. These selves are not autonomous; they are not independent. The controlling self is not a superego in a singular sense as implied by Freud; it has nothing to do with ancient kings such as Oedipus. It is rather a place, a union hall in a factory where you can still hear the machines grinding, processing flows of desire, of matter, or of information, cutting these flows, and breaking them down in random and unexpected ways. The controlling self could also be imagined as a group of citizens at a town meeting, or a group of parents and teachers at a PTA meeting. The composite self that shows up at any of these meetings is different every time.

The self of the fortunate individual is thus, not a single autonomous entity, but a multiple one. It is more like the Congress than the White House. It is a self that exists in the world of Fortuna, where things and people are varied, diverse, flexible, adaptable, and changing, just like Fortuna herself. "A self," says Skinner, "is a repertoire of behavior appropriate to a given set of contingencies." We behave differently at an office party and in a classroom. Writes Skinner: "Two or more repertoires generated by different sets of contingencies compose two or more selves. A person possesses one repertoire appropriate to his life with his friends and another appropriate to his life with his family, and a friend may find him a very different person if he sees him with his family or his family if they see him with his friends."

These words have a familiar echo, and could almost have been written by Montaigne. He preceded Skinner in debunking the vanity of autonomous man. It is a constant theme of Montaigne's thought that man (women and men) shares his reponsibilities, his rewards, and his punishment with the circumstances (Fortuna). Just as Skinner deflated the pretentious claims of autonomous man, Montaigne fought against man's prideful delusion of perfect rational control. "The means I take to beat down this frenzy, and which seems fittest to me, is to crush and trample underfoot human arrogance and pride; to make them feel the inanity, the vanity and nothingness, of Man" wrote Montaigne.

Four hundred years ago, even as Montaigne was building on the new Renaissance idea of "self," he was already beginning to tear it down. And so, just as the Renaissance witnessed the creation of individual Man, each one at the center of his or her own solar system, culminating perhaps in the figure of Louis XIV, the Sun King (the despotic Self par excellence), now, in this last part of the twentieth century, we are witnessing a nuclear fission within the old unitary self which creates thus, the possibility of many selves. There is no such thing as the "real me." When we go "looking for ourselves," we find a crowd. We also waste our time.

The body is a place shared by many selves. The idea that a "real" self can always be found behind each role is false. There is no such thing as a real person, a real me, a real self, which just happens to play many roles. The search for identity that characterizes the "Me generation" and the "Me decade" are rightly seen to have been a waste of time. We have to discard the metaphor of the theater of the mind once and for all, whether it is the ancient theater with Oedipus and his phantasms, or any theater with "real" people hiding inside their roles. We have to get rid of the myth of the little person (the self) inside the big person, running his body and thinking for him. "The picture which emerges from a scientific analysis," writes Skinner, "is not a body with a person inside, but of a body which is a person in the sense that it displays a complex repertoire of behavior."

The new idea of man which is emerging is that of the fortunate individual. The term "fortunate" is taken here to mean "emulating the characteristics of Fortuna." Since the abstract idea of Fortuna embodies variety, diversity, uncertainty, adaptability, mobility, and other related traits having to do with chance, it follows that in order to be successful, the fortunate individual should embody all these characteristics as well. The fortunate person never asks "Who am I for ever and ever?" but rather "Who am I now, at this very moment and in this place?"; she or he does not say "What role am I playing?" unless she is an actress. A good actress will tell you that she is always amazed and frightened by how a role can grip her. She becomes the character she is playing and she'll become a different character tomorrow.

The fortunate individual lives at peace with apparent inner contradictions and inconsistencies. Wrote Montaigne: "Whoever supposes, to see me look sometimes coldly, sometimes lovingly, on my wife, that either look is feigned, is a fool." The body (or person) of the fortunate individual is made in the image of his or her Fortuna. It is a changing and discontinuous body, as Montaigne saw it long before modern psychologists: "We are wrong to try to compose a continuous body out of all this succession of feelings."

HOW TO BECOME A FORTUNATE INDIVIDUAL

What advice can we give, then, to people who desire to become fortunate individuals? First, we should accept our inner inconsistencies. "We are," wrote Montaigne, "I know not how, double within ourselves, with the result that we do not believe what we believe, and we cannot rid ourselves of what we condemn." We should be proud of our complexity. It will be nearly impossible for thinking machines to duplicate this essential confusion of internal multiple dialogues, the multilog that makes us human. There is nothing wrong with being, at some time or another, or even at the same time, a little bit mystic, a little bit agnostic, a little bit reactionary, a little bit left-wing, a little bit macho, a little bit homosexual, at some times a hero, at others a coward. Men should not feel ashamed of crying and women should feel comfortable with exhibiting strength. Also, we should not be ashamed to make use of people, parties, or ideas that clash against each other and appear on the surface to be contradictory. Fortunate individuals can make use of this diversity because they are not owned by anything or anybody. Wrote Montaigne: "In truth, and I am not afraid to confess it, I would easily carry, in case of need, one candle to Saint Michael and one to the dragon."

John F. Kennedy, ironically was both an unfortunate leader as well as our first "fortunate" one. As Roger Rosenblatt wrote in *Time* magazine (2/27/83): "When caught in a reversal of a former idea, John F. Kennedy used to counter, 'I don't think that way any more'." The fortunate individual uses the attributes of Fortuna for his or her own good advantage. That happy inconsistency of Fortuna which contributes to freedom and tolerance becomes the best asset of the fortunate person. Rosenblatt continues: "Consistent people are often said to be most in control of their lives, but rather than possessing consistencies, it is their consistencies that possess them; and they probably are less in control of themselves than more erratic and volatile people."

Fortunate people, moreover, are people who can be good friends; they may be mad at you at one moment but they never hold a grudge and will soon forgive you because they recognize that all of us are different from day to day. New selves rise within us from one moment to the next. "When I scold my valet," wrote Montaigne, "I scold him with all my heart; my imprecations are real, not feigned. But when the smoke has blown away, let him need my help, and I am glad to do him a service; I instantly turn over the leaf. When I call him a clown or a calf, I do not undertake to sew those labels on him forever; nor do I think I contradict myself when I presently call him a fine fellow."

It is interesting to note that our prototype of the fortunate individual, Montaigne, is quoted in the current press on this very subject of consistency. Continues Rosenblatt: "The consistent mind mocks and distorts life itself, blasphemes and perverts everything in a universe that insists on motion. 'Myself I may contradict,' Montaigne conceded, 'the truth I do not'."

The criterion of inconsistency becomes a most valuable asset when a fortunate individual judges others. Because there is no real self but rather a variety of possible selves in each of us, the judgments that fortunate people make about others will not be general, absolute, and final but balanced and temporary. Fortunate people can always find something to praise in anyone. Absolute praise and acceptance as well as absolute blame and rejection are foreign to their way of evaluating people. "Should we not dare say of a thief that he has a fine leg?" wrote Montaigne, adding these famous words: "And if she is a whore, must she also necessarily have bad breath? For my part, I can perfectly well say: 'He does this wickedly and that virtuously'." For all his errors, we should not be afraid to admit that Nixon may be one of the greatest living American statesmen today as well as a valuable expert in foreign affairs. Wise and fortunate people in power would be well advised to consult him and draw on his extensive experience. As controversial or distasteful as this may sound to some, this is the message of the Fortuna philosophy.

LOVE OF HUMANITY

The Fortuna philosophy involves more than excusing the bad aspects of a person and praising his or her good sides. The fortunate individual forgives and loves the whole person. When something bad happens to the rich and mighty, we may not initially feel inclined to have much sympathy for them because we may think, perhaps erroneously, that their fall has been cushioned by material means. But, as in Nixon's case, the fortunate individual will sympathize with the plight of someone fallen on hard times even if we suspect that the individual already had more than his or her share of good fortune.

Fortunate individuals

- love humanity
- are tolerant
- learn to manage their reactions to circumstances
- try to modify their environment
- live at peace with inner contradictions and inconsistencies
- embody variety, diversity, plurality, multiplicity, uncertainty, flexibility, changeability, and mobility

---

Love for humanity is a distinctive feature of fortunate individuals. Fortunate people are remarkable because they hate no one and therefore have little reason to fear anyone. This lack of fear, even in the face of death, is communicated to other people who then look on fortunate people with kindness or at least without fear, suspicion, or hostility. "Moreover," writes Montaigne, "I hate no one; and I am so squeamish about hurting that for the service of reason itself I cannot do it." Some self-righteous people may take exception to the idea of being good to everybody, and Montaigne is perfectly aware that he has made himself vulnerable to criticism when he claims that he hates no one. He wrote that he did not care which of the two ways, good or bad, he might be judged. To illustrate this point he borrowed this paradox from Plutarch: "He could not possibly be good, since he is not bad to the wicked" and "He must certainly be good, since he is good even to the wicked." In the final analysis, while we cannot control what others may think of us, and while their judgments of us may be contradictory, we can manage our own actions and the way we think of ourselves.

The love of fortunate people for others goes beyond the simple truism that everyone has something good in them. When Fortuna touches others, or when something bad happens to someone, fortunate people sense vividly how easily it could have happened to them. We are all bathing in the same sea of circumstances, in the same sea of Fortuna. Sidney Hook, Emeritus Professor of Philosophy at New York University wrote these words in *The New York Times* of September 3, 1976: "The older I grow the more impressed I am with the role of luck or chance in life. The Puritan father who remarked to his son as they observed a man being dragged to the gallows: 'There but for the grace of God go I,' put in the language of religious piety what even the most skeptical of disbelievers also recognizes."

We have three ways in which to view chance. First as the Puritan who believes that everything is directly under the will of God; second as the disbeliever who recognizes the scientific fact that chance is an integral part of the universe; third as the moderate skeptic who takes a middle-ground position acknowledging the existence of both God and chance. Fortunate people can be any of these three kinds. Regardless of which of these three possible ways of looking at chance is taken, fortunate individuals realize that God, or Fortuna, Fortuna working alone, or under the overall supervision of God will love us most when we keep in mind that we should be cautious, that we should be vigilant — because the man being taken to the gallows could be us. The believers among fortunate people are told that, "God helps those who help themselves." We have a responsibility for contributing to our own happiness, and a role to play by managing ourselves and changing our environment.

CHANGING OUR ENVIRONMENT

Sometimes it is a matter of pure accident that we escape harm as we go through our daily lives. Knowing this, one of the major ways that fortunate individuals improve their chances for happiness is by changing their environment. The world is already very much man-made: the surfaces upon which we walk or ride, our means of communication, our health and sanitation facilities. More and more, our environment is being shaped in ways that allow us to live comfortably with the uncertainties of Fortuna. The wise, fortunate individual will go beyond such simple tricks as not buying apple pie if he or she wishes to diet and become slimmer. For example, who knows what could happen to many of us if a gun were available at a moment when we enter into a fit of anger? Might we not reach for it as a violent "self" takes over our physical body? We must be clear about what happens in such a situation: It is not that a violent "self," like a little devil, rises from inside of us and orders our hands to grab the gun and shoot. A more accurate, although more difficult way to comprehend these circumstances, is to realize that a new situation occurs where the person, plus the gun, plus the causes of the anger, all constitute a machine that pulls the trigger. As Gregory Bateson writes: "What thinks is the total system which is man plus environment." Skinner would say the same thing except he would not say "what thinks" but "what behaves." Both agree on this point, however, that, "the unit of survival is organism plus environment." So the lines between the individual and the gun are fictitious and purely artificial when we are dealing with the question of "what happened."

What we should do, then, is to anticipate that such combinations of circumstances could occur. We can alleviate the danger involved in their occurrence by taking preventive measures: not owning guns, not raising one's voice, or avoiding contact with things or persons that may cause the anger. A wise move would be to get rid of guns in the house and to get rid of atomic weapons in the world. Their very existence is a cause of anxiety. Fortunate people are ready to admit that accidents can and do happen. Fortunate people thank Fortuna for the good things in their lives and thereby cure themselves of folly and pride. As Professor Hook, quoted above, continues: "When we realize what we owe to luck, it tends to cure us of overweening pride, of smugness and self-righteousness. For whatever our achievements, we will note that they are not a consequence only of our worth, or of our efforts and virtues alone."

It should be stressed that fortunate people are not self-centered. Fortunate individuals are good to others as a result of their being good to themselves. Because the Fortuna philosophy has been treated here in terms of advice on how to become a fortunate individual, we should not conclude that the less fortunate are "the others" about whom we do not care. Quite the contrary. Making Fortuna an integral part of our lives develops in us a strong sense of kinship with the rest of humanity. "A realizing sense of the role of luck in life," writes Professor Hook, "makes for modesty towards one's own accomplishments and for sympathy and compassion towards others who are less fortunate. It reinforces our feeling of kinship with others when natural or social disasters strike. It strengthens our will to cooperate in the face of danger. When it is necessary to do justice, it opens our hearts to appeals for mercy."

Finally, while fortunate individuals are impelled, for all these reasons, to be generous and merciful to others, their first responsibility still continues to be to themselves. We can best help others when we are strong ourselves. We become stronger by interacting vigorously and frequently with the environmental forces of things, events, and people. After these experiences, after acquiring more wisdom and endurance for living successfully in the world of chance and uncertainty, we will learn to treat these forces like friends. We recognize, however, that we cannot ever become so strong and steady as to forget their existence. No plan can be absolutely fail-safe, just as no one is still trying to build unsinkable Titanics. For all our yearnings for safety we cannot lose sight of uncertainty. We must learn how to live happily with uncertainty itself. Montaigne, our prototype of the fortunate individual put these ideas in poetic terms: "And I found that with my endurance I had some foothold against Fortuna, and that I would need a great shock to throw me out of my saddle. I do not say this to irritate her (Fortuna) into making a more vigorous attack on me. I am her servant, I hold out my hands to her; in God's name let her be satisfied." And so Montaigne, who felt at ease with the poetic vision of a Fortuna who works "in God's name," demonstrates the optimistic and trusting attitude of fortunate individuals. He holds out his hands to Fortuna, evoking the image of the Pietà with which we commenced this chapter, he abandons himself finally into her arms.

THE MATRIX FOR CHAPTER 19

	A	B	C	D	E	F	G	H	I	J	K	L	M	N	O	P	Q	R	S	T	U	V	W	X	Y	Z
A	16	20	20	7	2	7	2	5	2	15	4	7	20	13	13	6	4	12	18	17	7	13	17	5	6	13
B	16	18	13	3	16	2	17	7	18	10	16	2	6	15	11	7	14	12	20	4	6	2	7	14	6	7
C	3	13	2	8	8	17	10	13	12	6	3	12	13	2	17	8	17	12	18	15	8	8	13	5	20	5
D	9	8	13	2	12	2	7	11	18	5	13	7	18	10	5	4	3	8	6	14	2	3	4	13	2	16
E	9	7	20	3	8	6	10	6	7	8	2	15	10	16	13	10	15	2	12	13	3	12	17	20	13	4
F	7	11	15	9	4	6	14	17	20	13	13	17	7	12	8	11	8	18	20	7	18	12	18	17	9	6
G	5	6	6	20	11	5	3	5	16	11	17	9	6	10	7	9	14	10	2	18	20	4	14	16	20	6
H	5	9	14	7	16	12	15	16	20	5	3	2	9	3	7	10	12	13	9	11	14	14	12	4	8	2
I	16	16	13	8	2	16	14	9	20	20	18	10	6	6	17	18	4	17	15	15	17	9	15	15	4	15
J	20	14	10	6	20	8	15	4	7	13	17	2	20	13	4	14	13	7	6	18	10	18	20	20	14	7
K	3	12	6	20	20	14	8	9	11	18	2	9	2	7	20	20	12	15	18	16	13	13	6	8	9	9
L	7	17	3	10	4	6	6	7	6	18	13	10	16	5	11	5	9	18	3	3	13	15	5	11	10	10
M	6	9	14	8	11	5	7	14	4	2	11	16	18	16	16	9	9	3	20	14	18	14	12	20	15	20
N	8	18	13	7	10	18	4	10	20	7	14	15	3	8	9	7	2	7	6	7	18	4	14	20	4	4
O	5	15	7	4	3	17	15	13	17	6	7	8	4	18	12	7	14	7	11	6	17	5	15	3	10	17
P	12	20	14	10	2	6	16	15	20	16	15	5	10	14	13	10	14	3	2	20	10	2	9	2	6	3
Q	14	13	14	14	5	4	10	18	6	3	5	9	14	16	8	13	7	10	17	16	6	14	6	3	3	7
R	2	3	12	14	9	15	8	2	18	14	17	14	10	4	7	5	14	15	3	5	2	8	8	3	14	13
S	5	4	12	8	7	13	5	18	18	11	4	18	3	13	17	15	20	14	4	3	9	12	7	4	14	10
T	15	13	4	14	13	9	11	2	5	17	15	17	4	12	9	7	6	14	10	14	12	7	6	13	17	9
U	16	10	10	15	15	3	7	14	18	9	13	3	12	15	9	10	14	2	2	14	20	4	16	8	4	14
V	2	3	12	14	2	11	3	10	18	20	5	10	3	6	15	8	5	6	16	14	2	10	11	8	20	15
W	6	4	8	14	20	6	15	12	5	16	7	6	20	7	18	12	3	20	13	11	18	5	13	8	20	10
X	8	18	12	10	9	17	3	17	13	9	18	18	5	17	9	6	18	12	15	6	8	15	20	9	9	10
Y	12	2	6	9	20	17	18	14	15	15	12	4	17	2	17	3	12	7	4	5	16	9	17	20	15	17
Z	14	4	3	9	12	13	5	14	13	2	15	9	11	11	15	20	17	8	5	5	14	14	17	17	6	11

On the chart, find the place where the initials you've chosen intersect. Read the chapter whose number appears at that intersection.

20

LET US KNOW

Every morning when we wake up, we are a new person, different from the one we were the day before. We are modified daily by the things that happen to us and the influences that touch our lives. As we change, we begin to react differently to people and events. We begin to deal differently with the circumstances of our lives. This change may be precipitous or gradual.

Did you use the tables at the end of each chapter to find your path through this book or did you read the chapters in the order in which they were printed? The choice we offered you at the beginning was a test. It was a way of finding out how comfortable you were with the role of chance and uncertainty in your life at the time you began reading.

If you could do it all over again, would you choose differently? Has your introduction to Fortuna, through this book, changed your attitude toward chance?

It's possible that reading this book may be one of those events that changes your life. You may discover that you have a new, more sensitive relationship with the forces of chance. Maybe you've been putting some of the ideas of this book to work for you and you've begun to look at Fortuna's good face, welcoming the accidental in your life rather than running away from it. You may have discovered a new and different way of dealing with the opportunities which come into your life. You may have discovered the key that unlocks those opportunities which before were inaccessible to you.

If so, maybe you've become a fortunate individual, a lucky person. Maybe you've begun to successfully practice the Fortuna philosophy in your life. If something unusual has happened to you as a result of reading this book, we'd like to hear about it. It can happen!

Write to the address below and tell us of your experiences. Your responses will remain confidential. If they are referred to in our ongoing investigations into the nature of chance or in future publications, it will be done anonymously unless you give us your permission to do otherwise.

G.I.F.T.
(Group for the Investigation of the Fortuna Theme)
c/o Collier Associates
875 Avenue of the Americas
Suite 1003
New York, New York 10001

BIBLIOGRAPHY

Bateson, Gregory. *Steps to an Ecology of Mind.* San Francisco: Chandler Pub. Co., 1972.

Blum, Harold F. *Time's Arrow and Evolution, 2nd Ed.* Princeton NJ: Princeton University Press, 1951.

Boethius. *The Consolation of Philosophy* trans. Richard Green. Indianapolis: Bobbs-Merrill, 1962.

Born, Max. *Physics in My Generation.* New York: Springer-Verlag, 1969.

Carter, J. B. *The Religion of Numa and Other Essays on the Religion of Ancient Rome.* London: MacMillan, 1906.

Cicero. *De fato* trans. H. Rackham in *Cicero in 28 Volumes.* Cambridge: Harvard University Press, 1967.

David, F. N. *Games, Gods and Gambling: The Origins and History of Probability and Statistical Ideas from the Earliest Times to the Newtonian Era.* London: Griffin, 1962.

Dawkins, Richard. *The Selfish Gene.* New York: Oxford University Press, 1976.

Deleuze, Giles and Guattari, Félix. *Anti-Oedipus: Capitalism and Schizophrenia* trans. R. Hurley, M. Seem, and H. Lane. New York: Viking Press, 1977.

Eichner, Hans. "The Rise of Modern Science and the Genesis of Romanticism," *PMLA,* vol. 97, no. 1 (June 1982), pp. 8-30.

Fowler, W. W. "Caesar's Conception of Fortuna," *The Classical Review,* vol. XVII (1903), pp. 153-156.

Fowler, W. W. "Fortune (Roman)," *Encyclopedia of Religion and Ethics,* vol. VI, ed. J. Hastings. New York: Scribner's, 1914.

Hall, A. Rupert. *From Galileo to Newton.* New York: Dover, 1981.

Heisenberg, Werner. *Physics and Beyond.* New York: Harper and Row, 1971.

Heisenberg, Werner. *Physics and Philosophy.* New York: Harper and Row, 1958.

Hofstadter, D. R. *Godel, Escher, Bach: An Eternal Golden Braid.* New York: Basic Books, 1979.

Hofstadter, D. R. and Dennett, D. C. *The Mind's Eye: Fantasies on Self and Soul.* New York: Basic Books, 1981.

Jeans, Sir James. *Physics and Philosophy.* New York: MacMillan, 1943.

Kline, Morris. *Mathematics in Western Culture.* Oxford: Oxford University Press, 1953.

Kristeller, Paul Oskar. *The Classics and Renaissance Thought.* Cambridge: Harvard University Press, 1955.

Lorenz, Konrad. *On Agression* trans. M. K. Wilson. New York: Harcourt, Brace and World, 1966.

Machiavelli, Nicolo. *The Prince* trans. W. K. Marriott. Chicago: Encyclopaedia Britannica, Inc., 1952.

Martin, Daniel. *Montaigne et la Fortune: Essai sur le hasard et le langage.* Paris: Honoré Champion, 1977

Mill, John Stuart. *On Liberty.* Chicago: Encyclopaedia Britannica, Inc., 1952.

Monod, Jacques. *Chance and Necessity* trans. A. Wainhouse. New York: Alfred Knopf, 1971.

Montaigne, Michel de. *The Complete Essays of Montaigne* trans. Donald M. Frame. Stanford, CA.: Stanford University Press, 1948.

Naisbitt, John. *Megatrends: Ten New Directions Transforming Our Lives.* New York: Warner Books, 1982.

Patch, Howard R. *The Goddess Fortuna in Medieval Literature.* Cambridge, MA: Harvard University Press, 1927.

Patch, Howard R. "The Tradition of the Goddess Fortuna in Roman Literature and in the Transitional Period," *Smith College Studies in Modern Languages,* vol. III, no. 3 (April, 1922), pp. 130-177.

Petrarca, Francesco. *De remediis utriusque fortunae* trans. C. H. Rawski in *Petrarch: Four Dialogs for Scholars.* Cleveland: Western Reserve University Press, 1967.

Prigogine, Ilya. *From Being to Becoming: Time and Complexity in the Physical Sciences.* San Francisco: W. H. Freeman, 1980.

Rogers, Carl R. *On Becoming a Person.* New York: Houghton-Mifflin, 1961.

Rollin, Betty. *Am I Getting Paid For This?: A Romance about Work.* Boston: Little, Brown, 1982.

Rousseau, Jean Jacques. *The Social Contract* trans. G. D. E. Cole. Chicago: Encyclopaedia Britannica, Inc., 1952.

Schrödinger, Erwin. *What is Life and Other Scientific Essays.* Garden City, NY: Doubleday and Co., 1956.

Skinner, B. F. *Beyond Freedom and Dignity.* New York: Knopf, 1971.

Sophocles. *Electra* and *Oedipus the King* trans. Sir Richard Jebb. Chicago: Encyclopaedia Britannica, Inc., 1952.

Van Marle, Raimond. *Iconographie de l'art profane au Moyen Age et à la Renaissance.* The Hague: Martinus Nijhoff, 1932.

von Foerster, H. "On Self-Organizing Systems and Their Environments," *Self-Organizing Systems* ed. Yovits and Cameron. Oxford: Pergamon Press, 1960.

Weaver, Warren. *Lady Luck.* Garden City, NY: Doubleday and Co., 1963.

ABOUT THE AUTHORS

DR. CATHERINE LILLY was born in Detroit, Michigan. She did her undergraduate and graduate work at the University of Michigan, completing her Ph.D. in 1971 with a thesis on the theory of numbers. She is now Chairperson of the Mathematics Department at Westfield State College, Massachusetts, where she is a full professor. Dr. Lilly has published several professional and popular articles in publications ranging from *Self* to *New England Mathematics Journal.* She lives in a small New England town with her son and three cats.

DR. DANIEL R. MARTIN was born in Madrid, Spain. He came to this country in 1960, and received his B.A. in French from the University of Illinois, Chicago, before going on to Yale University to earn his M. Phil. and Ph.D. degrees. He is now professor of French at the University of Massachusetts at Amherst, and a popular lecturer in the Five College area. Dr. Martin has written two books on Michel de Montaigne.